Scripture Windows

Toward a Practice of Bibliodrama

PETER & SUSAN PITZELE

Ben Yehuda Press
Teaneck, New Jersey

Published by Ben Yehuda Press
122 Ayers Court #1B
Teaneck, NJ 07666
http://www.BenYehudaPress.com
ISBN13 978-1-934730-75-1

Second edition   19 20 21 / 5 4 3 2 1   20190109

With thanks to

Zerka Moreno, who gave me the tools;
Rabbi Steve Shaw, who opened doors;
Rivkah Walton, who saw a method;
and Lisa Goldberg, who helped
me find the words.

Irrefutably, indestructibly, never wearied by time, the Bible wanders through the ages, giving itself with ease to all men, as if it belonged to every soul on earth. It speaks in every language and in every age. It benefits all the arts and does not compete with them... More than two thousand years of reading and research have not succeeded in exploring its full meaning. Today it is as if it had never been touched, never been seen, as if we had not even begun to read it.

—Abraham Joshua Heschel,
God In Search Of Man

Contents

Foreword to the Re-issue of "Scripture Windows"   xi
Preface   xvii
Bibliodrama: an appetizer   xvii
What is Bibliodrama?   xix
Why Bibliodrama?   xx
Origins   xxii
Scripture Windows: design and format   xxiv

Part I: The Short Form

1. The Vocabulary of Bibliodrama   2
    White Fire   2
    The Move from Commentary to Bibliodrama   7
    Redefining Familiar Terms   11
    The Bibliodramatic Form   13
    Bibliodrama: The Tools   17
2. First Steps   29
    The Role of the Interviewer & Matters of Control   31
    Dipping In   33
    Bibliodrama with Objects   38
    Getting Inside the Head of...   44
    Who Are You?   45
    Closure & Review   51
3. The Elements of a Scene   53
    Sculpting   54
    The Encounter   65
    The Encounter between Parts of the Self   77
    The Encounter Between the Human and the Divine   78

Part II: The Longer Form

4. Text Selection and Text Preparation   83
    Text Selection: Three Criteria   84
    Text Preparation   90
    The Eight Questions   90
    Preparing for the last scene: 92
    Preparing and then letting go   94

5. The Warm-Up   95
    Antidote to Anxiety: The Director   95
    Stage fright: Yours   96
    Centering Exercise   97
    Articles of faith   98
    Antidotes to Anxiety: The Group   101
    Stage fright: Theirs   101
    Guidelines   102
    Confidentiality   104
    The Director's Prologue: Sample Script   104
    Prologue to the Bibliodrama of Joseph in Egypt   106
    A Prologue Analyzed   109

6. Action Phase I: Ease of Access   111
    Trance   111
    Scene One: Opening Moves   113
    Scene Two   120

7. Action Phase 2: Depth of Field   126
    Developing the Drama   126
    Director's Aside: Criteria for When
       to Get Players on Stage   135
    Back to the Scene   136
    Director's Aside: Doubling on Stage   141
    The Encounter   144
    Director's Aside: Strategies and Options   145
    Director's Aside: God-Talk   148
    The Climactic Scene   152
    Director's Aside: Managing a Challenge   155
    Director's Aside: Limitless Possibilities   160

Director's Aside: Letting Go   165
Director's Aside: Handling Emotion   166
8. The Sense of an Ending   **170**
9. Reviewing   174
    De-Roling   175
    Sharing 176
    Exegesis 178
    Other Sources 180
    Processing   181
10. Curtain Call   183

Part III: Appendices

Appendix 1: A Code of Bibliodrama Ethics   188
Appendix 2: God In The Drama   190
Appendix 3: Participant-Centered Bibliodrama   194
Appendix 4: Troubleshooting   196
    1. What to do if someone will not stay in role   196
    2. What to do if group members are inappropriate or
       distracting   197
    3. What to do if someone uses qualifiers like "maybe" 200
    4. What to do if someone becomes emotionally
       overheated   201
    5. What to do if someone tries to take over
       a Bibliodrama   202
    6. What to do if someone wants to bring in
       traditional commentary   203
    7. What to do if...   204
Appendix 5: Bibliodrama From The Pulpit   206
Appendix 6: Some Conventions for Closure   209

Epilogue: A Critique Of The Method   212
Afterword   215
Postscript   217

Acknowledgments   218

Foreword to the Re-issue
of "Scripture Windows"

I

This re-publication of *Scripture Windows* offers us a chance look back at the role this book has played in the transmission of the method of Bibliodrama, and also to offer some reflections on what may be the value of the work for those who practice it and those who experience it.

But before offering some thoughts about Bibliodrama, I personally wish to correct a serious omission in the history of the method, even as it is contained in the original edition of the book, namely the role Susan Pitzele played in its development.

Because Bibliodrama developed from Psychodrama, in which I had been trained, and found its first reception in the Jewish world, to which Susan was not a native, the role of the director-facilitator naturally fell to me. Susan simply did not have the same opportunities to present the method that I did. But her influence on me cannot be overstated. Her oversight and insight affected the evolution of Bibliodrama, its methodologies and its values. In particular Susan kept in view Bibliodrama's capacity to address non-Jewish communities and to engage with Christian scripture.

If, as I like to think, Bibliodrama is a kind of feminine methodology, perhaps even feminist in its somewhat challenging posture towards hier-archical-patriarchal interpretation, then the method has Susan to thank. I see her influence in Bibliodrama's gentleness of approach; its interest in the mirror dimension in which participants reflect on how their role-playings show them aspects of their own stories; in how when the drama is done, the sharing of these insights of reflection can build community and trust; and most of all in her sense, through her own experience, of what is spiritual in this method, both for the director and for the participants.

No one has played more bibliodramatic roles than Susan. From the very first, in all manner of public demonstrations, in classrooms, in houses of worship, Susan has been in attendance and ready not only to play a role, but to model the process of de-roling and sharing that make possible the exploration of a text that can lead to an experience of community and to genuine growth of spirit for individuals. That growth is expressed in a greater capacity for empathy and compassion, a greater respect for the power of Scripture to lead us to new understandings, and even a way of forming a relationship with the figures of wisdom and prophesy who can play a part in one's everyday life.

So here at the beginning of this fresh publication, I want not only to write Susan into the record, so to speak, but place her name with mine on the cover of the book about Bibliodrama-Bibliolog[1].

—Peter

---

[1] Beginning here in the United States in the 1990s in a predominantly Jewish context, the method, and the book we wrote to describe it, took root in Germany, where Bibliodrama came to be called "Bibliolog". Much has now been writ-ten about the method in German, and a network of trainers has developed in Europe that has brought Bibliolog all over the continent and as far distant as a Zulu community in South Africa. The application of this method to Christian scripture has been seamless and its adoption in Christian communities and seminaries fruitful.

II

Scripture Windows has been translated into German, Korean, Hebrew, Finnish, and Russian—and parts of it into several other languages. This attests to the range of interest this method of biblical work has evoked. In unanticipated ways Bibliodrama squirmed out of our hands and was carried to distant places and into many hearts. We have the sense of parentage, but not of possession.

We have decided not to revise the text, though in both nomenclature and approach the method has evolved. The original book has proved itself useful to many people from many different quarters, and we are happy to let it continue to be useful in its original format. The introduction we offer here represents our shared articulation of Bibliodrama as an aspect of religious life. These reflections are the result of 30 years of experience. This is likely to be the last best place for us to say something about what this method means to us and what we see it has meant to others.

Bibliodrama is, basically, a way to place oneself *inside* the biblical cosmos and to locate aspects of that cosmos in oneself. This connection—stepping into the shoes of biblical figures (characters, objects, figures of speech)—brings the Bible alive and home to one's life.

As we have often said, the most oft-quoted response of a participant to Bibliodrama is, "I will never read the Bible the same way again." What had been for many a book read at some distance—read with an interpretive, moral mind-set, read out of creedal obligations rather than personal discovery— becomes through Bibliodrama an embodied experience, a lived and felt identification that brings the biblical story to life and to our lives.

Scripture Windows is a book designed for people who wish to learn how to offer this experience to others. The method was never meant to be restrictive; the book was never intended to offer rules; and many men and women have used it well as a springboard for their own creativity, adapting it to many different contexts while preserving its essential feature: speaking **in the first person singular as the biblical figures**.

What the book does not do, for it cannot, is offer an understanding of the experience of participants. This is varied, of course, but in our opinion it has been too little researched. We wish to venture to say something about that here.

The phrase "I will never read the Bible the same way again" may be the most common comment heard after a session, but another, less heard but implicit, is "I will never read my own story the same way again."

The function of sacred texts and rituals is **religious** in the etymological sense, that is they serve to tie the individual back again into a cosmos that contains and transcends the personal.

The Latin word *ligare* (showing up in our word *ligament*) means to tie or bind. Sacred texts are records of the human experience of an all-inclusive Mystery. Individuals and cultures throughout human history have known themselves to be embedded in a vast interconnected web of life that can only be brought into the human community through story, metaphor, and play. That which cannot be expressed in logic may be captured in the dream-languages of myth-image. Religions are the repositories of these images, and when, as happens, these images reify into texts and the texts ramify into interpretations, when religious experience becomes routinized into norms, the myth-images lose their power. The re-animation of these images is essential to religious life.

The bibliodramatic experience in its own way offers this re-animation; or to change the metaphor, Bibliodrama seems to open a two-way channel between our own stories and the mythic narrative of the Bible. Both seem to gain in the process, and the result is that not only is the Bible never to be read in the same way again, but one's own sense of oneself is no longer alienated from that mysterious source from which the myth-images of the Bible come and to which we belong.

Thus for us the method of Bibliodrama has served three purposes:

One is its capacity as a hermeneutic to open the text to ever-fresh interpretation. This is what we mean when we use the image of *the window* in our title. The method opens new windows on the text.

Two is its capacity to show each of us his and her own face reflected in that window. This is what we refer to as *the mirror* dimension of Bibliodrama. When I step into the shoes of a biblical character, I can hear my own story reflected back to me in my portrayal. In that moment my personal identity undergoes a strange diversion, and I see myself as situated *within* the mythic, a participant in and not an observer of it. One could say that I am "mythologized," and this mythologizing brings about a new kind of self-knowledge.

The third function is religious. In this sense Bibliodrama is an instrument of repair.

The separation between our minds and the text, which is endemic to acts of reading words and interpreting them, is a kind of tear in the fabric of wholeness. We sense ourselves not only outside the text, seeing the text as the object of our attention and analysis, but outside of the Mystery the text bears and offers to us. This experience of being outside, of inhabiting a dualistic condition, is briefly but profoundly overcome in the act of participating in a Bibliodrama. For a moment, as I assume the role and the role assumes me, I am no longer separated. In that moment I am returned to an original wholeness, or, perhaps better said, I regain for a moment my innate capacity for a direct and unified connection.

The reader will notice how persistently we use words that begin with the prefix *re-*:

re-ligion, *re*-pair, *re*-animation, *re*-turn, *re*-flect, *re*-gain. The prefix comes from the Latin where it carries the meaning of *back* and *again*. The prefix tells us that we must go back again and again, crossing from the state of separation to the state of connection. This is the essential *re*-petition that *re*-vives.

For this reason Bibliodrama is fundamentally *re-creational.*

Anyone who has heard us teach Bibliodrama has heard us say, as our final words, "Have fun." And anyone who has gone on to learn the method and participate in it has known what this "fun" is. The fun of which we speak is contained in the lovely doubleness of the word *recreation*. In its common sense, the word means something that is *not work*. Recreation is synonymous with play, leisure, and the unproductive.

On the other hand, the word means to create again, to refresh not by resting but by some activity that is paradoxically a not-doing. The act of re-creation *re-minds* us—that is to say puts us back into our right minds again—so that we may be able to engage in the work of the world with a sense of wholeness.

In that sense one could say that re-creation in both senses of the word is the process of the 7th day of creation, the Sabbath. In the Jewish tradition the Sabbath is a day in which it is good to study the sacred, for on the Sabbath one approaches the sacred not from the outside but from the inside. On the Sabbath, Scripture is experienced in a different way. Its luminous magic, its depths, its delights glow and the white and black fire are unified in a sacred flame and our separateness can be consumed in it.

In this, its third purpose, we experience through Bibliodrama what religion is for and why it is precious. The religious person is not necessarily someone who belongs to a particular faith tradition—though the fact that religion is communal in its historical sense seems important. The religious person is someone who finds a way of going back again and again into the Mystery that dissolves separateness. For those of us who recognize the Bible's potential to offer re-entry into Mystery, Bibliodrama can be a vehicle for a religious life.

—Susan & Peter

Preface

Bibliodrama: an appetizer

A class is in progress: a group of fifteen adults are seated in a circle, studying the Bible. We have been reading the story of the Garden of Eden and have come to the end of that story, to the lines that say:

THEREFORE THE LORD GOD SENT HIM FORTH FROM THE GARDEN OF EDEN TO TILL THE GROUND FROM WHENCE HE WAS TAKEN. SO HE DROVE OUT THE MAN (Genesis 3:23-24).

Rather than talking about this episode and giving our ideas about it, I propose to the class that we step into it and play it out....

"Let's look at this scene in a bibliodramatic way," I suggest. "Let's see what Eve has to say about this moment of expulsion." The class, familiar with this approach from previous experiences with me, accepts this suggestion with nods of assent. "So I'd like you to imagine that you are Eve at this moment in the story. Tell us, Eve, what is this like for you?"

Hands go up, each hand a potential voice of Eve.

"I am furious at the deception God practiced on us, the temptation, the duplicity, the curse. It will take me a long time, if ever, before I trust God again."

"Driven out is right. I don't want to leave. I straggle. I hide. I look back. All I know is being left behind."

"You know, it says in the story that God 'drove the man out,' but nothing is said of me. Here is another place where I feel invisible. This whole thing is always between God and Adam."

"But that's the point," says another participant. "You see, I am not being driven out. It's Adam who is all nostalgic and depressed. I can't wait to get out of here, any more than I could wait to eat the apple. Eden is a place where I have no part to play, no future. It *has* all been Adam and God. In this world we're going to there's going to be lots for me to do."

"So you feel...?" I ask.

"Excited. I have a sense of power and possibility. There's something coming. I have a purpose. I am to be 'the mother of all living.' Now that's a part to play.

"Not a bad exchange, if you ask me," someone adds by way of comment.

Another hand is raised, a man speaks as Eve: "It's even more than that. In a certain way, I don't really leave Eden at all, ever. Only Adam leaves. He really is banished. He's never going to know again what it feels like to be part of life in the way he is here. He goes into exile. But a part of me stays here. A part of me can go back. The garden is the womb, and I have that inside me."

"Can I speak for Adam?" another participant asks. "Sure."

"I do feel the curse falling directly on me. Eve is not included in this expulsion. And yet she does come with me. Why?"

"I choose to go."

"Yes, but why?"

"I choose because it is what I want. I want out and I want a life with you. We were created together. Whichever way you want to think about how we came to be, it is clear that we belong together."

"I was angry at you because you caused us to lose the Garden."

"Well, I was angry at you that there was no place in that Garden for me, even for us. It was all you and God."

"So you deliberately..."

"Well, we have to give the serpent some credit."

"Where is that serpent anyway?"

"Here I am," says one of the group members, playfully easing himself from his chair to the floor.

"Are you coming with us?" Eve asks.

"He'll be nothing but trouble," says Adam. "You heard what God said about 'enmity' and 'bruising'."

"Well," says the serpent, "you heard what God said about eating and dying. And here you are."

"I don't understand," says Adam, looking genuinely bewildered, "you're not saying that God is not to be trusted...are you?"

"Let's just say that with God you cannot always trust your human sense of things. Nothing is ever quite the way it seems."

"Let's take him with us," says Eve. "I think we're going to need him."

What is Bibliodrama?

Most simply described, **Bibliodrama is a form of role-playing in which the roles played are taken from biblical texts.** The roles may be those of characters who appear in the Bible, either explicitly and by name (Adam or Eve), or those whose presence may be inferred from an imaginative reading of the stories (Noah's wife or Abraham's mother). In Bibliodrama, the reservoir of available roles or parts may include certain objects or images that can be embodied in voice and action (the serpent in the Garden or the staff of Moses). Places can speak (the Jordan River or Mount Sinai). Or spiritual figures may talk (angels, or God, or the Adversary). Then there is a host of characters from the legendary tradition (Lilith or the five perverted judges of Sodom) who can be brought onto the bibliodramatic stage. Finally, as an extension of the process in a different direction, there are the figures from history who have commented on the Bible (Philo, Augustine, Maimonides) whose presence and perspectives may be imagined and brought alive by an act of role-playing.

As I have developed it, then, **Bibliodrama is a form of interpretive play. To honor it with a venerable Hebrew name, Bibliodrama can be called a form of** *midrash.* The Midrash—used with the definite article and a capital "M"—is both a product and a process classically associated with the exegetical works of the rabbis of late antiquity. For the rabbis, this interpretive engagement with the Bible manifested itself in word-plays, analogies, and even puns that intensified the active experience of reading texts. Midrash is derived from a Hebrew root that means to investigate or explore. In the Midrash the written text is closely examined for meanings and insights that will enrich our understanding and enhance our relationship to the Bible. In a more generic sense, however, midrash—now in lower case—may be extended in time to later ages and to our own. From a more liberal perspective midrash may include extra-literary acts of interpretation such as movement, song, visual art, and drama, which, like their classical forebears, serve to illuminate meaning in the biblical narrative.

Why Bibliodrama?

In our time, a vital interest in religion and scripture exists within three different and often antagonistic communities. There are the religiously devout for whom the scriptures are an unquestioned and replenishing source of doctrine, law, and moral imperative. There are the academics and literary scholars—many of whom see the Bible as a patchwork of writings embodying complex literary, textual, archeological, political, social, and historical agendas—who give their professional lives to studying and teaching religious texts. And finally, there are creative men and women—writers, artists, poets, actors, musicians—who still find inspiration for works of imaginative creation in the shaping myths of the Judeo-Christian culture.

But outside of these three communities, it is clear that the Bible is losing its meaning for regular people—and has been doing so for several generations—even though the stories and images of the Bible still run in our veins and haunt our dreams. The spiritually awakening, the spiritually hungry—to say nothing of the ordinarily literate—do not, by and large, turn to the Bible for nourishment and direction. They do not see it as a mirror and window for their souls.

The popular culture, in spite all its talk about myth and soul, does not encourage us to revisit our inherited traditions and rediscover there the soul-myths we so deeply need. Few of our contemporary guides and spiritual pundits, not professionally associated with the pulpit or the business of religion, look to the Bible for those archetypes of human experience and feeling that might connect our struggles for meaning and continuity with the quests of our ancestors. We are so busy distancing ourselves from "patriarchy," from "institutional religion," indeed from the past itself, that we do not recognize how the old biblical figures are still able to tell us something about who we are, where we've come from, and where we're going.[2]

It is not my purpose here to make a case for the Bible and the place I think it should have in our culture. **I am writing for those who are currently trying to teach the Bible to children or adults in religious communities or outside of them, in schools, academies, seminaries, or in the home.** In whatever context, these people—I will say *you*, my reader—are teaching the Bible to people who no longer take the book's value for granted. We can no longer rely on a shared belief that the Bible is the great code, the supreme text of moral and spiritual pedagogy, the prerequisite for a literary education. The authority of the Bible and the respect it once conferred on those who taught it are gone in all but the most orthodox sectors of faith. Unhoused from its haven in the church or synagogue, the Bible is in exile and must make its case, if at all, without benefit of clergy.

The Bible now shares the fate of all the great literature of the past; it is not so much embattled as ignored. People don't care and don't see why they should. As a result, and more than it ever did before, the Bible relies on teachers. The clerical collar, the rabbinic pulpit, the Ph.D., the list of publications: All these count for relatively little in the current scene and

---

[2] To give only a few examples. The popular and influential psychologist James Hillman, who has probably done more than anyone to bring the word "soul" and "myth" back into our cultural vocabulary, hardly ever refers to the biblical repertoire of archetypal images. In this he is followed by his foremost student, Thomas Moore. And in their attempts to develop a mythopoetic imagination for contemporary men, both Robert Bly and his ally Michael Meade prefer the European fairy tale to the far more vexing and culturally central myths of the biblical tradition. Among contemporary feminists the Bible is, by and large, anathema.

will count for less in the future. **Today and tomorrow the Bible will need teachers who are passionate as well as literate, savvy as well as scholarly, street-wise as well as book-wise, and who can, without degrading it, make the Bible come alive as living myth, relevant, disturbing, and still capable of taking our breath away.** We who love the Bible will have to learn new styles, new lingos, new steps. If we fail in that, then in its final reduction the Bible will become only a whetstone for the fanatical.

Bibliodrama, then, is a tool for teaching the Bible and for forming a unique kind of learning community. It is to traditional literary and biblical interpretation what avant-garde theater is to the Broadway stage. It is not meant to supplant traditional biblical study any more than the avant-garde seeks to or ever could supplant classical drama. But in a climate where men and women who teach Bible are in need of new equipment to meet new needs, Bibliodrama has its place.

Origins

It evolved from an unlikely seed.

In the spring of 1984 I was invited by Dr. Samuel Klagsbrun to substitute teach a class for him at the Jewish Theological Seminary, where he was on the faculty as professor of pastoral psychiatry. I found this request intimidating and one I could not refuse. It was intimidating because I had at that time no particular Jewish learning whatsoever, and the august Seminary scared me (visions of exposure and ridicule: "Who do you think you are?"). But much as I would have liked to, I could not refuse his request, because Sam was not only my employer; he was my mentor and my friend. His course on leadership, in which he was asking me to teach a single class, was considered by many students an invaluable opportunity to examine the pragmatics of pulpit life.

As nervous as I can ever remember being, I walked into his class at the Seminary that day armed with two skills. I had a Ph.D. in English literature, so I knew I could at least read carefully. And as a trained clinical psychodramatist I had the ability to involve people in a role-playing experience. In that class I brought these two skills together, a shotgun marriage of necessity; I focused on the story of Moses and the struggles he might have felt at different moments in his career. Students selected incidents from the life of Moses that they felt revealed some telling aspect of his leadership; I had them take the part of Moses, speaking in response to my questions as if they were in his shoes.

It was the longest hour of my life. But at the end, much to my surprise, students told me with evident sincerity and enthusiasm how useful and interesting the experience had been both as a way of humanizing a leader of mythic stature and as a way of exploring their own conflicts and concerns.

On this occasion I heard the word "midrash" for the first time. I was told that there was an immensely long tradition of commentary, story-telling, and imaginative interpretation of the Bible called midrash that sought to fill in the gaps in the narrative, address textual contradictions and inconsistencies, and weave in applications to contemporary life. Though until fairly recently a learned and historical enterprise confined to the study of The Midrash, there had developed in modern times an appreciation for midrash as an ongoing and inexhaustible form of biblical interpretation and commentary. There was, I learned—and my reading began to confirm it—something folkloric about midrash. It belonged to a still evolving oral and literary tradition that responded to the Bible in fresh ways. Without knowing it I had stumbled into a conversation with the Bible that had been going on for thousands of years.

From this casual beginning a new phase of my vocational life began. I was invited back to teach another class, again to employ the methods of role-playing to open up dimensions in the biblical narratives. I began to read and to study; I became increasingly caught up in this method of pluralistic and communal interpretive play. One opportunity to teach and learn with others led to another. Over the years, I have been asked to demonstrate this dance between text and drama in synagogues and churches, in seminaries and classrooms, in retreat centers and therapeutic communities. In response to the conditions I found in those places—levels of knowledge, willingness to play, the range of ages and backgrounds, the familiarity with the Bible, the degrees of reverence, observance, openness, and many other variables—I have created Bibliodrama in the form I am describing here.

Scripture Windows: design and format

Scripture Windows is the first attempt to provide a praxis of text-centered or midrashic Bibliodrama for an English speaking audience.[3] I am not by any means its inventor, though the writing of this book may foster that illusion. Bibliodrama already belongs to diverse practitioners working in a wide range of contexts; any attempt to systematize Bibliodrama is bound to be incomplete. And this is as it should be with a medium so inherently creative and so intimately connected to the purposes of those who employ it. As more people try their hands at it and adapt it to their own talents and audiences, the form is likely to evolve in healthy ways. So the subtitle of this book, with its indefinite article, *Toward a Practice of Bibliodrama,* is intended to represent Bibliodrama only as one man's art and one man's scope. Indeed, my own work is changing all the time.[4]

---

[3] For a brief discussion of other forms of Bibliodrama and an attendant bibliography, see Part III, section 3: "Participant-centered Bibliodrama."

[4] Even the orthography of the word requires a note. Used with a small "b", bibliodrama is the application of action methods—psychodrama, drama therapy—to any piece of writing. In its generic form, bibliodrama is used both hermeneutically and as a creative instrument. The first person whom I saw conduct a full scale bibliodrama was my father, Merlyn Pitzele, who directed an exploration of Hamlet at the Moreno Institute in 1980. My first exposure to Bibliodrama—now used with a capital "B" and indicating the application of these same methods to a biblical story—was at the hands of Claire Danielssen, Ph.D., who, in a retreat conducted in Tivoli, New York, in 1981, explored the story of the baptism of Christ.

Well after I had started my own experimentations, which began in 1984, I came across the "Mimesis" work of Sam and Evelyn Laeuchli. In the form in which I saw it,

Scripture Windows **is written with an imagined reader in mind who has seen Bibliodrama and wants to learn more about how it is done.** You, my reader, are reading this book in the hopes of learning more about this multidimensional form, though in this necessarily two-dimensional medium.

You will note that the discussion of Bibliodrama in this book draws its examples entirely from Genesis and Exodus. These stories are shared, albeit differently interpreted, by Jews, Christians, and, in some cases, by Moslems. In drawing my examples from these books I have looked for materials that might interest readers from all three traditions. Most of my practice has been within the Jewish community, so you may notice a Jewish milieu or context for the examples I provide, but Bibliodrama is by no means limited to that context.[5]

Also, you will observe that many of the examples in Part I focus on female figures in the Bible. The reason for that is twofold. In the first place, as two generations of feminist biblical critics have been reminding us, the Bible is dominated by masculine characters. No small part of the work of transforming our relationship to the Bible, feminist readers insist, is to elicit the voices and experiences of women that are hidden or buried in the text. Bibliodrama is, if not a feminist methodology, then a method of

---

Mimesis was not Bibliodrama *per se*, because of its not usually making use of written texts nor serving the ends primarily of textual interpretation. If, however, it was more interested in the self-reflective rather than the interpretive dimension of hermeneutical play, it had a great deal to offer as an example of mythic drama in a contemporary idiom. Later still I read of Arthur Waskow's development of "drashodrama," and I recognized again that there were many people playing experientially with similar materials in similar ways. My own development in this method, as it grew out of my psychodramatic practice, is to be found in my book *Our Fathers' Wells: A Personal Encounter with the Myths of Genesis*, Harper SanFrancisco, 1995. The only book I know of in English that illustrates B/bibliodrama in much of its variety is edited by Bjorn Krondorfer: *Body and Bible: Interpreting and Experiencing Biblical Narratives*, Trinity Press, Philadelphia, 1992.
[5] Twice I have been invited to teach a course at the Union Theological Seminary in New York. There I have engaged students in bibliodramatic explorations of the Gospels. There is, so far as I know, no real tradition of midrash as such in Christianity, though there is a recent book by Bishop John Spong, *Liberating the Gospels: Reading the Bible through Jewish Eyes*, that argues that the gospels are midrashic. If my students at Union are any indication, then there is, at least in some quarters, a recognition of how creative hermeneutics—midrash in everything but name—can help non-dogmatic Christians find a sense of connection to their sacred stories. Bibliodrama has yet to reach an Islamic audience.

interpretation that lends itself to a feminist project, and I want to suggest, at least by a few examples, how that work can be done. In the second place, the long Bibliodrama that occupies Part II of this book pertains to the story of Joseph and is therefore dominated by a male figure. The illustrations in Part I are meant to provide some sense of balance to the book as a whole.

This book is divided into three parts.

Part I, called The Short Form, consists of three chapters. It begins with the ABCs of Bibliodrama and moves to a discussion and illustration of ways of doing Bibliodrama appropriate for the beginner. It introduces a set of concepts and a vocabulary that attempt to give us some shared language for understanding the strategies and methods of this craft. In *Scripture Windows* as a whole and in Part I particularly, I am trying to lay some groundwork for a discipline, to provide numerous examples of Bibliodramas, brief and contained, so that you can grasp the rich, playful possibilities of this work. For many readers interested in ways of getting started quickly, Part I will be an end in itself.

Part II, called The Longer Form, consists of five chapters in which I recount and analyze a Bibliodrama that might last as long as an hour or more. That account is riddled with asides and comments designed to take you into my thinking, my choices, my understanding of the bibliodramatic event.

Part III, The Appendices, contains a working Code of Ethics for bibliodramatists and a series of very brief essays focused on specific issues and concerns.

Two final remarks:

Bibliodrama, or at least this practitioner's version of it, draws inspiration and technique from a variety of disciplines: from psycho-drama, drama therapy, literary theory, feminism, and the mythopoetics of the men's movement. In writing this manual I have felt it necessary to develop some kind of specialized vocabulary in order to call your attention to certain techniques and to the elements of the form. But I am afraid that in coining a language for Bibliodrama I am creating jargon that will distance Bibliodrama from the very people I most hope will find it accessible and useful. In the end I have seen no way around giving some formality to the form, and my fear that I have written the kind of book I might myself be loath to read is one of life's little ironies.

Second, I want to say in the strongest terms that **this book cannot be taken as a substitute for the experience of Bibliodrama nor for a hands-on experience of training and supervision.** *Scripture Windows* **is meant to accompany such experience, not to replace it.** Increasingly, experiential learning opportunities are being made available by me and by others I have taught. At present, however, there is no credentialing of bibliodramatists, so word-of-mouth and your own careful assessment are the best guarantors of quality.

Part I

The Short Form

1

The Vocabulary of Bibliodrama

Text-centered Bibliodrama is a creative and expressive mode of biblical interpretation; it is a kind of dramatic play. Bibliodrama has its parameters, but it also open and adaptive to new audiences and new directions. In different hands the form assumes different shapes. **There is no one right way to conduct it.** At the same time, there is a set of conventions, some of which I am forging, that define this form of biblical exploration. This chapter is intended to provide a general overview of the bibliodramatic event, its tools and terms, and to offer a vocabulary for this practice. In this chapter and in those that follow I provide numerous examples to illustrate the method (and I would encourage you to base some of your own first efforts in directing on any one of them). These examples are based on actual moments in actual Bibliodramas that I have directed over the years.

White Fire

The seeds of a bibliodramatic enactment are to be found in a way of reading the Bible. You read the words on the page, and you read *into* the spaces between the words on the page. This way of reading is the beginning of your journey toward becoming a facilitator of Bibliodrama.

There is a traditional Jewish commentary that talks about the Bible as having been composed in black and white fire. The black fire is seen in the form of the printed or handwritten words on the page or scroll; the white fire is found in the spaces between and around the black. The black fire is fixed for all time; the white fire is forever kindled by fresh encounters between changing times and the unchanging words. The black fire establishes the canonized object we can all see before us; the white spaces represent the endless potential for the fresh interpretation of that object. Bibliodrama takes place in the open spaces of the text for which the black fire, the black letters, are the boundaries.

To prepare yourself to conduct Bibliodrama you must become a student of biblical commentary. This does not mean necessarily that you steep yourself in the study of traditional rabbinic midrash, though for those working in a Jewish context such knowledge will certainly enhance your ability to conduct Bibliodrama in a rich dialogue with the past.[1]

But you must develop a certain kind of interpretive imagination; and you can do that, for example, by reading contemporary feminists whose biblical studies and stories, written in a contemporary, sometimes wonderfully irreverent idiom, open up vistas of possibility.[2]

---

[1] For those like myself who need the classical texts and legends in English, there is *The Midrash*, in multiple volumes and published by Soncino Press in London. There is Louis Ginzberg's collection of stories published in five volumes under the title *Legends of the Jews*, or in one volume, *Legends of the Bible* (both Philadelphia: Jewish Publication Society). See also Bialik & Ravnitzky, eds., *The Book of Legends* (New York: Schocken Books, 1992). I have found useful Rabbi Moshe Weissman's *The Midrash Says* (New York: Benei Yakov Publications, 1980) and David Curzon, ed., *Modern Poems on the Bible, An Anthology* (Philadelphia: Jewish Publication Society, 1994). This list is partial, to say the least.

There is very little Christian "midrash." You can see the midrashic imagination at work in the literary rather than the religious tradition. There are the medieval miracle plays, on the one hand, and *The Last Temptation of Christ*, by Nikos Kazantzakis, on the other. In between you can find Christian midrash from Milton's *Paradise Regained* to the novels of Taylor Caldwell. Film, in explicit and implicit ways, draws on the themes, images, and stories of the biblical tradition. *The Robe* and *He Who Must Die*, to name only two films, contain many penetrating glimpses into biblical character and story.

[2] See for example: Susannah Heschel, ed., *On Being A Jewish Feminist: A Reader* (New York: Schocken Books, 1983); Carol P. Christ and Judith Plaskow, eds., *Womanspirit Rising: A Feminist Reader in Religion* (San Francisco: Harper and

There are also films—from *East of Eden* to *The Ten Commandments*—that rework biblical myths in challenging ways. Wherever you find them, you need examples of how the interpretive imagination has found fuel for the white fire. The purpose of such study is not only to learn from the masters; it is to liberate your own imagination, to give yourself permission to embroider and to embellish the text, to invent new interpretations and inspire others to do the same. Nor is reading in volume always necessary; sometimes a single instance of poetic license is enough to throw open the doors of your own creativity.

I remember reading Lawrence Kushner's book *The River of Light* and coming upon his account of a midrash on the story of Abraham and the three mysterious visitors who come to him before the destruction of Sodom (Genesis 18:7ff). The biblical text tells how Abraham, in the zeal of his hospitality, "ran to the herd, took a calf, tender and choice, and gave it to a servant boy who hastened to prepare it." The traditional interpretive tale Kushner recounts unfolds in the space between the words "ran to the herd" and "took a calf": When Abraham "ran to the herd," he selected a choice calf that then ran away from him. Abraham pursued the animal. The fleeing calf ran into a cave. Abraham followed it there and was drawn into the depths of the cave. At the far end he saw an opening and, looking through it, gazed into the Garden of Eden. In the recess of the cave he saw the burial places of Adam and Eve. Only then was he able to "take" the calf, return to camp, and "give it to his servant boy." Abraham did not forget the place. Later, after the death of Sarah, he haggled with the Hittites for this very plot of ground and purchased it as a place to bury his wife. There he, too, would be buried, and generations to follow him as well. The cave would be called Machpelah.[3]

In recounting this now I can still feel the amazement of my first reading. The visionary and poetic license of this midrash freed me from whatever might have hobbled my own interpretive energies. Through this single window of scriptural interpretation I saw that the country of

Row, 1979); and Alicia Ostriker, *The Nakedness of the Fathers: Biblical Visions and Revisions* (New Brunswick: Rutgers University Press, 1994).

[3] Lawrence Kushner, *The River of Light: Spirituality, Judaism, Consciousness* (Vermont: Jewish Lights Publishing, 1995).

commentary was vast, anonymous, democratic, and inexhaustible. There I could join an endeavor of explication and discovery that had been in progress for thousands of years. Profound readers had been there before me; many of their achievements were in the record books; but the field welcomed new discoveries. As Abraham Joshuah Heschel wrote of the Bible, in words I quoted as the epigraph for this book: *"More than two thousand years of reading and research have not succeeded in exploring its full meaning. Today it is as if it had never been touched, never been seen, as if we had not even begun to read it.*

Reading creative interpretations of biblical texts permitted me my own creative response to the same material. I did not need to be a learned scholar or a sophisticated literary critic. Many of the interpretations to which I was drawn in my reading and which I was helping to create in Bibliodrama had the quality of folklore; they were based on engaging and human ways of asking and answering questions about the Bible, and even a child could do that. (I was to discover through Bibliodrama that children sometimes asked and answered questions more piercingly than adults.) For all the time I had put in as a sometime professor of literature, I had never been invited to create with the creator. I could tell you a lot about *Hamlet*, but no one ever suggested that a legitimate form of Shakespearean commentary might be to write my own soliloquy. Yet here was the Bible, a text more sacred than Shakespeare, and there existed a tradition of interpretation that sanctioned a participatory creativity.

It is, then, with the ability to read creatively that Bibliodrama begins. It begins in the mind of a reader who discovers what the biblical stories leave out, the gaps and the spaces in the tales, and who imagines ways they might be filled.

What actually occurs when you begin to read in this way is that your reading slows down. You begin to see each verb and predicate as a cinematographer might see them. You become aware of the ways you are unconsciously filling in detail the narrative itself does not specify. You begin to imagine various different ways that filling in might be done. You start to ask questions about the gaps and spaces so that you can become aware of the interpretive possibilities they provide.

For example, take the following verse:

WHEN THE WOMAN SAW THAT THE TREE WAS GOOD
FOR EATING AND A DELIGHT TO THE EYES, AND THAT
THE TREE WAS DESIRABLE AS A SOURCE OF WISDOM, SHE
TOOK OF ITS FRUIT AND ATE. SHE ALSO GAVE SOME
TO HER HUSBAND, AND HE ATE. (Genesis 3:6)

As I slow my reading down I am immediately aware that the verb "took" does not tell me *how* she took: Quickly? Carefully? Snatchingly? Furtively? Slyly? Eagerly? Wonderingly? etc. Each adverb inflects the verb and thus characterizes the action and the actor. The verb "ate" is similarly without a modifier. Having taken, how does woman eat? Does she weigh the heft of the fruit in her hand? Bring it to her nose to smell? Lick its skin? Nibble? Bite deeply and consume the entire fruit? Pick a fresh piece for Adam? And what about the space between "ate" and "gave"? Where is Adam? How long does it take her to find or reach him? Does she simply and wordlessly hold out the fruit to Adam, who, in a moment, takes it and eats? Is there a conversation between the two of them? What might it be? As you zoom in on the scene you supply detail upon detail; you begin to tell a story within the written story. The white fire begins to burn. To imagine this scene in all its particularity is to realize how much the biblical narrative leaves out.

For many readers of the Bible these kinds of questions are novel; for some they may seem heretical. Depending on your religious orientation as well as your religious education, you may be utterly unused to thinking this way about the Bible. Where might such ways of imagining not go? That way blasphemy lies.

In answer to such concerns I can only point to the remarkable legacies of interpretation that challenge normative, naïve, and simplistic responses to the Bible and point us to deeper and more complex possibilities. We may be delighted as well as surprised to discover that the Bible can retain its power as a sacred book not because its authority is never questioned, but because the questions it raises have the authority to lead us to some of the most important issues of our lives. The story of Eve's eating the fruit is, after all, a story in which the themes of temptation, disobedience, and courage are all woven together. Surely we know these issues in our own lives, and perhaps can better understand ourselves as we imagine a drama for Eve.

The Move from Commentary to Bibliodrama

Most forms of commentary are ways of talking *about* the biblical text. Those ways may be literary, historical, theological, etc., but what characterizes all of them is that the first person singular—the speaker whose words we hear on the page or in the classroom or in the sanctuary—remains outside of the literary object. He or she walks around the biblical text, commenting, analyzing, speculating. The relationship is *I* to *It*. The object is mute; it has no voice other than that with which it has already spoken. **In Bibliodrama, on the other hand, I confront the work as an *I* to a *Thou*.** Our fundamental hypothesis is that the biblical narrative has more life in it, more voice in it than is captured by the words on the page. I, the reader, meet the biblical narrative as if I were meeting a living being. I speak to the images and characters in the Bible in an unmediated address. The questions that I ask of the text I ask as if the text could answer me back directly in its own voice. **The move from commentary to Bibliodrama occurs when the text is given a voice and answers me back.** This answering occurs when I, as reader, step into the story; I *become* the biblical character, speaking *as* that character, not *about* him or her. I imagine and tell his or her story as if it were my own. **In Bibliodrama, passive readers becomes active players; we assume roles.**

Voicing: Bibliodrama presumes a dimensionality in biblical characters and events, a depth beyond what is written. It treats Bible as a living history, a human story. In Bibliodrama the story is still being lived; the future of its characters is still unknown. If I want to know more about a biblical character, or even a biblical image or object, I can address it with my questions. I can then play the role of the biblical character and respond to those questions. In this role-play, the character or the image questioned now has the ability to use my voice (or, in a group, the voice of another participant) for response.

The technical term *voicing* will be used in this book to describe

the act of speaking in the first person singular, in the role of a biblical character or object. Voicing is a form of role-playing. Like all dramatic presentations, voicing takes place in the immediate present: The character is speaking here and now.

Underpinning all bibliodramatic play is this simple formula: The readers go into role (by voicing or acting) and become players, and the story unfolds in the present tense. The primary task of the facilitator is to help people stay in role and to keep them speaking in an unfolding present.

For example, all the questions I proposed above concerning Eve's eating of the fruit and giving it to Adam and then his eating of it could be answered in an indirect and speculative fashion: "I think Eve snatched the fruit off the tree and bit into it in a furtive way." *Or* "I think woman really savored this moment. She looked over the tree to find a really choice-looking piece of fruit, gently twisted it off its stem, brought it to her nose to smell, to her cheek to feel, to her tongue to lick. Having decided to eat it, she was now in no hurry and prolonged the pleasure. Perhaps she still felt a little afraid, and so her finickiness was both dalliance and delay." *Or* "I think Adam was watching the woman from behind the bushes. As soon as she ate, he was there with his hand out." *And so forth.*

As imaginative and insightful as these responses may be, they are not bibliodramatic, or at least they are not couched in bibliodramatic terms; they are indirect. The interpreter is not in role, and the story is not in the present tense. The reader's *I/eye* still stands outside the story looking at it as something that happened in the past. But once the same questions are answered in the present tense and answered as a form of dramatic soliloquy, as *voicing,* then Bibliodrama occurs.

For example,

I listened to the serpent. I thought for a while. I went away and returned to the tree many times. Each time I went away and came back I was that much closer to touching, to plucking, to tasting, to eating. I could see the whole sequence in my mind, though I could never imagine the effect. Then finally one evening, just as the sun was setting, I did it...

Even in the writing (writing as voicing) of this little dramatic monologue I found myself taken by the voicing to places I had never been before in all my thinking *about* this moment. The time of day, for example, came unbidden from my impersonation, and in my written role-play I realized how, as Eve, I wanted the coming darkness to shield me, shield me from God, perhaps. I wanted to go to Adam half-hidden.

This example may for a moment puzzle the reader who is looking for the two minimal criteria for Bibliodrama: character in role, story told in the present tense. Here we have a character in role, but the tense is past. Yet we are in the present, for we are in the presence of an Eve who is alive, remembering. One question we may always ask is "So, Eve, you are looking back on these events. How do you feel about them *now?*" Though Eve has been narrating what she did, we can always find her in the present, for her *tone* is present. In this tone we might hear her feelings of regret or shame; she might tell us of the rekindling of her excitement; she might speak of feeling nostalgic or defiant. No matter how filled with the past, spoken memory takes place in the present.

Take another example: the moment where we read of God fashioning woman from the rib of the sleeping Adam:

> So the Lord God cast a deep sleep upon the man; and while he slept, He took one of his ribs and closed up the flesh at that spot. And the Lord God fashioned the rib that He had taken from the man into a woman; and He brought her to the man. (Genesis 2:21-23)

Again, as we read in a slower mode the spaces appear. Where are we? Did Adam dream in this deep sleep? If so, what might he have dreamed? In that moment of her first creation, is woman awake beside the sleeping Adam? If so, what might that moment be like for her? We note that she is "brought" *to* Adam. Where *from?* And what is the moment of their first meeting like for each? All these questions can be the basis for Bibliodrama.

As I begin to read this incident bibliodramatically, I take this newly created woman's point of view. In doing so I endow her with a fuller measure of consciousness than she has explicitly at that moment in the story. I bring her alive in a present moment. *Tell me, Eve, what is this experience of birth like for you?*

> I am Eve...no, not yet, not yet Eve. I don't have that name. That
> name will be given to me by someone or something else. No. Now
> I simply am. I hum with a sense of myself interfused outside and
> inside. I am the sound of my blood circulating in my body and the
> song of the birds over my head. I am the feel of the air on my skin
> and the feeling of joy in my heart. I am the taste of breath in my
> mouth and the pervading sense of my own awareness. I am the
> scents of this fragrant garden and the aroma of my own pores...

In this fragment of a soliloquy I have given myself permission to
use my imagination as a means of entering the text and the figure of the
woman within it. I become for a moment not merely a reader-critic but a
reader-creator. In the most intimate way I join myself with the imagination of the Bible, let myself be led by it to new forms of insight.

**Bibliodrama is an extension of literary interpretation in the direc-
tion of an original and dramatic creativity.** Like other forms of literary
analysis, it respects the closed nature of the biblical text; the words in the
Bible are canonized and immutable; the black fire cannot be modified. But
in the spirit of midrash it searches for sub-stories and voices within that
existing text; it plays with narrative inconsistencies, unanswered questions,
puzzling juxtapositions. It plays with white fire. Bibliodrama licenses
fresh invention and original storytelling, placing these in the service of
illuminating the text.

In a playful way we might ask the Eve-on-the-page to tell us what
it has been like for her to be bibliodramatized. She might say something
like this:

> Wow! As a character frozen in the narrative tableau, I suddenly
> feel you imagining a story within my story. I am not alone
> any longer.
>
> I am given a voice where I have been frozen by the canonized
> tale into silence. I feel in some ways rescued, seen, given new life.
> Nothing can change the words of my fate. I cannot revise the set of
> events in which I am contained. But my experience of my condition
> may be given a voice. Through you, and only through you as my
> alter ego, can I be heard in this way, as a living being. You can tell

the ways I feel within my fate. You may even imagine alternative fates for me—a friendship with Lilith, a conversation with God—played out as fantasies that can never be transposed into the changeless shape of the story. Only with you, my bibliodramatic reader can I wake to these possibilities.

Redefining Familiar Terms

The vocabulary of Bibliodrama is borrowed in part from the theater; in part it is borrowed from psychodrama; and in part it is my own coinage. For most people, terms like stage, player, audience, action, role, etc., conjure up the kind of theater for which we buy tickets and then sit in an anonymous and passive assembly. The very word "theater" refers both to dramatic production and the building within which such production is housed; so to think accurately of Bibliodrama as a kind of theater requires some redefinition of terms. In a somewhat schematic way, I want to provide those bibliodramatic definitions now.

Stage: I will use the term **stage** repeatedly in this book, but the word does not mean the same thing it does on Broadway. In scripted theater the stage is usually raised above and separated from the audience. In non-scripted theater, of which Bibliodrama is a part, there is no such formal theatrical environment. The bibliodramatic stage may be anywhere: in the front of a room, in the middle of a circle of seated onlookers. At times the group and its entire space become the playing space or stage.

The entire space may become a stage because Bibliodrama dissolves the clear or absolute boundary between audience and actor. With certain contemporary exceptions, most plays leave the audience in their seats; no one paying money to go to the theater expects to act onstage. But in some forms of improvisational theater, and especially in Bibliodrama, the players are drawn from those who attend, though attending does not require acting. This kind of theater is designed to shift a person from observer to participant and back again. At one moment you may be sitting as an audience member—with all the comfortable anonymity that provides—and in the next moment you may be invited to be an actor who has a voice and interacts with others in spontaneous ways. The sense of risk for all involved is greater in improvisational drama, in Bibliodrama, since the participants are not trained performers and do not have the benefit of a script. Concomitantly, the task of the director is complex; he or she must be supportive, must coach and encourage the players as much as shape the action and develop the plot. As hard as it is to be an actor without a script, it may be even harder to be the director, for you have an ensemble to look after and the sense of a dramatic and aesthetic whole to manage.

Actor: So the term **actor**, which has such a clear meaning in formal theater, loses its distinctiveness in Bibliodrama. I like the word "participant" as well as actor (I use the terms interchangeably) because it has in it the word "part," a theatrical term. Those who attend a Bibliodrama are potential participants, and they may play a part in any number of ways. There is, as I will make clear later, a range of participatory possibilities, from involvement from your seat within the audience-group to getting up on "stage."

Script: As I have already indicated, there is no **script** for Bibliodrama. Or, to put it more precisely, the script derives from Scripture, and the performance is built upon its foundation. That performance, being improvisational, is made up of some combination of the life experiences of the participants, a collective reading of the text, the interactions of the players with one another in action, and the choices of the director or facilitator in orchestrating the play. The story will never be the same twice. There would be, even if it were transcribed, no invariable script, only a version that came into being out of the particular interplay of group, text, director, and the moment of production.

Director: The Bibliodrama has its **director**. The director's competence will be based on skills of study and preparation, and on the experience and practice of improvisational play. Whether good directors are born or made is an open question. Probably a bit of both. But the mix of skills is unique and a little daunting to the beginner. With time and practice a good director learns to play many parts: scholar, gypsy, actor, poet, therapist, humorist, actor, raconteur, and dramaturge. There is even a shamanic potential in the role when the director guides participants deep into the inner worlds of biblical archetype.

The Bibliodramatic Form

Though Bibliodrama may take many shapes, it is not without a few formal principles, a few distinguishing methods. I begin here with an overview of the structure of the bibliodramatic event in its text-centered form. This form should be followed whether the Bibliodrama lasts a few minutes or runs over an hour.

Bibliodrama is composed of three parts: the warm-up; the action; and the review.

1. The Warm-up: I will use the term **warm-up** in this book to refer to the part of Bibliodrama that precedes the action. It begins when you first take up the Bible in the privacy of your study, and it ends when the group with whom you are conducting a Bibliodrama starts to assume roles. At that point the action of the Bibliodrama begins.

In the first phase of the bibliodramatic warm-up you warm up to your role as facilitator or director.[4]

You quarry a narrative block from the Bible. You begin to size up the possibilities for bibliodramatic interpretation embedded in it. **The**

---

[4] In the interests of clarity, I keep the distinction clear here at the outset but will use the terms almost interchangeably as I go on. By "facilitator" I mean to designate a person with a lesser degree of skillfulness or ambition in handling group dynamics or emotion-laden materials. The facilitator is a relative novice who prudently does not try to do too much, who does not select stories with too strong an element of grief or rage implicit in them, who does not try to sustain a drama for too long a duration, and who does not probe too deeply into the affective layers of the role-playing. The "director," on the other hand, is some- one more fully trained and practiced in both the theatrical and the therapeutic dimensions of Bibliodrama. Such a person will often have formal training in psychodrama or drama therapy. At this point, and for the opening moves that follow, the term facilitator—one who makes things go easily—is appropriate.

warm-up covers the development of some kind of game plan, a list of questions, a sense of order and agenda. What will you read? What will you tell? What will you play? Along the way you may study commentaries. You engage in a cognitive and exegetical process (an apprenticeship to the black fire) that kindles an imaginative process (an envisioning of the white). You are measuring your anxiety and doing what you can to allay it. You are talking to friends; you are bouncing ideas off of colleagues; you may read or write in a journal or in other ways prepare yourself for the work. Unlike the conventional director, you have no script beyond the text itself to study, so you cannot block scenes in anything but a preliminary way; you cannot rehearse actors. More in the spirit of the dancer or athlete, your warming-up is a kind of psycho-physical process (thinking, reading, pacing, writing, talking) in which you limber and prepare your imagination to engage in this work. (See Part II, chapter 1 for a fuller account of these stages of text selection and preparation.)

The warm-up then carries forward toward its **second phase.** Now you begin thinking about the specific group you are hoping to engage. You give consideration to time constraints that will in part shape what you can do. You survey the limitations and possibilities of the space you will be working in—sanctuary, classroom, social hall, home, or out of doors.

The second phase of the warm-up formally begins when the facilitator enters the playing space and actually meets the group. Now your task is, on one level, to transform an audience into a group, to break down the passive expectations of theater or the right answer/wrong answer mind-set of the classroom, and to open people up to the participatory possibilities of Bibliodrama. You orient people to what you are doing, sketch out the rules of the game, allay certain fears about participation *(no one has to participate; you can always decline, can always simply observe)*. You may talk about yourself if you wish, tell a story if you wish. In short, you do whatever you need to do to let the group see you in a new role (as a bibliodramatist, though you do not need to use the term) and to begin to get comfortable with the idea of being in a new role themselves (creative players rather than students). **The second phase of the director's warm-up blends into and becomes the warm-up of the group.** (See Part II, chapter 2, for more detail about the warm-up process.)

2. The Action: The **action** phase begins when a member of the group first gives voice to a biblical character. Voicing *is* role-playing.

It is important to understand that "action" may involve no action in the usual theatrical sense of gesture and formal, rehearsed movement. When participants, sitting in their seats, simply speak as if they were characters in the Bible, they are, for definitional purposes, in action. Even when participants do not move from their seats—do not get up and gesture, move, and in other ways "act"—they are even by slight changes of posture or position, by facial expression, by tones of voice, *acting* bibliodramatically. They are in role, and from this it follows that everything they do can be seen as bibliodramatic acting, as interpretation. As facilitator you need to see them as actors and to view their gestures and words as parts of their renderings of the text, as ways of giving meaning and sense to the story. You need to help them be convinced of, as well as convincing in, their parts. You need to remember they are amateurs and improvisers who need your support and guidance.

Action, as gesture and movement, may both accompany the verbal and be, in some cases, an end in itself. Though text-centered Bibliodrama places a primary emphasis on voicing, on verbal interpretations, on soliloquy and spoken encounter, there is an important place in it for the body. Even by its smallest motions the body can discover and present interpretive insights. Downcast eyes, a foot tapping nervously on the floor, a hand turned palm up: all these are gestures that may be worth their weight in words. The more open people are to using their bodies in expressive ways, the livelier the Bibliodrama. Thus "action" may comprehend a wide range of possibilities.[5]

At a certain point the action is over. The time you allotted for the action phase of the Bibliodrama is up, or the passage you set out to explore

---

[5] There are a number of dancers and performance artists who are experimenting with motion and music as forms of midrash. Hardly more than a partial list, the following come immediately to mind. Dancers and choreographers: JoAnne Tucker, Liz Lerman, and Miriam Minkoff. Musicians and composers: Elizabeth Swados, Margot Stein, Gila Rayzel Raphael, and Judy Fried. Performance artists: Shawn Zevitt, Rob Huffer, and Deborah Baer Mozes. And among the poets and writers, to name only two: Alicia Ostriker and Marge Piercey.

has been covered. In some way—and I will have suggestions for how later in the book (Part III, Chapter 6)—you bring the action phase to a close. You let a curtain fall. You are ready then for the final part of Bibliodrama.

3. Reviewing: **Reviewing** refers to everything that happens from

the end of the action phase through the closure of the bibliodramatic event. During the review participants should be discouraged from speaking any further in role; by definition, to speak in role would be to go back into action. Time must always be reserved at the end of the bibliodramatic process for reviewing. Just as the warm-up is the bridge from our usual ways of talking to one another and about the Bible to a bibliodramatic mode, so reviewing is the bridge from bibliodramatic speech and play back to our ordinary (non-roleplaying) modes of speaking to one another and about the biblical story. Depending on the depth and duration of the action phase, reviewing may require that a strong shift in tone and mood be made in order to put behind us the realm of our make-believe and return us solidly to our ordinary identities.

Reviewing must begin with de-roling but after that need follow no particular formal sequence but often contains the following five elements: (a) de-roling, (b) sharing, (c) exegesis, (d) consulting other sources, and (e) processing.

De-Roling: In **de-roling** the facilitator helps people who have been

playing parts get out of their roles. Often very little is needed to accomplish this. Sometimes, if the role-playing has been intense or protracted, people need a chance to "shake out" the performance part and to be reminded of who they are in the here and now.

Sharing: In **sharing** the facilitator helps participants talk about

what it was like for them to play certain parts, what they might have felt in the playing, what they might have seen about themselves. In sharing, a person always talks about him or herself, not about anyone else; otherwise sharing might take on an intrusive or critical quality.

Exegesis: **Exegesis** can be part of the review when you, as the

teacher, wish to connect the bibliodramatic work to the meaning of the text you are working with. Bibliodrama can serve more traditional methods of explication. When, in the reviewing phase, you emphasize the Bibliodrama as commentary, you resume your role as teacher rather than director, and the group naturally moves from the role of players back to that of students.

Consulting Other Sources: It becomes very interesting to consult **other sources** after having engaged in Bibliodrama because often the play will have anticipated the insights of the masters or given them a fresh twist. We are often in a better position to appreciate traditional commentary when we have made our own. By consulting other sources you give the group the chance to recognize their participation in a millennial conversation about text and meaning.

Processing: **Processing** refers to the option of talking about the way the Bibliodrama was conducted. Often, as facilitator, you are making choices about what directions you will take; sometimes a class will want to ask you why you chose to concentrate on one character rather than another, why you explored one set of interpretive possibilities over others. Or players, now out of role, may want to talk about what it was like to act in this improvisational form, the energy they felt among them, the excitement, the questions this kind of interplay can evoke. Or, because there is an artistic quality to Bibliodrama, people may want to discuss point of technique, talent, or beauty. Processing is even more important for a group of people in training to learn facilitation skills. Processing gives them a chance to break down the bibliodramatic event and to understand the craft of the work.

Bibliodrama: The Tools

No props or devices are needed to accomplish the bibliodramatic illusion. However, there are a number of tools that can help the would-be director get people more engaged in the action.

The only physical props I consistently use are **empty chairs;** these can be employed to concretize an idea, to block a scene, or to symbolize an internal state. Another tool involves the use of the director's verbal skills in a technique I call **echoing.** In echoing you, as the director, use your voice to elaborate what the players say and help them sustain and deepen their role-playing. And a third tool is **doubling,** a method by which more than one person can develop a biblical character at the same time. My purpose here is simply to identify these devices briefly with a few examples. Later they will be illustrated in the context of both short and longer descriptions of Bibliodramas.

1. Empty Chairs: The use of empty chairs can focus a group and concretize a situation in all phases of the bibliodramatic event. The "empty chair" may not be an indispensable part of every bibliodramatist's arsenal, but it is certainly essential to my own style of direction.

As the director you face your group or class or congregation. Let's say that as part of your warm-up with them you want to explain what Bibliodrama is. You set out two empty chairs, placing one behind the other. "This first chair," you explain, "represents the words on the page. We can all see them; we all agree on what those words are. This second chair"—now pointing to the chair concealed behind the first—"represents all that these words can mean and allude to, all the things that these words open up and invite us to imagine or speculate about. Here"—positioning yourself beside the second chair and patting it with your hand—"here we find the subtexts and the undeveloped dimensions of the story that we can explore in action. This second chair is the realm in which Bibliodrama takes place."

Or, as director, you want to develop various dimensions of a single biblical character....

Let's say the group is exploring Eve and Adam as they depart from the Garden of Eden (Genesis 3:24). The group has explored Eve as she presented herself in exultation, in fear, and in regret, but you feel there is another side to Eve in this moment. You place a chair in front of the group and say, "This chair represents all that we have heard about and from Eve so far, but I wonder"—and here you place a second chair behind the first—"if there might be something still missing. I wonder if someone would come here and sit in this second chair and find Eve's anger, or her shame, her guilt, or her sense of betrayal."

In this second instance **the empty chair serves both to concretize a dimension of the character and to provide a staging point for its expression.** Using the chairs also cleanly demarcates the playing space from the group space, the stage from the audience. In coming to sit in the chair a person moves from audience to participant, from self to role; and then, returning to her seat, that person steps out of the role and becomes part of the audience again.

Empty chairs can be used to block a scene before people actively play the parts. For example, in a scene from the time when Adam, Eve, Cain, and Abel lived together before the murder of Abel...

Four chairs can be brought out onto the playing space to stand for each of the actors in this drama. You and the group can play with the relationships between the characters. Simply by their arrangement—the corners of a square, or two chairs side by side facing two chairs side by side, or three chairs together with one off alone, or four chairs in a square but all facing out—the chairs tell a story. Once the chairs are arranged and set, their positions help the players warm up to the parts. When they come to sit in the chairs and assume the roles of Eve, Adam, Abel, and Cain, something is already determined by the blocking of the scene that will hint at unspoken feelings, alliances, and oppositions. Used in this way, the chairs suggest an interpretive direction for the scene and give the players some information and hints to warm them up to action. Of course, rearrange the chairs and new bibliodramatic interpretations present themselves.

As we all know, chairs are, by their nature, stationary; the performance possibilities for someone seated upon them are limited. To sit in a chair placed in the "playing space" within a group may seem at first not so very different from sitting in your seat in the group-audience. The difference can be crucial, however, because the chair in the playing space is often a platform of sorts, helping people move from voicing a part—which they have been doing while seated in the group—to enacting a part in motion and gesture on the bibliodramatic stage. The chair is a safe place on stage that initially requires no "performing" and no performance skills to occupy. As a director, you will find that persuading players to leave the safety of their seats in the audience and move to an empty chair up front is far easier than getting them directly to their feet and into spontaneous and more expressive action on the stage. **The empty chair can be the launching point for a more physically enacted drama.**

2. Echoing: Very often at the beginning of a bibliodramatic exercise participants are shy and slow to enter into action. No matter how well you have conducted the warm-up, people feel a little intimidated at the challenge of calling upon their spontaneity and voicing the roles. Their shyness is seen in their silence or in the brief responses given to your questions. Their voicings may be terse and tentative at first. Sometimes they fall out of role, and you, as the director, can almost hear the hiss of the energy escaping through the cracks in their partial participation. **The technique of echoing helps the facilitator to engage players more fully in the voicing of their parts.**

Let me illustrate echoing first by an example.

My text is the familiar scene in which Eve, having eaten the apple, prepares to bring it to Adam. I am interested in what occurs just before the Bible tells us that "SHE GAVE IT TO HIM AND HE DID EAT" (Genesis 3:6).

In our warm-up we have retold the story up to this point. We have talked about the geography of the scene, discussed the conversation with the serpent. Now comes the moment when I wish to move the group from their warm-up into action, from discussion to **voicing**.

"So," I say, "here you are, Eve. You can all be Eve at this moment (we'll call you Eve though in fact you don't really have your name yet). You have plucked and eaten the fruit and you have a piece—*the piece?*—in your hand, and you are on your way to Adam. I can only imagine what might be going on inside of you. But I wonder, could you take us back a moment and recall what happened after you ate the fruit? What was it like? How did you feel? How did it taste?"

Reading this, you can see how I have summed up the moment, decided the specific point of entry into the Bibliodrama, and cast the entire group as Eve. Anyone can speak. At the same time you will notice that I am beginning this drama in the past tense. Recalling something is a more distanced modality than experiencing it in the present moment. Here I am using recollection to warm people up to the moment when Eve actually has the fruit in her hand and is on her way to Adam. That is the present I am aiming for.

Silence greets my invitation. It is important for the director to be able to wait. Sometimes this is the hardest thing to do. But in the silence people are struggling with this unfamiliar assignment. At last a few—usually only a few in the beginning—decide to venture. Seeing an upraised hand or two, I might repeat my final question: "How did it taste?"

I recognize a participant. "Good," she says.

I say, **echoing**: "It tasted very good. It tasted as good as it looked." Pause.

"Better," says this participant, with a mischievous smile. I nod. "Yummm," I say, echoing. "Anyone else?"

Another hand is raised; I recognize this person, a man: "Actually, it tasted very different from the way it looked. It was hot, spicy, I guess."

I say, **echoing**, "I was a little surprised. I thought it would be sweet, but it burned my mouth a little."

"Yes," the same person says, "I felt a little frightened. It was strong tasting. Dangerous. I wanted something to drink. Maybe water."

"Thank you," I say. ("Thank you" tends to be my style of marking the transition from one player's contribution to the next. The tone is never dismissive, but genuinely appreciative. No one knows better than the director how much s/he depends on the willingness of the participants to venture into play.) Pause. Another hand goes up. "Yes?"

"It was actually rotten inside. You know, like an apple that looks so red and sweet, and then you bite into it and it's mushy and brown."

I say, **echoing**, "I was almost sickened by it. I didn't eat another bite. I felt like I'd been fooled."

Picking up on my echoing, the participant elaborates. "I thought this garden was good and that everything in it was good and safe. I guess I was wrong." "Yes," I say **echoing**, "I felt betrayed. This was the first time that something was different from the way it seemed. Until this moment appearance and reality had been unquestionably one."

Then spontaneously from the group someone says, "No sooner did

I eat it than I wished I hadn't done it. I did feel a little sick. I knew I had done wrong. I had done evil." I do not need to echo here; the response has its own fullness.

"I was scared," says someone else.

In order to get this person to amplify a little, I **echo** her words and then lead her a little. "I was afraid," (I **echo**) "because..." (I **lead**).

"Because God will be mad."

I say, echoing, "As soon as I eat the fruit I feel afraid. I know God must be watching me, and I know I have done something wrong."

If you examine these echoing responses, you will note at least two things about them. One, in echoing the director actually goes into role with the role-player. I think of this move as siding with the participant for a moment. And two, in echoing the director extends and deepens the role-player's response. The art of echoing has to do with how well the director is able to match the voicing of a participant, then give it an inflection of feeling that takes the player's expression to another level. But it is important that the director do this without taking the role away from the player but rather that he give it back heightened and clarified. You want the role-player to feel that you really get what s/he is saying, but not that you could have done it better and that s/he is unnecessary.

Rarely does a player remark on my echoing. Occasionally someone will ask, "Who are you?" genuinely confused for a moment by my ventriloquy. At such moments I say something like this: "I am only making sure I heard you. I'm stepping into the role with you for a moment." That seems quite sufficient.

There are other times, however, when the question "Who are you?" is the expression of annoyance; players may feel that I am trying to take over their parts, or they feel bothered by my appearing to have to change their words. When confronted by this kind of recoil from my echoing, I cease doing it—not in all cases, but whenever I feel it is not welcome.

All through this account I am aware of what is not getting through in the transcription. It cannot be obvious in reading this account how much the participants find echoing supportive. Through the coaxing and coaching quality of echoing players gain confidence, feel heard, take risks, and entertain more fully their own glimpses of the character. It is important to remember that participants begin the bibliodramatic game without a sure sense of the rules and without any clear sense of my role. They often come from the world of right answer/wrong answer, and echoing often serves to clarify for them what my initial role is here. One of the things they are learning is that I appear to have no agenda except to draw them out further in this form of play. I accept whatever they say. I attempt to hear what they most mean to say and help them say it better while in role. I join them. **Echoing is, in effect, a moment in which I play their role with them, and by joining I lend my voice, my interest, to their performance.**

I said a moment ago that I appear to have no agenda beyond drawing the players out further into play. This matter of agenda is complex and needs a few more words.

Because in the work I do I am interested primarily in demonstrating the methodology of Bibliodrama and its power to generate new insights into the Bible, I do not usually have an agenda beyond the technique itself. My goals are for the process to work, and what I most want to hear from participants afterward is that they feel they will never read the Bible the same way again. Mission accomplished. However, educators and men and women of the pulpit are not always so free; they are often interested in using the method to teach something. They may indeed have agendas, moral, spiritual, or didactic. They may have themes and topics they are using Bibliodrama to illustrate. Yet even in those cases facilitators must find ways of being supportive to tentative participants. Too strong or pointed an agenda will have the effect of making people feel they should be looking for right answers rather than entertaining the responses, the feeling-insights, that spring to mind. Just how you negotiate between the freedom of the form and the point of the lesson will come with practice, but I warn you against trying to use the form too didactically. People may feel like puppets rather than players.

Let's return now to the scene as it moves on.

A participant has just said the fruit was actually "rotten inside." It had looked inviting, but it was not. **Echoing,** I had said, "I felt I'd been fooled."

"Yes," says the same person, "I feel exposed and alone and afraid. My first thought is 'Adam.'"

Here I feel no need to echo. There is a certain gathering of energy noticeable in the lengthening of people's responses, the inclusion of references to feelings, the imaginative detail. I can feel us entering into the story, and echoing has served to propel us gently forward. Quite naturally, without any prompting from me, we are in the present tense.

"Yes," I say to the group as our playing of the scene now moves toward the encounter with Adam, "tell me, Eve, why are you going to Adam? Why don't you keep this little secret all to yourself?"

"I want him in this with me."

Echoing, "I want him in this with me because…"?

"Because if something bad happens, I want it to happen to both of us."

Echoing, "I don't want to be in this one alone."

"Hell, no," says another participant. "Face it, this is like getting high. I can already feel it, and it's much more fun to do it with someone." No echoing needed, the level of spontaneity is delightful.

"For a while I don't know what to do," says another participant.

Echoing, "Yes, I'm confused. On the one hand…"

"Yeah, on the one hand I feel all sorts of things stirring in me, pleasure, and knowledge, and guilt, and fear, and a new way of seeing the world."

"On the other hand…" I prompt.

"On the other hand I have done something I have been told—at least by Adam and through him by God—will have mortal consequences. It's fatal. And for the first time I understand that I will die. Maybe not right away, but I understand now that I will not live forever as I would have done before I ate."

"So I feel…", leading, leaving open the space.

"I feel a huge sense of responsibility, I guess. I mean, is it right to involve Adam? What I did, I did; I have only myself to hold accountable. But to give it to Adam…well, wouldn't that be a kind of murder?"

With a little coaching and support the Bibliodrama is now well launched. There are already many strands to follow. Managing all these different interpretations isn't easy, and managing them skillfully takes practice; but even if, in the hands of an amateur, the process becomes somewhat chaotic, the text has already begun to open before our eyes. We are doing Bibliodrama together, and echoing has helped make that happen.

In many ways, echoing is simply an extension of the art of listening. To echo well you have to listen well, not just to what is being said, but also what is being implied in a player's voicing of a part. I have pointed out how the director speaks *as* the player, not *to* him or her. This is critical. **Echoing is the repetition of an actor's words enhanced by the creative insight of the director.** If I were to use empty chairs to demonstrate echoing (to use one technique in the service of another), I would place one behind the other. In the first chair are the words I hear from the participant; in the second chair are the feelings and thoughts I imagine might lie behind those words. In echoing I give voice to the participant's second chair, or I lead the participant toward a fuller voicing of the part.

You have also noted, I am sure, that echoing often makes use of a prompt word or an incomplete sentence that the participant then finishes. For example, when one participant said, as Eve, that she felt "scared," I echoed, "Scared" with the added prompt word "because..." as an invitation to further elaboration. I am encouraging the participant to fill in the blank and step further into imagining, in this case, the cause of Eve's fear.

Sometimes, of course, my echoing turns out to be wrong. My sense of the unexpressed meaning does not coincide with what players meant. When that happens players will almost always correct me, and that correction can serve to get them a little bit clearer about what they were trying to say or help them elaborate what they first said. On the other hand, **echoing is not always essential to the Bibliodrama nor appropriate for every player.** It is a skill that takes practice, and you should know that you can conduct a lively and valuable bibliodramatic experience without any echoing or with very little of it.

Voicing and echoing often go hand in hand. For that reason, echoing is usually most useful at the beginning of a Bibliodrama or as part of the opening of a new scene. Echoing helps people warm up further into action. In fact, at this early point in the Bibliodrama the process seems to consist of a series of interchanges between the director and each participant, rather than dialogue that flows between participants. That kind of dialogue usually develops later in the action phase of this work, when people are more fully warmed up, when participants have invested themselves more deeply in roles and are willing to play them out in a scene.

At such times you can step aside and let the action flow spontaneously.

3. Doubling: Though the timing and management of the technique called doubling take some practice, doubling itself is easily explained. Think back to the Bibliodrama scene in which Eve gave Adam the apple. The Bibliodrama involved an exploration of Eve's state of mind in that moment, and rather than inviting people to role-play other biblical figures—Adam, God, the serpent, the attendant cherubim—I let Eve alone hold our attention. Without naming it at that point, I was illustrating doubling. In doubling the director does not move the Bibliodrama either in the direction of various interactions among characters or toward the development of a single coherent characterization; s/he stops time and allows variations to be presented.

Doubling is a way to get two or more voicings and versions of a character in play at a single dramatic moment. One of its great virtues is the way it allows observers to become participants, if only for a single line; in these short chimings-in, so to speak, people who might not be ready for a more demanding level of role-playing are able to sample and support the process.

Doubling is an option you as the facilitator invite the group to try; it is an option you introduce; but once it is introduced, group members may be free to offer doubling statements spontaneously at various points in the proceedings. Observers may leap in with a phrase or a brief soliloquy and step out again without feeling stage fright or the burden of having to stand in for a fuller development of their characterization. **Doubling serves to keep the Bibliodrama open to fresh insight from the group as a whole.** It gives nonparticipants a way to move from the periphery to the center. I will be illustrating doubling often in the course of this book.

For now, a brief example, one that I used earlier as a bibliodramatic appetizer:

As the director, I can prepare the group to double a character—say, Eve at the gates of Eden—in the following way (picture here a class of about fifteen adults seated in a circle together):

"What I'd like to do at this point is see how many different possible Eves we might be able to give voice to in this moment. In Bibliodrama

this is called doubling and it can lead to a piling up or a piling on of interpretations that can be quite inconsistent with one another. Here's the
line that's our starting point:

> THEREFORE THE LORD GOD SENT HIM FORTH FROM THE
> GARDEN OF EDEN TO TILL THE GROUND FROM WHENCE HE WAS
> TAKEN. SO HE DROVE OUT THE MAN (Genesis 3:23-24).

I'd like you to imagine that you are Eve at this moment in the story.
Tell us, Eve, what is this like for you?"

"I am furious at the deception God practiced on us, the temptation,
the duplicity, the curse. It will take me a long time, if ever, before I trust
God again."

"Driven out is right. I don't want to leave. I straggle. I hide. I look back.
All I know is being left behind. I weep until I think I will turn to salt."

"You know, it says in the story that God 'drove the man out,' but nothing is said of me. Here is another place where I feel invisible. This whole
thing is always between God and Adam."

"But that's the point," says another participant. "You see, I am not
being driven out. It's Adam who is all nostalgic and depressed. I can't wait
to get out of here any more than I could wait to eat the apple. Eden is a
place in which I have no part to play, no future. It has all been Adam and
God. In this world we're going to there's going to be lots for me to do."

"So you feel...?" I ask.

"Excited. I have a sense of power and possibility. There's something
coming. I have a purpose. I am to be 'the mother of all living.' Now that's
a part to play. Not a bad exchange, if you ask me, for this shadowy life in
a garden where nothing ever changes."

Another hand is raised: "It's even more than that. In a certain way
I don't really leave Eden at all, ever. Only Adam leaves. He really is
banished. He's never going to know again what it feels like to be part
of life in the way he is here. He goes into exile. But a part of me stays
here. A part of me can go back. The garden is the womb, and I have that
inside me."

It is doubling that creates this rich montage of interpretive possibilities.
**In doubling we suspend the forward momentum of our reading to fan
out a series of snapshots,** in this case snapshots of Eve in different moods

and poses at this particular moment in her "life." Doubling is versatile: People can raise their hands and speak from their seats. Alternatively, they can come up on stage; they can stand beside the current Eve and speak or act what they wish to add. As the facilitator, I may choose to let one of these doubling Eves become the principal Eve. My choice to do this is guided by a number of factors: Do I sense this new Eve brings a greater degree of spontaneity to the role? A new and appealing interpretive wrinkle? Or do I sense the person in the role of Eve has had enough? **Doubling is useful in bringing new people into the action or in providing a graceful way out for those who want to quit the scene and return to being observers.**

In the chapters that follow you will notice how these various techniques are used, singly or in combination, to build the bibliodramatic event. As we proceed, I will highlight the director's (my) choices and methods in the various examples. Throughout this book my goal is to simulate, as well as I can, the actual climate of conducted Bibliodramas. However, there are so many nonverbal factors, so many nuances of response in the group and in individual players, so many ways the director can use humor and gesture to filter and guide people's participation, that I feel compelled to remind the reader that any version of Bibliodrama that has been transposed to the printed page is very limited. There is, in the end, no substitute for being a participant in a well-conducted Bibliodrama or for the learning one receives in an experiential training environment.[6]

---

[6] Of all the aspects of Bibliodrama difficult to catch in writing, the nonverbal dimension is the most elusive. Let me recount here just one incident that illustrates what I mean.

I was conducting a Bibliodrama with a group of seventh and eighth graders, and we were exploring the story in which Abraham is asked to sacrifice his son Isaac (Genesis 22). We walked through it with some understandable joking around and distraction, but I had and kept the kids in role. When it came to the final scene, the kids chose to interpret it not as the voice of God speaking to Abraham and telling him to stop, but as an angel sent by God actually to stop Abraham's upraised hand. (This interpretation is familiar to people who know some of the pictorial representations of this story, among them Rembrandt's The Sacrifice of Isaac, 1636.) At that moment, with the angel's hand on his, the young boy playing Abraham turned and attempted to stab the angel in the heart. This astonishing and psychologically plausible response was rendered not in words but in gesture, in spontaneous action. It was one of those action insights that

2

First Steps

Part II of this book contains a fairly detailed recreation of a full-fledged Bibliodrama, one that might last as long as an hour or more. It begins with the two phases of the warm-up and ends with the review.

---

are, like pictures, worth a thousand words.

There is a whole category of interpretation that goes under the heading "action insight." There are nonverbal commentaries a videotape rather than a book would illustrate more effectively. Action insight ranges from well-planned warm-up exercises in which participants are invited to represent characters or images by certain stylized or choreographed movements (dancers have a great deal to offer the bibliodramatist) to unplanned gestures such as that of the boy playing Abraham in the scene above. I once, for example, conducted a Bibliodrama scene done totally in mime with a group of art therapists; there, of course, all the interpretation was in physical action, none in words.

Then there was a moment in a Bibliodrama I conducted with a clergy group at an annual conference that focused on the meeting of the two unnamed brothers in the parable of the Prodigal Son (Luke: 15:11-32). The scene ended with the two men just reaching their hands toward each another in the most tentative and preliminary gesture of reconciliation. On another occasion, directing the same scene with different players, the two men embraced and began to weep in each other's arms.

Nonverbal gestures may be as small as a silence or the tilt of a head or as large as the dramatic exit of a player from the stage. In this regard, doing the stoning of the adulteress (John 8: 1-11), I watched one of the men in the crowd shake his head and wordlessly return to his seat in the group.

Where I can, I shall try to indicate the nonverbal level in the accounts that follow.

While I hope this presentation may be interesting to the reader and relevant for the advanced practitioner, it is not, for most of us, the place to begin; it is too complex.[7]

It would be misleading to suggest that text-centered Bibliodrama, in either its pure or its appropriate form, must be lengthy or complex. A single dramatic monologue or a brief dialogue, one sequence of doubling—any of these can make for an effective and memorable bibliodramatic event and a fine supplement to a class or a sermon. In some of its longer versions Bibliodrama may fulfill any number of functions:

It may, in addition to being a form of commentary and interpretation, function as a kind of theater, a mode of self-expression and self-discovery, a medium of group play, a means of building community. However, it is Bibliodrama in its text-centered form, as a vehicle of interpretive insight, with which I am principally concerned in this book, and in that form Bibliodrama is principally **a way of asking and answering questions about biblical narrative.**

For that reason, one may do a Bibliodrama that lasts only a few moments. It may be part of a more traditional discussion about the Bible, a kind of sidebar, an interpretive digression, a footnote. As a way of questioning the Bible, Bibliodrama should always be adapted to the needs and

---

[7] Most of the time I try to keep text-centered bibliodramatic work short rather than long. For one thing, much of my work has taken place in the synagogue, seminary, church, and classroom. In these venues the timeframe is fairly restricted. For another, when the bibliodramatic work is text-centered, the action phase of the work need not be lengthy in order to produce some exhilarating insights into the biblical narrative. And the longer the bibliodramatic event, the more likely it is to tap into and to stir up the emotional depths of the players, which is not the primary aim in this form of Bibliodrama.

When, however, the contract for the work is explicitly meant to open the inner territory of the players, then an hour or even two hours is too short a time. I have conducted three-day bibliodramatic events where self-exploration was as much the interest as the exploration of the text. I have co-led a week-long Bibliodrama in which the various resources of writing, meditation, study, and action were built and blended into a sustained, coherent experience in self-discovery and group dynamics. Obviously for such extended bibliodramatic forays, the director needs to be an experienced facilitator of group process and comfortable with people's emotional range and spontaneity. Even then the director may benefit from a collaborator who has similar training and expertise.

resources of the class or group. The teacher who is interested in getting students to read in this way can always control the volume and length of the bibliodramatic event, biting off just what s/he can chew. What follows in this chapter is a set of bibliodramatic moves that progress from the simple to the more complex, from the closed to the more open, from the cognitive toward the affective.

The Role of the Interviewer & Matters of Control

In all the sample exercises in this chapter you will note that **the facilitator's primary function is to ask questions.** Nothing fancy here; no complex scenes to set; no clashing encounters to engineer. What I hope to show is how Bibliodrama can be sprung from the page and set running by the common art of the interview. In this process the facilitator plays the role of the curious, the naïve, or the challenging investigator.

There is a temptation in this work, even for a novice, to get caught up in the process. Yet there are many ways of insuring that the group and its play remain at an appropriate level and that you, as the facilitator, retain control of the process. These include:

Choice of text. What you read and play has a great deal to do with what people will be brought to think about or feel. Clearly scenes of intense grief or conflict always run the risk of plunging the facilitator and the participants in over their heads. But even there the drama can inch forward rather than gallop ahead out of control, depending on the questions asked.

Questions. The questions you ask are like prompts; they send the participant off in certain directions. Look closely at the questions asked in this book, and ask what they seek to elicit from the respondent (emotion? information? thoughts? playful invention? external detail? relationship?). Examining the questions in this way will give you a clearer sense of how fundamentally Bibliodrama is shaped by the kinds of questions the director asks.[8]

The use of echoing. The way you, as a director, echo the participants has a great deal to do with the temperature of the drama. Certain ways of echoing can lighten the mood, inject a note of understatement or irony, or even allow for comedy by evident exaggeration and caricature.

Returning to the text. Another way to put on the brakes, if you feel the process is getting away from you, is to return to reading the Bible. The virtue of bibliodramatic work is that it always takes off from a particular place in the biblical story. The written words are there to return to as boundaries, as markers. If the group seems to be skidding in ways you are not comfortable with, you can always pull them back with words like, "Well, let's remember where we are in the story. Let me read this passage to you again, and let's think about what we have been learning about the story."

All of the exercises outlined in this chapter focus on practicing this basic skill of interviewing. They are intentionally short. You will see how, through the questions asked and the time devoted to the play, you can modulate the experience of Bibliodrama.

---

[8] There is a form of bibliodramatic work that Dr. Sam Laeuchli and his wife Evelyn Rothchild have pioneered called *Mimesis*. As a form of mythic play, *Mimesis* engages other group members in the task of questioning, of interviewing, the people who are in role. This often takes the form of something rather like a press conference with one or more of the role-players being grilled by interested interrogators. This is a very lively and involving form and, when applied to the Bible as a form of Bibliodrama, makes for a heady atmosphere of challenge and confrontation. The single greatest drawback, in my view, is the loss of directorial control such a method entails. Though that loss of control may lead to a higher degree of spontaneity in the group, it also lowers the sense of safety felt by players who are asked probing, often invasive questions by their inquisitors. I have used this method, however, and in the right settings, especially with children, have found it to be an excellent approach. Its great virtue is the way it broadens the investigation of biblical material beyond the director's necessarily limited capacity, for a serious drawback of the director-centered model is the burden it places on the director to plot the entire Bibliodrama.

Dipping In

As I have said, Bibliodrama need not occur on a formal stage; it does not require trained actors. It does not even require a group, for bibliodramatic play may be conducted alone in the theater of one's own imagination, or on paper as a kind of literary, play-writing exercise. Basically the word "drama" used in this context is meant to suggest an active, participatory engagement with the Bible. Once you see the inviting spaces in the narrative, once you enter and begin to fill them, you are involved in an exercise of creative interpretation.

What follows are some illustrations of reading bibliodramatically set in the context of a more traditional (indirect) learning mode.

Let's say we have been reading the story (Exodus 3:1-10) of the birth and adoption of Moses. In talking about the text, we may have been using a variety of approaches: historical, looking at the social condition of slavery; political, thinking about repressive regimes; feminist, discussing the role women play in the opening chapters of the book. We may be noticing literary motifs, studying the Hebrew, talking about our own experiences of feeling trapped, threatened, exiled. All these are part of a familiar repertoire of Bible study.

But then, as the teacher, I might invite the class to zoom in on Moses' sister, Miriam. I might begin warming the group up to a bibliodramatic approach to the story without necessarily telegraphing my intention. (Sometimes there is less resistance to a method if it seems to emerge naturally from the context of study.) I might invite the group to imagine what it might have been like for Miriam to see a baby brother born in the time of the edict. Some discussion might follow, and we are still only speculating (we are talking *about* her, not yet *as* Miriam) until a moment comes when I say, "I wonder what Miriam would say to us if she could tell us about this time in her life." I say this in almost a musing manner, and I let the silence hang a bit, see whether a head comes up or whether anyone takes the cue. Then, making my question fully direct: "Would anyone like to speak for a moment as Miriam? Tell us, Miriam, what is this time like for you?" Here, in slight shifts, I move from thinking about

Miriam (*I wonder what Miriam would say...*) to thinking as Miriam (*Tell us, Miriam, what this time is like for you*).

Worst case? No one speaks. I have never seen it happen, but it is any facilitator's fear. If no one says anything, then you as the teacher might wish to offer your own speculation as Miriam. You might begin by saying, "Well, this is what I think Miriam might say if she were here to tell us her story: 'This is a cruel time for me. I am caught between impossible choices. On the one hand, I cherish this little baby. On the other hand, his every cry threatens my life and the lives of my brother and mother and father."

Then you might say, "I wonder if there is another Miriam here who might have something else, or something different, to tell us?" You hope that your words have primed the pump. But let's say that again no one picks up on it. The silence that greets you may be the silence of resistance, but it also may be a silence that is suddenly filling with the enormity of what Miriam's family and other families faced at that time. With no one else willing to play at that moment, you let go of the game, perhaps with some words like, "Well, it was just a thought to talk to Miriam, to imagine her words; it's just another way of interpreting the story. Maybe we will try it again sometime." And you go on with the study session, having planted a seed.

More likely, someone does respond to your invitation, or does offer a variant Miriam to the one you proposed. "I think Miriam would be afraid," someone says.

Hearing this, you notice by the phrasing that the speaker is not quite in role. "Miriam would be afraid" instead of, "I, as Miriam, am afraid." Your task here is to shift it into direct speech: "So you are Miriam, and you are scared," you say gently, moving the student into the role.

Or you may accomplish the same end by echoing. "I am Miriam," you offer, "and I am scared."

"Well, yes." The participant's assent comes with a slight shrug and a nervous laugh. Where is this going? This is different.

"And why are you scared?" you ask, interviewing now, but in a tone that is caring rather than confrontational. Students—adults perhaps more than young people—are so used to thinking there is a right answer that even in a method so evidently open as this one they may still feel cornered by any interrogation. You take the role of the concerned friend rather than probing teacher.

"Well, she's scared because..."

"I'm scared because...," I say, insisting gently that the role be played.

"All right, I'm scared because this little baby could get us all in trouble. In big trouble."

"Yes," I say, echoing, "My parents broke the law, and we have to hide this baby. Otherwise we could get into trouble. Isn't that right?" I ask, referring back to the participant.

"Yes. I mean, what if he is discovered? What if it's found out that we are hiding him?"

"What could happen?" I ask, interviewing.

"I don't know, and I don't want to think about it. They're killing babies out there. All I know is that we have to be very secret, very quiet."

"We could be arrested," someone offers.

"My mother and father could be killed," says someone else. "I could be arrested or killed," says a third person.

"Ah hah. So every time the baby cries, what do you say?"

"Shhhhhh. That's what I say. That's what we all say. We are all talking in whispers."

"It's hard," I say.

"Yes, it's very hard. Any day they could come and search our house; they could find us out." There is a certain shrillness now, and I think it time to back off.

"Thank you," I say to this participant. "So perhaps this is one of the things Miriam might tell us if she could speak to us today." And I see how the class wishes to move from this point.

"You know, I never thought of Anne Frank before," says one of the members of the group, "but in some ways this Miriam, or maybe it's the baby Moses, reminds me of her."

"In what way?" I ask.

"You know, hidden, hiding, scared."

And we smoothly resume our other ways of talking about the story. In short, you return to doing what you and the class are familiar with doing. The bibliodramatic moment—a brief foray into a different kind of discourse—requires no more closure and review than what naturally emerges from the class as it goes back to its usual ways of discussion.

Or take another example.

In Genesis 30:21 we read of the birth of Dinah. As a class we have been looking at the development of the family of Jacob, at the ways the names of the sons in the Bible give a sense of complex family dynamics, of the rivalry between Rachel and Leah, of marital tensions. We may have been talking about ancient Near Eastern marriage customs, about the economics of arranged marriages. I may be looking at issues of blended and extended families as we know them today. We may be talking *about* many things. And then I may introduce the following question, again in the spirit of speculation.

"You know," I may say, "I have been wondering about the birth of Dinah to Leah. There are four women in this household."

Note: As I begin to talk about this story I begin to talk in the present tense; I begin to talk in a way that suggests the outlines of a human drama elicited from a careful reading of the story.

"There is Rachel; there is Leah; and there are the two surrogate mothers, the serving women, Bilhah and Zilpah. So here is the moment when finally instead of someone saying, 'It's a boy!' someone says, 'It's a girl!' I'm wondering how the various women in this story might react to this birth."

Note: This speculation is still in the warming-up mode. But I am beginning to lay out the possibility of action: The phrase "it's a girl" lights up momentarily a scrap of a scene.

Here some student might say, "Well, I'll bet Rachel is really jealous."

"So," I say, "pretend for a moment you are Rachel. Tell us how you feel." The invitation to the bibliodramatic method.

"You mean you want me to talk as Rachel?"

"Yes. Exactly. And someone here might like to talk as Leah, or as Bilhah, or as Zilpah. What would you women be thinking, if not saying aloud?"

"Well, as Rachel, I would be jealous as hell." The phrasing "as Rachel I would be" is still distanced and conditional; it's close to the bibliodramatic style, but not quite.

"You *are* jealous." With this emphasis I draw my participant into role and into the present tense.

"Damn right!" she says, responding to my energy. "Why?" I ask, shifting back into the naïve interviewer.

"Well, now there's this really pretty little girl in the house, and she's Leah's, who's already had...I don't know...a lot of sons. And now Leah has one more weapon to use against me. I can't have babies. I feel really alone and like a failure, and there's something about this innocent little girl that makes it all harder to bear. I don't know why."

"And Leah? what do you think about having this little baby girl?" I look around the class for someone to take up my question. It never fails; someone will.

"Well, if sons won't do the trick, maybe a little girl will." "The trick? What do you mean?" I ask, **interviewing**.

"Yeah, you know, winning my husband completely over, controlling the family, getting the better of my sister."

"Aha," I say; and then, **echoing**, "As Leah, I have lived in my sister's shadow since the beginning. Nothing has worked, really, to get Jacob to see...to value me. But this little girl—well, fathers often have a very special thing with daughters." I look to the woman who just played Leah, checking to see if I am on the right track. She nods.

I go on. "And what about the serving women? Bilhah, you are Rachel's; Zilpah, you are Leah's. Anything to say, or are serving girls supposed to keep quiet?"

"Well, I'm Bilhah, and all I can say is it's going to be lonely for this little girl. No one to play with. Growing up in a family of all boys."

"As Zilpah, I want to say that I feel very drawn to her."

"You are very drawn to her. Why?"

"These boys have been hard to mother, hard to love, all that fighting and squabbling and rivalry. This little girl...maybe she will be free of that. Maybe she will be special. I'm going to love and protect her. She brings us together, at least Bilhah and me."

"Thank you," I say, meaning it, for this little bibliodramatic excursion has given me a sense of something I didn't have before, of the possible bond between the serving women and their gentle concern for the baby girl.

"I wouldn't want to be Dinah," a student says, and rather than asking that student to speak as Dinah and thereby continuing the Bibliodrama,

I simply ask why not, and the discussion returns to its usual level of talking *about* the story. "Well, you know what's going to happen to her. She's is going to…"

These examples are intended to give you an idea of the ways Bibliodrama may be introduced as part of a reading of text, almost as a kind of digression. If, as the teacher, I am matter-of-fact about proposing it, then my casualness will communicate to my class that this is "no big deal." I can feel out the class, try out the process, and return at any moment to talking *about* the story or characters. The bibliodramatic method opens a door; it may lead nowhere, but it may lead to other doors, some brand-new even to me. Talking about the possibilities of the novel, the American writer Henry James wrote in his *Art of Fiction* of "dramas within dramas and innumerable points of view." Some dizzying sense of those perspectives may threaten to overwhelm us as we begin to read bibliodramatically. But the text on the page is always there as the mooring to which we can return if we start to get a little lost in our interpretive variations. We can always find our place; we can always return to the black letters and to the exact word or phrase from which we began.

Bibliodrama with Objects

Certain schools of modern dream interpretation suggest that the best way to understand a dream is to imagine that we are every part of it, not just the dream-self or dream-protagonist. We are all the other characters, and we are also the dream's images, objects, plots, and relationships. It makes perfect sense, of course, since it is our mind that spins out the dream web in all its detail.

I find this perspective useful in freeing me to think of objects as having consciousness, and in this regard I sometimes think of the Bible as God's dream within which everything has meaning and a charge of life. I often use these analogies to introduce a class or a group to a bibliodramatic exercise in which we find a voice for objects in the Bible and have them speak to us.[9] I like to use an object-oriented exercise as a way of introduc-

---

[9] Kushner's *River of Light* includes a parallel development of this same idea.

ing people to the experience of role-playing, but it is an introduction that has some distance built into it. We are not, after all, looking directly at personal feelings, though we are personalizing objects.

Here is an example of an exercise that I have used with moderate sized groups (under twelve) when I want to hear from—or at least open up the possibility of hearing from—everyone in the group. This exercise may be used as an end in itself or as means for warming a group up for a longer Bibliodrama. I offer my words in italics to show what it is I might actually say:

"The Bible is full of objects—stones, swords, wells, mountains, staffs, arks of different kinds. You get the idea. Think of an object in the Bible that interests you, or perhaps one that just pops into your head for no good reason that you can see. Raise your hand when you have such a object in mind."

I proceed in this fashion so that people make a commitment to an object without having to think about having to present it. *Now imagine you are that object. Introduce yourself to us in the following way: 'I am...Moses' staff.' If you are not comfortable with this exercise, please feel free just to watch and listen."*

Most of the members of the group in turn—some with a smile, some with a giggle, many without much expression, some with a certain playfulness—introduce themselves in this manner.

"I am the staff God gives to Moses."

"I am Rachel's tears."

"I am the serpent in the garden."

"I am the rope used to bind Isaac on the altar."

"I am the Tree of Knowledge."

"I am Miriam's well."

"I am the little idols Rachel stole from her father."

"I am the little reed ark that carried Moses down the Nile."

"I am the stone Cain used to slay Abel."

"I am Sarah's tent."

"I am the ram caught in the thicket on Mt. Moriah."

"I am the golden calf."

"I am a candlestick in the tabernacle."

And so it goes.

The exercise gains momentum and energy as it proceeds. We feel that these objects have stories to tell. The task of the facilitator, depending on the time available, is to elicit some of these stories.

So as a next step one might ask, "Do any of you wish to tell us anything about yourself?"

Here is an example of what I heard a woman say in an adult Torah group: "I am the reed ark that carried Moses down the Nile."

"Tell me more about yourself," I said, starting to **interview** her in the role.

"Well, what do you want to know?"

"Who made you?"

"I don't know." This response is not at all unusual and represents an important and challenging moment for the facilitator. The participant is, for a moment, caught in a dilemma. It is not yet clear whether she can give full rein to her imagination, making up a story out of whole cloth, or whether she has to adhere to the information—or lack thereof—in the Bible. The task of the facilitator at this point is to encourage her to invent the story, or to supply the information she might need in order then to embellish and invent.

"Well, someone must have made you, and though your story is not told in the Bible, perhaps you can let us in on some of your secrets." Or "I know we do not know anything in a factual way about you, but in this exercise you are free to make up a story. I'll ask you a few questions, and you can just see what answers come to mind." Or "Sure you know. Maybe you're afraid you'll get them into trouble, that the Egyptian authorities will trace your story and arrest those who arranged for Moses' escape. Don't worry; none of us here will reveal a word of what you tell us." The important thing here is, in the spirit of play and invention, to encourage the role-player to let her imagination respond.

"OK. Moses' father made it."

"Made me," I say, gently correcting the speaker back into role.

"OK. Made *me*."

"Did he talk to you while he was making you?" (Beginning to **interview**.)

"Not actually aloud."

"But you could read his thoughts?"

"Not his thoughts, his feelings."

"Ah hah. And what were those feelings?"

"He was sad, and he was angry."

"I see. And did you know what you were being made for?"

"Yes."

"And that was...?"

"To carry the little infant down the Nile." "How did you feel about this assignment?"

"It was a huge responsibility. I wanted Moses' father to be very careful, to weave me well and to caulk me well. I did not want to leak or tilt over."

"And did he build you well?"

"Yes, very well."

"I have many more questions I could ask you, but I have other objects here to meet who, like you, have come to tell their stories. But before I leave you, is there anything else you want me to know?"

"Yes. I want you to know what it felt like to carry him down the river." "What was it like to carry the baby down the river?"

"It was like being his mother."

"Ah hah. If I understand you, you are saying..." (and here I echo) "'I was like a second mother to Moses.'"

"Yes, a second womb. I held him safe and warm. I rocked him gently. I whispered to him. And I was the one who gave him his name."

"And the name that I give him (echoing) is...?"

"Moshe...it means 'the one who is drawn out.'"

"Out of...?"

"Out of me."

"How important you were."

"Yes. And I was sad to let him go, but I had done what I was made to do, and I was glad. But then I was empty."

"Well, thank you for sharing your story."

This kind of interview depends in part on the facilitator's ability to ask questions, but not entirely. The interviewer's skill of asking naïve and simple questions helps the participant get into the part and to sustain the role, but often participants will embellish quite spontaneously. The more you see the participant as the object, the easier it is for the player to get into playing the part. It may help to remember that there is, often unconsciously, a reason the choice has been made, and sometimes all you need to do is invite the participants to tell their stories. One doesn't have to maintain a complicated dialogue with the object to get the benefit from this bibliodramatic exercise.

You can probably see how working with objects can limber up a group's bibliodramatic imagination. The insights that come from playing objects have a certain charm; there is something childlike in this far-fetched play. While to some it may appear frivolous, to others it can be liberating and yield insights both into the text and into the player. It is also an excellent form in which to practice interviewing.

Another way of working with objects, either sufficient in itself or as a prelude to a Bibliodrama, is to arrange the objects in various ways. You might notice, for example, that there are two objects from Eden, two from the story of Abraham's sacrifice of Isaac, two from Rachel's story, several from the Exodus. You could group the objects according to the stories they belong to, or arrange them in their narrative sequence from—in this case—the Tree of Knowledge through Miriam's well. Objects may then share a story or sense of their relationship with other objects. Interesting juxtapositions open up surprising interpretations; conversations between objects are full of insight, humor, and pathos. In the course of the exercise participants discover how connected they are to these objects; through them they are able to question, quarrel, comment on the story in which they are embedded.

Always you need to leave time at the end for the review. Participants and observers need a chance to comment on the process, to share what the experience has been like, what they learned. It may be surprising how much excitement this simple, safe exercise generates. Its momentum can lead to archeology, history, to an examination of traditional commentaries, to a heightened sense of literary technique, and to self-reflection.

This exercise may be brought to a close in any number of ways. For example, if people have stood to group or arrange themselves in some kind of tableau, I will thank them. I will call attention to the time and to the other things we still have to do and ask them to take their seats again, noting as they sit down that they are to be themselves again. Or if people have been seated and several people have not yet been heard from, I may suggest that before the next class they might want to write out what it is they did not get a chance to tell.

In the reviewing phase of the class in which the woman played the reed ark, she expressed her surprise at how vivid the scene had become for her. "I could really see Moses' father bending over in candlelight and weaving the basket. It was amazing, and as the basket I had feelings, too. It was harder to say goodbye to the baby than I said while I was playing."

And another group member, speaking to her, said, "I never thought about the ark before as a kind of second mother, a womb. I mean, I guess it's obvious, but it made me realize how many times Moses was mothered and passed on. The little ark is like a metaphor for how transient his childhood must have felt for him."

These comments have a degree of adult sophistication. But this exercise lends itself well to a class of young kids, to families, and particularly to intergenerational groups. Kids may not have the same ability to comment on the objects afterward, but they are less inhibited in representing them in the first place.[10]

I'll never forget the kid who, playing Joseph's coat, said, "It was scary when the brothers tore me into pieces and splashed blood on me. They were so mad. Like wolves."

---

[10] A minister once said of Bibliodrama that it created "a level playing field." What he meant was that this method does not privilege knowledge or booklearning and therefore exclude the less literate. While he was a man who certainly prized booklearning, he recognized in Bibliodrama a tool for drawing into a valid discussion of the text people who were, or felt themselves to be, biblically illiterate. And he also saw the ways Bibliodrama could lead toward an increased desire for literacy in texts and sources. In Bibliodrama it is possible for men and women, boys and girls of all ages and familiarities with the Bible to enter into an interpretive community together in which what is valued is imagination, empathy, and certain expressive abilities.

Getting Inside the Head of...

Another bibliodramatic gambit with built-in distance—and therefore safety—involves "getting inside the head" of someone *outside* the biblical story.

For instance, one can establish a bibliodramatic sketch with the "Redactor" as a dramatic figure. The "Redactor" is the name commonly given to the anonymous master editor who created the Hebrew Bible in its canonized form. Much scholarly discussion and biblical literary criticism involves an attempt to second-guess the Redactor, to understand his (or her) reasons for making certain editorial and artistic choices. It is possible, and actually quite enlivening, to bring this anonymous and voiceless Redactor into a discussion. (You can do the same thing with the gospel writers: Interview Matthew, Mark, Luke, or John about why certain things are said and others left unsaid.)

To give an example:

We have been looking at the moment in which Esau and Jacob meet after years of separation. We have noted that the "Redactor" uses an unprecedented series of dots—the cantillation—over the Hebrew word for "kiss." Pointing this out to the class, I then say: "Imagine for a moment you are the Redactor. Why these little marks?"

"I put them there to call attention to the beauty of this reconciliation."

"They are like little teeth marks to tell you Esau's kiss was actually a bite."

"I put them there..."

Or take another example.

We have two different versions of the creation of man and woman at the opening of Genesis. Why? Or, in the story of Cain and Abel, there is something left out between the lines in Genesis 4:8 that tell of the brothers talking and the act of murder. Why the ellipsis? In all these examples there are puzzles that only the author or master editor could explain. I propose to the class that they imagine themselves as the Redactor. I address them as follows: "Redactor, can you tell us: Is this just a mistake, a place where you just got confused? Is this a place where two different stories or traditions existed, and you are trying to respect them both and sacrificing narrative consistency? Or what?"

You will be amazed at the inventiveness of students when challenged to account for a textual anomaly, and because there can be many people playing the role of the Redactor, the possibilities for a solution to our questions remain open and speculative. The virtue of the method is not only that it stirs up our inventiveness, but also that it makes the distant authorial figures—the Redactor, or the gospel writers, or any of the prophets, for that matter—more present.

There are other minds you can enter when reading the biblical narrative. For example, in a class studying Rashi—the great Torah commentator of twelfth century France—ask students to get inside Rashi's head the more fully to explain one of his comments. Or ask students to invent a comment that Rashi did not write down. Contemporary Christians can look at biblical stories through the eyes of liberation theology or the prophetic imagination of a Martin Luther King. In Bibliodrama these voices can be embodied, brought back to life, extended beyond their time and the confines of what they wrote, and therefore be brought into relation with one another. Augustine can talk to Aquinas, Buber with Maimonides.

And finally there are the voices and perspectives of historical and contemporary readers who are not represented in our classroom or group. For example, in a class of high school kids reading the story of young Moses, I might say, "Imagine you are a Jew living in Germany in 1938, in the time of Hitler, and you are reading this story. Tell us what it means to you." Or "Imagine you are a slave on a plantation in the South in 1859 and you are hearing this story. What do you think it would mean to you?" You get the idea.

Who Are You?

One last set of "short takes" will round out this survey of opening moves and simple bibliodramatic gambits. Earlier in this chapter we saw what it was like to invite people to choose and to role-play objects. Now we take the same approach but apply it to the playing of biblical characters.

There are three primary ways to go about this. The most common is **the open-ended**, where you simply invite participants to be anyone they choose. Then there is **casting the text**, where you invite participants to choose a character from a particular text or biblical story, usually the one you have been studying. And in a third approach, called **group characterization**, everyone is invited to play the same character and, in that way, to liberate as many different versions of that character as the class can create. This is, in effect, a doubling exercise.

1. Open-ended: The warm-up for this exercise is very similar to the one I used above for objects. Once again it is best to take the process in two stages. In the first stage, people are asked to think of a biblical character that interests them, or one that pops into mind and seems to intrigue them. Then, in the second stage, people are asked to introduce themselves to the group *as* that character. You might say something like this:

"Having selected a character that interests you, now step into the shoes of that character and introduce yourself to us. If you don't feel like trying this out, just say, 'I pass' when your turn comes."

As in our play with objects, you can group the characters by a variety of criteria: according to their place in the Bible, by status (from chief to slave), by the amount of space they take up in the Bible (from Moses to characters who make a single appearance), etc. There are all sorts of fascinating permutations of this exercise. For example, you can place an empty chair in the center of the room and tell the players that this chair represents God, and that they are to stand as near to or as far from that chair as they feel represents their closeness to or distance from God. Characters may then be questioned about their feelings, relationship, history with God. Once these tableaux are created, the facilitator's task is to interview the participants in role and to help them tell the group a little about themselves. Often other characters will take part in asking characters questions.

Once in a class where there was a Sarah and a Hagar, the two woman struck up a conversation after my simply asking them if they had anything to say to each other. I didn't have to do anything else.

This open-ended form of Bibliodrama may be very playful. There are all sorts of ways of following up on this kind of process, whether having people do some writing, some study, or even—as I did one summer in a group that met daily for three hours over a week—having people make masks for their characters and present them in a dramatic (and in this case public) group presentation-performance.

It goes something like this.

Having begun by asking people to choose a character and then to become that character, you can then have them locate that character in time and space. For a woman who chooses Miriam, the play proceeds in the following way:

"You tell me you are Miriam. So at what point in your story are you coming before us?"

Sometimes the participant may answer immediately and with certainty. "I am Miriam; I have just seen my brother's wife, Zipporah."

Other times, when a player, though in role, draws a blank about the particular moment, you may need to present some of the options. "I am Rebecca," says a participant.

"You are Rebecca? OK. Where do we find you in your story? At the well? Seeing Isaac for the first time? Pregnant with the twins?" etc.

"I am getting ready to leave my father's house."

"Ah ha, I see. You are in Haran. And where are you at this very moment as you are speaking to us?"

"I am leaning against the door frame of my father's house. The stranger who came looking for a wife for Isaac is saddling the camels. I can feel the cool of the darkness of my family's house on one side of my body as I stand here; the hot sun warms the other side of my body. I am saying goodbye. I don't know where I am going or what I will find, but I feel I am leaving one world to enter another. I am excited. I am scared. I am ready."

The fullness and quality of this response is not unusual. Once the player discovers the particular moment in which the role-play takes place, s/he often unearths a trove of descriptive details and feelings.

Or another Rebecca, in the same group, at a later point in her story:

"I am Rebecca, and I, too, am standing in a doorway. I have just sent my son Jacob away to Haran with the promise that I will send for him when Esau's anger has subsided. But I wonder if I will ever see him again, and I wonder whether anyone will understand my loss, my sacrifice, to gain for him what God has promised. Sometimes I wish I had never come here."

"Yes," I say, to lighten the tone a little, "I've noticed that God asks people to do some pretty hard things. Let me reassure you, Rebecca, your two sons will work it out."

2. Casting the Text: This method of character presentation can be a very useful accompaniment to the study of a particular biblical story.

Let us say, for example, we have been reading Exodus 18. It begins with the account of the arrival of Jethro, who is Moses' father-in-law and also a priest of Midian. This old man brings with him Moses' wife, Zipporah, and their two sons, Gershom and Eliezar. This family comes to meet Moses in the wilderness encampment just after the Israelites have defeated the Amalekites.

You might introduce a bibliodramatic exercise in the following way: "So, class, we have been reading this story pretty carefully. I'd like to invite you to do something a little different. Let's make a list on the blackboard of all the possible characters who might appear—even if unnamed—in this episode."

"Moses."

"Jethro."

"Zipporah."

"Gershom and Eliezer."

"Miriam."

"Aaron."

"Moses' mother."

"How about his father?"

"Joshua."

"A soldier."

"OK. That's good. Let's create some interpretation together. I want you to select one of these characters and, for a moment, to become that character. I'd like to get your perspective on what happened today in camp. Raise your hand when you know who you are. You can pass if you don't feel like doing this." Again hands go up. Not all. Not all need to play, and I need to make sure people feel free to watch. People warm up differently to this kind of work; there are always fast starters, usually enough of them to get things moving. But it's a good idea, as well as good teaching, to check in at various points to see if any of the people who were quiet at the beginning would like to ask a question or in some way get involved now that the enactment is beginning to move.

In the process that follows I again play the role of the interviewer, asking questions as if I had a microphone in my hand. Though I know the story, I pretend to a certain naïveté. That naïveté keeps me fresh and open to the surprising things I might hear. The better I can imagine myself there in the scene in the camp, the more lively and curious I become as interviewer. I may have heard certain rumors for which I am trying to get confirmation. "Is it true that Moses kissed Jethro but not his wife?" Or "Is it true that Jethro told you, Moses, that what you were doing was 'not right' when he watched you judging the people?" Or "Gershom, what was it like to leave Midian where you grew up to come to see your father here in the wilderness?" Questions, questions, questions: These are the means by which the bibliodramatic facilitator gets people involved in the play.

The scene of Moses' family meeting in the wilderness can easily become a full-scale Bibliodrama. To keep it short and study-centered, ask characters only one or two questions about themselves and what they see going on around them. Also, be sure to ask everyone who appears in the scene and whose part has been taken. In that way the method of casting the text has latitude but does not go into depth or detail. You end up with a slightly richer feel for the entire scene.

3. Group Characterization: Finally, you can ask everyone in the group to be the same character. (This is, in effect, an exercise in doubling.)

Take, for example, a class that has been studying Genesis 12, the departure of Abram (not yet Abraham) and his clan for Canaan. You could introduce the exercise in the following way:

"You know, I have always wondered what Sarai thought of this venture. All we are told of her is that she is Abram's

wife and that she is barren. I wonder how many different
versions and voices of Sarai we can discover together. Imagine
yourselves as Sarai. Your husband has told you what God has
proposed to him to do. Tell us what are your reactions. Raise
your hand if you want to give us your side of the story."
"I have no voice or say in this matter at all. You say my
husband has told me what his God calls him to do. You
are wrong. My husband doesn't tell me anything. He
just announces that we are going, and we go."
"I am a different Sarah. Or Sarai. My barrenness is difficult for
me. I stand out here among my kinswomen. I think maybe this
journey will be important for me. My husband has told me
about the summons of God, and I felt it hinted at a promise
for me that we will have a family. I am excited to go."
"I am scared to go. We are leaving what we know, our homeland,
our gods. Who is this God who talks to Abraham? This
God has no name. No idols. Abraham is putting his trust in
something he cannot see; and I am putting my trust in him."
"I don't know why we are taking Lot along. Sometimes
I feel this young man looks at me very strangely.
I feel a little scared of him sometimes."
"I have said so many goodbyes as a woman; this is just one
more. A woman goes where her husband goes. That's
the way it is. I wonder if we will ever settle down."
"It's so funny to me how the Bible tells our story. As if it were
Abram's decision for us to go to Canaan. I had been having
dreams and hearing a voice call us to leave his old father and the
old idolatry for years while we lived here in Haran. But no, Abram
felt he had to take care of his father, couldn't leave him alone.
He told me I was a foolish woman; he told me that the voice
I heard was in my head. So I waited. My barrenness, I knew, was
God's way of telling Abram that our lives were not and could not
be complete here. Then finally God spoke to him. I could only
laugh. What took you so long? I've been ready to go for years."
And so it might go. I make no attempt to harmonize these different

versions. The point is to open up possibilities and to let us see how many different facets there are of a character in the Bible. Once Sarai has been subjected to this kind of kaleidoscopic interpretation, we can, if we wish, turn to other figures in the story and get a multifaceted cluster of insights into their states of mind.

Closure & Review

In the examples in this chapter I have not said much about the closure and the reviewing process.

Closure: Closure, the final moments or phase of the action process, is really the discovery of a way to end. **As facilitator, you look for a certain grace in the ending, a certain flourish, like the skater giving a finish to her exercises, like the storyteller closing up his tale.** Closure is the slow fade of the last shot or the swift drop of the curtain. The pace of the closure is something that gives the action-work a chance to settle, a wrapping up of loose ends, a silence that falls after the last words are spoken. Sometimes narrating the subsequent events of the tale just enacted will allow for closure; sometimes returning to the text enacted for a rereading will do it. In Part III, section 6, I will say more on this subject.

When, as in the case of most of the preceding examples, the bibliodramatic forays have been brief, you don't need much closure. A simple "thank you" on your part will often be adequate to acknowledge what the participants have done. In longer exercises, of course, more closure will be necessary; you'll need more time to wrap up a scene and to find the rhythm of a conclusion.

Review: Reviewing, by definition, is what occurs after the action phase of the role-playing. It cannot begin until the players are themselves again. After all but the shallowest excursion into Bibliodrama, the facilitator has to mark the end of the bibliodramatic event and then to provide a chance for people to look back on the experience. The facilitator must allow them to put it in perspective, to mine it for its learning, to integrate it into their present understanding of themselves, one another, and the Bible. This is the review.

The warm-up and reviewing phases are not necessarily of equal duration. Many Bibliodramas are catalyzed by the briefest invitation, the slightest warm-up. In groups that have been together over time, Bibliodrama may arise almost spontaneously. And it may take on sudden power. **Reviewing needs to be seen in relation to the phase of action, as a counterforce to its duration and intensity**. The facilitator needs to reserve time for debriefing and de-roling. The review need not be elaborate, but it is always necessary. Any time people play with consciousness—in this case stepping into imaginal dimensions, tapping into their own spontaneity and depths—reviewing is essential. It helps everyone to cross back over the threshold and return to ordinary consciousness, ordinary time.

Think of these short takes as building blocks. Many of them are excellent places to make your first venture into bibliodramatic interpretation. Though my accounts are not designed to be scripts, they can be used as models for your own first steps. In the next chapter, we will start to put these elements together to make whole scenes. Later still, in Part II, we will be putting scenes together to make the longer form of a full Bibliodrama. As we build up the craft of working with text, players, time, and emotion, you will need new skills in addition to those of asking questions and echoing the responses. For those of you reading as practitioners, you may want to set up a group of people with whom you can practice these skills.

3

The Elements of a Scene

In more complicated forms of bibliodramatic play, new roles and skills are required of the facilitator. For the various strategies described in the last chapter the term "facilitator" does quite well; however, for what comes next—a set of more dramatic and interactive forms of biblical exploration—I will start to use the term "director." **As Bibliodrama grows fuller and more complex, the person conducting it must be, in addition to a skilled reader and an imaginative interviewer, someone who can begin to think of stage-managing and scene-building, of coaching player-actors and blocking action, of generating a higher level of tension by arranging dramatic encounters. This fuller sense of theatrical responsibility takes the work to another level and merits the titl**e *director*.

The elements of a scene may be approached and practiced as bibliodramatic events in their own right. In time, and with a growing mastery, they may be blended to create one-act or multiple-act plays that have an aesthetic shape as well as interpretive vitality. In this chapter I will be looking at two key elements in a scene that can begin to move participants out of their seats: **sculpting** and **the encounter**.

Sculpting

Without naming it as such, I have already introduced sculpting in a rudimentary way when we imagined taking a group of characters and arranging them in the order in which they appear in the Bible, or grouping them according to their relation to one another within the same story. Sculpting is a term taken from certain family therapists who, of course, lifted the term from the plastic arts. In a therapeutic context sculpting asks members of a family to group themselves spatially in order to show their dynamics. "Create the family dinner table" is an example of a task given to a family, which will show, by their seating positions, something about relationships. We would see who sits next to whom, across from whom, etc. Another invitation for sculpting might invite family members to pose for a picture: "You are being grouped for a family portrait; show me how you pose."

Once group members are on their feet, as opposed to voicing their roles from their seats, your task as director begins in earnest, for when people stand and move they begin to create a space for play, and you have, in effect, a stage. (Whether it is raised or not, whether it is defined as such or not, a "stage" comes into existence as soon as someone "acts" rather than talks—sings a song, recites a poem, strikes a pose.) **On stage the whole body becomes an expressive element; any movement may take on meaning.** The participant becomes more self-conscious; a certain performance anxiety, a "stage fright," can creep in and constrain spontaneity. And just as the group members become "actors" once you have them on a stage (even if they are immobile), you become their director. You must begin to think about how to choreograph entrances and exits and how to position people in relation to one another. In order to practice this task of managing more than one body on stage at a time, exercises in sculpting can be helpful. And like all exercises in Bibliodrama, they may be interpretive ends in their own right as well.

When I was a child at camp, my favorite counselor, Angelo, taught our bunk a game called "Statues." Angelo was always the Statue Maker. He stood at the center of our circle (and in forming a circle we were, without knowing it, creating a stage). When it was your turn you went up to him and extended your arm. He grasped it by the wrist and then began to swing you around, slowly at first, then faster, spinning you around him until you were almost off balance. Just before you became airborn, he let you go, and while you were still reeling from the momentum the Statue Maker called out an object you had to become when you came to a stop: "tree," or "swimmer," or "lion," or "the grump," or "archer," etc. In the game, if you bumped into anyone while you were whirling on your way to becoming a statue, you were out. If you didn't achieve statue-dom before your momentum stopped, you were out. The game wasn't over until everyone had a turn. In sculpting, you, as director, are a kind of statue maker; but in sculpting, the statues are expressive not only in their own right, but also in relation to one another. The spinning, of course, is optional.

Ideas for sculpting will grow out of the reading and study of a particular text. Certain biblical scenes are written in ways that invite their rendering as tableaux. In such scenes, many of the characters appear. Often without being aware of it, we make a picture of a scene, sculpt it in our minds. Such scenes are natural starting points for bibliodramatic sculpting. All such sculptings are interpretive because in fact every arrangement of bodies in space (never mind for a moment pose and posture, just positions and distances and groupings) becomes a way of seeing the story.

Western art is full of this kind of thing. Stroll through a museum or page through book of Western art. Take, for example, the scene in which Hagar and Ishmael are sent away (Genesis 21:1-21). There is a haunting Gustave Dore lithograph of that scene. We see Hagar in the foreground with Ishmael clinging to her skirt; Abraham stands in the middle distance, an arm outstretched toward the retreating Hagar; and behind him Sarah in the background, brooding and triumphant, is seated in front of her tent with little Isaac clutched to her breast. Dore has, in effect, sculpted a biblical moment in two dimensions, an interpretation of Genesis 21:14. It would not be difficult for a novice director and a class of students to lift the same scene from the page and compose their own sculptural representation. Move the moment forward or backward in narrative time, and the relative positions of the characters, the spaces between them and the gestures appropriate to the moment, change. It is like looking at earlier or later frames in a film.

In bibliodramatic sculpting the simple act of embodying a narrative instant, mute and frozen as it is, gives participants and observers a palpable sense of the human dimension of a biblical story and its expressive potential. As players we feel something we do not feel as readers; even as witnesses to this tableau we sense interpretive possibilities not so apparent without the embodiment.

Some biblical scenes seem to have been written almost as recipes for sculpting. For example, take this moment from the wilderness story of the Hebrews:

> AND MOSES' HANDS GREW HEAVY; SO THEY TOOK A STONE AND
> PUT IT UNDER HIM AND HE SAT ON IT, WHILE AARON AND HUR,
> ONE ON EACH SIDE, SUPPORTED HIS HANDS; THUS HIS HANDS
> REMAINED STEADY UNTIL THE SUN HAD SET. AND JOSHUA AND
> HIS MEN DEFEATED AMALEK WITH THE SWORD (Exodus 17:12ff).

Once you render this scene sculpturally, you can see more vividly the transformation of a man into an icon; the players feel the passivity of their parts. We live, rather than read, the irony of being frozen as witnesses while those below us seethe in battle.

Another, far more complex sculpture, yet one that is fully articulated in the Bible, is the birth order of the family of Jacob (Genesis 29 and 30).

To sculpt this story one places Jacob at the center of the playing space, Rachel on one side, Leah on the other. Each woman is given her serving woman—Bilhah with Rachel, Zilpah with Leah. Then, birth by birth, one adds the children to the story, figuring out each time where the new child goes, who is shifted or displaced at each birth. Eventually one comes to the sole girl, Dinah. Then finally to Joseph. Done in this manner (without any words being spoken by the players), it provides the sense you cannot get by merely reading it of the crowding rivalry of the sons; of the gradual displacement of Rachel, of the dominance of Leah, of the isolation of Dinah; and, in the end, because of the birth of Joseph, of the entire family being dramatically reconfigured. Rachel is reunited with Jacob, placed at her husband's side; the precious Joseph between them as their bond, Leah at last deposed.

Almost any episode in a story can be thought of as a scene, and once you think that way, you can begin to see it. Seeing a scene involves making choices: Who stands where in relation to whom? This kind of seeing becomes part of the way the director practices reading and then teaches that kind of reading to a group. **In Bibliodrama the creation of a scene is a creative process that involves both the director and the participants. Together they discover the arrangement and content of a scene and in that way create the midrash together.**

There are scenes that lend themselves to sculpting that require a more imaginative reading of the text than those I have cited above. The cast of characters is not made explicit; one infers them from the context; one creates a Bibliodrama to include them. For example, in Genesis 21:8, we read of the weaning feast of the infant Isaac. As readers, we can fill in the cast of characters that might be found there. Abraham is easy enough to see; Sarah. But is Hagar there? Is Ishmael? Might Lot be invited, or has all contact between uncle and nephew been broken? Are certain Canaanites present? Is Abimelech there, who had been a patron and colleague of Abraham's in peace and war? And after we have brainstormed who might be there comes the next question: How are these figures positioned?

If you were an artist, how would you represent it? If you were a photographer, how would you arrange the figures for your picture? Where does the scene take place? Inside or outside? Who is there, and where do they stand? And because standing still becomes a stance (with its attendant inflection of attitude and feeling), one may see how stances further extend sculpting in the direction of expressiveness and interpretation. **Taking a position moves toward striking a pose.**

Let's walk through a sculpting and notice the ways a director shapes the emerging scene and coaxes the class to take part. Let's take as an example the moment in which Rebecca is preparing to leave home for a new life. It is a moment we visited earlier in one of our open-ended short takes. There, in the visual frame of that moment, we saw only Rebecca herself. But what if we pull back our focal length? Where is Laban, her brother? Bethuel, her father? Eliezer, Abraham's emissary? Does Rebecca have a mother? Who else might be there?

Learning to read bibliodramatically means learning to see what has been left out but might plausibly be brought in. We learn to see

characters, objects, scenery that, once seen, render the biblical moment in a fuller dimension. We employ a cinematic imaginationin this process, then freeze a frame. Once you, as the director, have seen these hidden elements in your own reading of text, you can then guide a group toward presenting them as a sculpted tableau, and you can invite a class, with their eyes, to see more than you have seen.

How might the sculpting process actually unfold? You might begin by saying something like this:

"You know, this moment of Rebecca's departure seems to me to have all sorts of unnamed characters in it. Remember when we asked who might be present when Jethro and Moses met? Well, let me ask the same question here. Who might be gathering to say good-bye to Rebecca? And I'd like us to put our answer into action; I'd like us to make a kind of tableau of this moment in the Bible. We'll take the story off the page and stand it on its feet right here; I think we'll see some things we can't see so clearly by merely reading the story. We can use this method as a way of creating an interpretation together. No one has to take part in what we're going to do. What do you say?" Heads nod, perhaps a little warily in some quarters, but no one objects.

"First of all, of course, there's Rebecca. Is there anyone who would come up here to stand as Rebecca?" Hesitation. People in the group are wondering what will be asked of them. The mere mention of "up here," however casual, generates a little anxiety; "up here" becomes the stage. "We are going to sculpt this scene together. There will be no speaking parts. You will just stand like a statue, though not so rigidly." It's a lot easier to go on stage if you know you don't have to speak or act. "Just stand there" is a direction almost anyone can follow without too much self-consciousness.

At last someone volunteers. I place Rebecca in the center of whatever playing space we are using.

"Her brother, Laban, might be there," someone says helpfully. "Good," I say. "Would you come up and stand as Laban?"

"I'd rather not."

"Fine. No one has to do this. We can put an empty chair for Laban if no one wants to stand here."

"I'll do it," someone offers. "Where should I stand?"

"Well, that's a good question. Suppose you stand as close to Rebecca as you feel close to her, or as far from her as you feel is your emotional distance."

This is the crucial element in sculpting: to use distance and position and even posture as ways of rendering information about feelings. "Space" becomes psychological and emotional.

The person playing Laban stops for a moment, thinking aloud: "If I remember right from later parts of the story, when Jacob comes Laban is kind of manipulative. And even in this story he seems sort of calculating. I'm not sure Laban is close to anyone. I think he'd stand a bit off to the side. Like here?" The player is tentative and looks to me as if I had the right answer.

"That looks good to me. If someone else were playing Laban, they might position him differently, but this is your Laban, distant, on the edge, where you can see everyone, maybe control things."

"Right."

"Fine," I say, wanting both to encourage the player to make his choice and to remind the group that we are seeing interpretation made concrete in a piece of stage blocking. Notice that in this exercise I am not asking the person playing Laban to speak as Laban.

The purpose here for me as the director and for the class is to work just with physicalizing a reading of the story. A silent movie. A set of stills. Though the words are just below the surface, I said there were not going to be any speaking parts, and I need to keep my promise.

"Who else might be here?" I ask.

"Bethuel, their father, is mentioned explicitly."

"OK, would you come up and stand where you think Bethuel might be, as close to or as far away from Rebecca as his feelings would place him?" And again the player thinks, talks a little, works it out, asks advice, finds a spot also at a distance from Rebecca and next to Laban. More interpretation, more insight into the story. Someone else might place the father closer. "OK. Who else?"

"There's Eliezer, the servant who has come to fetch her."

"Do you really think he'd be here, in this scene?" someone asks.

"I don't know. What do you think?"

"This is looking pretty intimate, you know."

"Doesn't it depend on when it takes place?" someone asks. "How so?"

"Well, if this goodbye takes place in the house, then it might be reserved just for the family. But if Rebecca is outside, say, getting ready to mount a camel, then Eliezer would be there."

"On the other hand," says another student, "Eliezer is there in everyone's mind. He's the future. I mean, you could have Abraham in this scene, sort of at the edge, a figure from Bethuel's distant past who is here through Eliezer."

"Well," says another student, "if you think that way, you could have Isaac here."

"Let's not get too far afield," I say, though I like very much this kind of thinking. "Is Eliezer in or out?"

"Let's put him in, but off to one side." Someone comes up to be Eliezer. He stands at the edge of the playing space opposite that occupied by Laban and Bethuel.

"Who else might be here?" I ask.

"It says in the text that she left with 'her maids.' So I guess there are serving women with her."

"Good," I say. "Let's have three people come up as the serving maids. If we were going to do this with speaking parts, they might almost be a kind of chorus for this moment." Three members of the class come up and stand on the "future side" of the playing area, where the servant Eliezer stands. They are ready to go. "Who else?"

"Well, the text says that Rebecca 'ran ... to her mother's household,' but no specific mention is made of her mother."

"Yeah," says another group member, "mothers are often left out of stories."

"So," I ask, "shall we put her in?"

"Yes," the group choruses, "let's put her in."

"Would someone volunteer to stand up and position yourself as the mother?" A woman stands up and moves onto the stage pensively, looking first at Bethuel, then at Rebecca. Her very process of getting into role, of deciding where to stand, is full of interpretive inflection. This moment of leave-taking with her daughter pulls her toward her husband and away from him at the same time. She keeps her own counsel and finally comes to stand very close to Rebecca, and the woman playing Rebecca, who has watched her "mother" enter this scene, spontaneously reaches out her hand. (This is where the game of statues is no longer a literal image for our process. These bibliodramatic statues move, and sometimes their smallest gestures provide action insights into the biblical narrative.)

"Shall we give you a name?" I ask of the mother.

"Yes, let's give her a name," says someone in the group.

"OK," says the mother.

"What is your name?" I ask. "Make it up."

"It's funny, but the name 'Dinah' popped into my head."

"Fine" I say. "You are Dinah." Nice touch, I think.

"Who else is in this scene?" Silence. "Are we done?" Like the auctioneer, I bring down an imaginary gavel in my mind: Sold! "OK," I say, "let yourselves settle for a moment into your parts. Let yourself notice how you are feeling about what is happening here and how you are feeling about other characters in this scene. Who are you farthest away from? Who are you closest to? Look around. And now, only if you want to, I would invite you to say one thing in character before we end this scene.

"Laban, what do you have to say, either in a one-line soliloquy or to someone else?"

"Can I do both?"

"Sure."

"Well, to myself I say, 'I always expected my sister would marry, but I never imagined she would move away from home.' And to Rebecca I'd say, 'Stay in touch ... somehow.'"

"Thank you," I say to this Laban, "and please, if you would, hold that pose until each character has had his or her say. Someone may want to say something to you." Then, turning to the man playing Bethuel, "Bethuel?"

"Well, I'm thinking kind of the same thing as Laban. She's leaving us; she really is leaving. I feel...sad, and I want to go over and give her a hug. May I?"

"Sure, then come back here to the place you first chose." Bethuel does this.

"Eliezer?"

"Well, this whole thing has been miraculous. I began this journey simply setting out on an errand for Abraham, but I end it feeling I have had an experience of his God." He pauses. "I have nothing to say to anyone here, but I am rehearsing what I will say to Abraham when I see him."

"And you three handmaidens?"

"I hope I'll find a husband where we're going."

"I hope Rebecca packed our little amulets and idols."

"I was having a nice little affair with Laban; this really breaks it up."

"And Dinah," I ask, turning to the woman who came up as Rebecca's mother.

"I don't know where to begin. I don't want to say anything." But here she puts her arm around her bibliodramatic daughter and pulls her to her. At first Rebecca seems stiff, but, feeling something in Dinah's hug, she lets herself soften to receive it and then seems for a moment to be holding her.

"Thank you, Dinah."

"And finally you, Rebecca. I am sure you have something to say to everyone, but what I want you to do is focus on what you are saying here to yourself."

If Rebecca were to speak to everyone, we would be moving into a full-scale bibliodramatic scene. This is not what the players contracted for, nor is it what I feel would be appropriate to set in motion. For a beginning practitioner it is enough to see is how you can keep the sculpting process manageable while still gaining a lot of mileage out of it as a method of interpretation.

Rebecca disengages herself from her mother and takes a step away from her. She looks at each person in the scene. Each meets her eye. Then she looks down. She draws a deep breath, then looks up at Eliezer: "*Hineni.* I'm ready."

"Well, thank you all. Will each of you take a deep breath?" They do, "And now will you begin to confuse our tableau, begin to walk, then to mill around?" They do this for a half a minute. "And now if you would each tell the person you meet your real name in real life."

"Robert."

"Sam."

"Ellen."

"Rebecca."

"No, your real name."

"My real name is Rebecca. It's why I wanted to play the part." We all laugh, and in this way the closure is accomplished, and when, as I do in a moment, I tell the players to return to their seats in the group, the reviewing can begin.

In the reviewing phase of a Bibliodrama like this I usually start with people in the group who were not part of the role-play and ask them to tell me things they saw or thought about during our sculpting. I have two reasons for starting with them. One, I want to draw them in as quickly as possible and to capitalize on their role as observers. Second, I want to give my players a little more time to de-role and to shift into a more cognitive mode.

The observers can talk about the placements, the poses, the feelings they heard, or the feelings they would have supplied if it had been up to them to play this character or that.

Then the players speak. Now it is important for them to talk *about* the characters and not *as* them. I do not want them going back into role.

In this instance, the most interesting part comes when the woman who played the mother, and who has been quite silent and pensive through this reviewing, tells us of having had her daughter move to Japan two years earlier. "It was very hard then, and it all came back to me now. I wanted to hold on and never let her go."

The woman who played Rebecca speaks up at this point. "I felt that at first when you hugged me, and I wanted to pull away. I was thinking, 'This is going to make it harder to say goodbye,' but then I felt for you. I understood, and I wanted to take care of you. Maybe your daughter felt that way, too."

"Maybe...yes, I think so."

"It's amazing, really," says the man who played Laban, "that in the next generation Rebecca is going to have to say goodbye to two sons, and one of them, Jacob, is going to come back here and take away my two daughters."

"Patterns," I offer.

"It happens in every generation."

"Then and now."

The group is now going in two directions at once. They are going back into the biblical narrative to notice the cycles of departure and return that make up one of the long, rhythmic lines of Genesis. And they are thinking about their own lives, daughters gone off to Israel, and perhaps their own departures from home recently or long ago. As the director, I hear how our stories are animating the biblical stories, how the two kinds of narratives, the lived and the written, are resonating with one another.

If, as teacher, I have an agenda to keep the Bibliodrama text-centered, I can steer the conversation in that direction. I might, for example, get the class to inventory other places in the Genesis narrative where a similar scene is played out either explicitly or implicitly. Or I might take the discussion of this particular passage to a deeper level of understanding. If I am comfortable with it and the group appears to be also, I can let the talk flow on in more personal directions, and I can be supportive to people as they tell pieces of their own stories. Time—How much time do I have left?—and comfort—Is the group all right with this type of personal sharing?—are the key factors in my guiding the review.

At every level, from playing objects to enacting characters in scenes, the fact is that bibliodramatic midrash necessarily draws some of its power from the substrata of personal history that run beneath our acts of interpretation. It is not my task as director to pull those deeper strata of memory and personal history up to the surface, nor to make them any more explicit than the participants volunteer. But neither is it my task to repress that information. My task is to trust the process, to make sure, by my guidance and restraint, that this work in interpretive play, which weaves text and self together, will do no harm to text or self. I want to maintain a double focus: to open the windows that give us views into the biblical narrative and to let, if people choose, other windows open as well. When the setting is right—when the group and the director both feel comfortable—then Bibliodrama can open windows into our own interiors, histories, dreams. When it does, the window of scripture becomes for a time a mirror in which we see our own faces.[11]

The Encounter

The encounter is the heart of the western dramatic imagination. Encounters are charged, layered, and human; they are built upon the point and counterpoint of differing voices, the meeting face-to-face of differing perspectives. The Bible is no exception; it, too, is full of scenes of encounter. In the Pentateuch alone we find them everywhere from the interchange of Eve with the serpent to the last words Moses addresses to Joshua. In between there is a whole host of encounters: Cain and Abel after the sacrifices; Abraham and God before Sodom; Rebecca comforting Isaac in his mother's tent; Jacob's reunion with Esau; Joseph and Potiphar's wife; Moses and Pharaoh; Aaron and the idolatrous Israelites; Miriam and the Cushite woman.

And ranging far beyond the five books of Moses we can find numerous examples of scenes of encounter—David and Jonathan, Peter and Jesus—in which the bibliodramatist may have a field day—encounters just waiting to be embodied into action.

In gaining the skills needed to create and direct an encounter, you must—again—start by reading and rereading the text closely. Gradually you will come to see encounters where you had not seen them before and to sense in them the potential for Bibliodrama. When we were looking earlier for sculptural possibilities in the text, we saw that there are moments in the biblical story in which the tableau is explicit (as in Jacob's extended family built up character by character in Genesis 29 and 30). And there are places where the tableaux, the sculptural possibilities, are implicit and require more imaginative insight to realize (as in the invisible and unmentioned figures whose presence we have to infer and enact in the

---

[11] Just here lies the difference between text-centered Bibliodrama and the bibliodramatic school that invites a deeper probing of the personal dimension. Unless a group explicitly contracts for this latter kind of work, then it is, from an ethical point of view, the responsibility of the director to maintain the focus on biblical interpretation, not on personal disclosures. It is a matter of what is kept in the foreground and what is kept in the background.

scene of Rebecca's departure). This is equally true of encounters—some are explicit in the text; others are implicit and take some penetration to recognize.

Here is an example of the staging of an explicit encounter. You can use it as a kind of model for how to direct encounters. Basically, you will notice the following steps:

1. First, one character is brought on stage and given his or her time to develop as a bibliodramatic character.

2. Then that character is frozen, so to speak, while you bring the second character on stage, interview him or her, and allow that character to become warmed up.

3. Then you bring the two characters together and support them in developing a spontaneous dialogue.

4. Look for the right moment to bring the encounter to a close; thank and de-role your players and engage the group in their closure of the scene.

Note: Doubling is often useful at the beginning as each of the two characters is amplified; but once the encounter begins, it is best to let the figures engaged in dialogue proceed without interruption. They need to own their characters and to play them out.

In Genesis 25:9 we read that "Abraham's sons Isaac and Ishmael buried him in the cave of Machpelah." The meeting between Isaac and Ishmael is explicit in the text, and therefore the movement from noticing it to enacting it can be made in a gentle, almost ruminative way. "I wonder what these two men actually might say to each when they meet to bury their father. Anyone have any ideas?"

"I think Ishmael would be angry."

"I think Isaac would be scared."

Notice that these responses are quite distanced; the class begins by talking about the characters in the third person. This is their warm-up.

For a first-time experience this is an easy and appropriate way to begin. There is no need to get people "on stage" right away. Engage your class in thinking about this scene as an encounter, questioning the biblical narrative and imagining it, taking little steps in personifying the characters. And even before thinking *encounter*, think *sculpture*.[12]

You might ask: "I wonder how Ishmael found out that Abraham was dead."

"I thought Ishmael had been sent away."

"He was. But there are stories that tell of Abraham visiting him, staying in touch."

"I know. I bet he—"

"Wait. Why don't you speak as Ishmael?"

Here, formally, I am initiating the action phase by asking a participant to talk as—in short, to voice—one of the characters in the Bible story.

"As Ishmael? All right. 'Call me Ishmael." (Laughter). "No, seriously, I heard about Abraham's death from Isaac."

"From Isaac?"

"Yes, he sent word that our father was ailing, and he thought I might want to see him before he died."

"And?"

"And I got there too late."

"Ah hah."

"I don't think that's what happened at all," someone else says.

"We have another Ishmael. OK, what do you think happened. How did you find out?"

We are **doubling**.

"My mother, Hagar, told me. She was keeping tabs on the old man, waiting for him to die so that I could return and claim my inheritance, the

---

[12] In fact, this scene may be done first as a sculpture in which one invites participants to brainstorm who might be there at the Cave. If Isaac is there, what about Rebecca? A careful reading of the text will show us that the twin boys, Esau and Jacob, are fifteen years old when Abraham dies. What then about Keturah, Abraham's second wife? What about the six sons they had together? What about Ishmael's mother, Hagar, and Ishmael's wife or wives, and his sons (Genesis 25:12ff)? To bring all these characters "on stage" is to provide the fullest setting and warm-up for the climactic meeting of Ishmael and Isaac.

one I had been cheated out of by Isaac and Sarah."

"So when you hear about Abraham's death from your mother, you… do what?"

"I get a band of men together."

"Ah hah, I see."

"I have another idea," says a third participant.

"Another Ishmael? Good. And what's your insight?"

"OK, I'm Ishmael. Abraham is a famous man. He was a king among the Canaanite kings. He remarried after Sarah's death, a Canaanite woman; he has a bunch of sons by her. Like me they're all disinherited. I hear about his death from one of them who wants me to come and help them oust Isaac."

"Wow," I say, amazed at the inventiveness of this group. "So you, Ishmael, are being asked to join a coup."

"Yes."

"And how do you feel about this?"

"Ready," says one person.

"Willing," says another.

"Ambivalent," says a third.

"Ambivalent?" I ask. "How so?"

"Well, on some deep level I love my baby brother Isaac. It wasn't his fault, his idea, to have me and my mother sent away. In fact, it wasn't Abraham's, either. That—that Sarah put him up to it. I'm going to pay my respects to our father; he loved us both; and I don't know what I'm going to do about his inheritance. I'm not sure what it is or whether I want it."

"And would you be willing," I ask of this participant, "to come and sit in this empty chair and play Ishmael in the scene that follows?" The participant seems a little dubious. "You can always step out of the part; we have other people who are willing to play Ishmael; we just need someone to start us off." Now, feeling this flexibility and support, the group member is willing to come to the stage and sit as Ishmael.

He has at his command now all the previous interpretations and insights the group has given us of Ishmael. (**Note: this marks the end of Step 1. The first character is developed and in role onstage.**)

"Now what about Isaac?" (**Beginning of Step 2.**) "Someone suggested Isaac sent for Ishmael, others imagine he will be surprised to find him at the cave. Do any Isaacs want to speak?"

"I do."

"You are Isaac."

"I am Isaac, and I am as ambivalent as Ishmael."

"Tell us more."

"Well, I lost my older brother. I always wondered what became of him. I've missed him. I wonder what it would be like to have grown up with him."

"Yeah," says another version of Isaac. Again we are doubling this figure, creating multiple versions of Isaac. "But I'm scared of him; I've heard he's a pretty fierce warrior, but at the same time I feel weak and scared and alone, and I'd like his strength, his support."

"I wonder if he blames me. I know it was my mother who put my father up to it, but I am the one who benefited from his being away."

"Yeah, I really benefited. I got to be taken up to the mountain and tied up on an altar," someone offers.

"Would you be willing to play out Isaac for a while?" I ask this latest voicer of the part.

"Sure, as long as you don't let him beat up on me." And with these words, half joke and half serious in their acknowledgment of Ishmael's likely anger, our Isaac comes to the stage. It happens that a woman has taken the part; she takes her seat on a chair I provide for her at some distance from Ishmael, facing him.

Step 2 is completed: two characters in role on stage.

"So," I say, turning to Ishmael, "you heard what Isaac said. He was starting to talk about being taken up on the mountain by his father. Do you have anything you want to say to him?"

(With this question I begin to stir the players toward a dialogue with one another: Step 3.)

"My father, too," says Ishmael, "and it was no picnic for me being his son. I got circumcised when I was thirteen. Did he ever tell you that? Did he ever talk to you about me?"

Spontaneously, by virtue of the slow and steady building of the scene, the two players—Isaac and Ishmael—begin to talk to each other (**Step 3 is underway**).

"I was old enough to remember you," says Isaac. "I remember the day you and Hagar left. I will never forget the look on my father's face, and there were times, later, if I displeased him, that I sometimes wondered if he would rather have sent me away than you."

"Did he ever talk about me?"

"Well..."

"Tell me the truth. I can handle it."

"No. He never did. But it was almost as if his silence spoke louder than words. After you left, and Hagar, he was depressed. I'm not sure he ever got over it. And things were never the same between him and my mother. You don't know what it was like to have him as a father. He was there, and he wasn't.

"Listen, Yitz, I know what it was like. He did what God told him to do. If I had been around, it would probably have been me he took up that mountain."

"Did you love him?" Isaac asks.

"I did, but I lost respect for him. He did what he was told. He didn't question his God enough. And when he gave in to Sarah, well, that was the last straw."

"Tell Isaac how you felt," I prompt.

"I felt hurt and angry. He disowned me. I hated him."

"He scared me." Isaac stops, and Ishmael doesn't say anything. I step in with a little encouragement.

"Ishmael, do you want to hear what Isaac is saying?"

"Yes, I guess so."

"OK, Isaac, go ahead."

"My father scared me. He was so old. He never played with me. That's why I missed you so much. But more than that, he seemed like he was in another world. He prayed. He walked alone into the wilderness. He wanted to teach me about his God, but I didn't want to learn. It wasn't just him who was scary; his God was scary, too. He told me once that God had destroyed the whole world in a flood."

"He told me that story, too. Right away I didn't want to have anything to do with that God. And then when Dad took out the knife—did it to himself first, then to me—I thought to myself, 'this man is crazy.'"

"Yes, I often wondered if he was crazy. And then he took me up the mountain."

"Tell Ishmael what that was like." Again I do some prompting, wanting to keep the energy between them going.

"I don't know whether I can."

"Try," says Ishmael.

"Well, it was like I was completely divided in myself. On the one hand, I felt like this journey was in some way the culmination of my life with my father. I knew he was taking me to his God and I was ... gripped by curiosity. It's like I really wanted to see this God of his who was more special to him than anything or anyone else. And at the same time I was terrified. I was a grown man. He didn't force me to go. I was drawn along by something in me that found this whole thing fascinating, irresistible."

"You know, Isaac, I just realized something," Ishmael interrupts. "I just realized what it means to have our father's inheritance."

"What does it mean?"

"I always thought the inheritance was his sheep and cattle and servants and gold. I always thought I had been done out of material wealth, and I came here in part to get my due. But I realize now that the inheritance is his God, is being...a servant, I don't know what...of being willing to do whatever this God asks you to do. My mother saw God in the wilderness, but He didn't ask her to kill me. I just realized I don't want the inheritance."

"I don't either."

"I can understand that, but I think it's yours. I hope you never have to sacrifice one of your sons."

"I never could."

The two players sit facing each other in silence. (What they have been creating between them has reached some natural point of closure, and I use it as the occasion to bring Step 3 to a conclusion.)

"This seems like a place where we could end this encounter," I offer. "What do you think?"

"Sure."

"Fine with me."

"I want to thank you both for playing it straight, so to speak. You have given us some real insights into the characters of Ishmael and Isaac and also one version of their relationship." Group members murmur their assents. "I'd like you both to stand up, take a deep breath, and introduce yourselves to the group by name" (**De-roling**). This they do, and I ask them to take their seats back in the group. As they resume their places in the group there are hands offered and pats on the back. Their work is appreciated.

"Before we talk about what L. and S. have given us in Ishmael and Isaac, and some of our own takes on these characters, I wonder if members of the group who have been watching this would like to say, as Isaac or as Ishmael, anything you think these biblical brothers might have wanted to say but did not get a chance to put into words."

In this way I create a move toward closure (Step 4), but I want to engage others in the process of play. At the same time, I want to let the two who have been playing these parts to have a chance to cool down. I encourage group members to voice the parts from their seats; I do not want to move into another encounter with a fresh Ishmael and Isaac on stage. In this case, it is a matter of both time and control. A lot has been stirred up, and I want to make sure there is time in the reviewing to hear from participants and observers alike and to make sure we have a chance to explore the interpretations we have created together.

"As Ishmael, I'd like to say that I came here with anger in my heart, but right now I feel something like compassion."

"As Isaac, I was scared of Ishmael, but I feel I have found a friend."

"As Ishmael, I envy the father that Isaac had. At least he had a father."

"As Ishmael, I have not been able to forgive Sarah or God."

"As Isaac, I wonder if we will have a future together." (There are other comments, but this gives you an idea of the kinds of things people say.)

"Thank you," I say to the group. (**Step 4 is completed.**)

The role-play is over; the reviewing phase is ready to begin.

The account of this encounter is, in part, a writer's fabrication; in part, it draws on many instances of my having directed this scene. When you do it, it will be different from this. The feelings, the insights, the interplay will take the scene in different directions. Sometimes Ishmael will actually need to talk to Abraham or Sarah as departed spirits (encounters within an encounter) before he can talk to Isaac. Sometimes the talk of the two "brothers" will never get past accusation and self-defense. It is gratifying when a scene works itself out toward a relatively harmonious closure, but the proof of the work, even when the ending is not so smooth, is in the insights into the text that the Bibliodrama has created. With that as your goal, any enacted exploration of this encounter is likely to yield new insights into the text. **But however the variations occur, the underlying pattern is the same:**

First one character is developed and brought to the stage.

Then the second is developed by the group, enroled, and brought to the stage.

Then they talk.

When their dialogue is done you bring the scene to closure.

For each subsequent player added to the scene you need to engage the group in voicing that character; you then select someone to play the character onstage; and you bring that player up and prompt a dialogue.

As always, I leave time for review. That is the time when players and observers are encouraged to talk about what this work has been like. What have we learned together? I want to keep the focus on the textual rather than the personal level, and so my questions will lead in that direction. As I have said before, **I never see it as my task in this context to seek out the personal associations.** To do so would be to create a climate that might make participants understandably uncomfortable. It might suggest that my agenda, hidden until now, was to bring about self-disclosure. People might feel they were being manipulated. **On the other hand, voluntary self-disclosure is very different from personal information elicited by the leader-director's questions. When volunteered, this information is a sharing prompted by a sense of personal safety and some inner readiness to tell others in the group something about themselves.** As you will see shortly, the personal often comes up unbidden. While I won't fish for it or feed it, I will welcome it and do my best to be supportive to those venturing to talk about their experiences of the Bibliodrama in these candid ways.

I begin by thanking the group and by appreciating their participation. Then I might ask, "What are some of the things that we learned about this story by doing it this way? Does anyone have an insight they want to share?"

People talk about many things. The different versions of Ishmael, the history of Arab and Jewish relations, the wish that ways could be found for these two peoples to really talk to each other. Maybe, someone suggests, the masklike quality of Bibliodrama would actually help the peace process. Some participants state that it was too polite, too nice. "I think there would have been much more anger between them." Some people are amazed that the passage exists at all in the Bible. "The story would have made perfect sense without their having met at the cave," someone says. "Maybe whoever wrote it wanted us to think of these two being reconciled in some way." (Here, if we had more time, we might hear from the Redactor.)

At a certain point, the man who played Ishmael talks about what it was like to move from an initial sense of hostility into... "Well, by the end I felt sorry for Isaac. I didn't want the inheritance. As a non-Jew, I guess I am going to have a different experience of God. Maybe 'chosenness' isn't such an overriding idea."

The woman who played Isaac remains quiet until the end. I ask her if there's anything she wants to share with us. "Not really. I've just been thinking a lot about my father. He died last year. In some ways he was like Abraham, serious, sometimes remote. I had a huge respect for him, but I didn't really feel close to him. I guess the Isaac I played here was a lot like me."

"Thank you," I say. "In doing Bibliodrama, we often find some surprising resonances between the story and our own lives. But as interpretation, what you presented had a real validity for me as an insight into the biblical Isaac. I actually felt that in some way it made perfect sense that he was the one who needed to hear it, who could most understand."

And as long as time allows, we will proceed in this way to review the work. The other steps of the reviewing process—bringing in other sources and commentaries, returning in a more exegetical spirit to reread the story and seeing what new light we have shed on it, and even processing the direction of the piece, the choices players made and how they felt in their roles; all these are also matters for the ending of the session, but I am not interested here in providing an account of these. My purpose has been to illustrate the conduct of an encounter.

Explicit encounters, such as this one at Makhpelah, arise very naturally from the text of the specific story you are studying. Implicit encounters take a little more digging, but once unearthed can be directed along the lines of the scene above. Here are some examples of implicit encounters.

- Noah and his wife talk aboard the ark (Genesis 7:24-8:1).

- Abraham's farewell dialogue with his father Terah (Genesis 11:3212:5).

- After Jacob cheats him of his blessing, Esau leaves his mother and father and goes to live with Ishmael (Genesis 28:9). What do these two men, who after all have a good deal in common, say to each other?

- Rachel is dying in childbirth (Genesis 35:16-20). Might she not wish to have a final conversation with her sister Leah? If so, what might the two women say to each other?

- At some point after his return to Egypt, as the would-be liberator of his people, Moses meets the woman who adopted him, the princess, in the palace of Pharaoh (Exodus 5:1). What do they say to each other?

- Aaron and Moses speak after the episode of the Golden Calf (Exodus 32:21-25).

- Aaron and Miriam talk together about the Cushite woman Moses has brought into his tent (Numbers 12).

Implicit encounters, once seen by the director, can then be introduced to the group in a speculative mood. *"I wonder what these two might have said to each other...."* Alternatively, the director can invite a class, while reading a story together, to look for all the implicit encounters buried in a text. Or s/he can place two empty chairs facing each other in the front

of the class and name a character for one of them—Sarah, for instance—
and ask the class who in the story we are reading might have something
to say to her.

**There is a third kind of encounter, what I think of as a constructed
encounter. Constructed encounters are those that cut across the Bible
and bring together characters from different narrative zones who might
have some interesting things to say to each other.**

Here are some examples:

- What would Sarah say to Rachel as one barren woman
to another?

- What would Abraham say to Moses?

- What would Dinah say to Zipporah?

- What would Tamar say to Dinah?

- What would Cain say to Ishmael?

- What would Isaac say to Jesus?

In order to create such dialogues, the director needs to set up a kind
of playing space that allows characters to step from their particular stories
and meet in a neutral dimension. There are certain localities in the Bible
that suggest this kind of dimension. The Cave of Machpelah, for example,
is the resting place of Abraham, Sarah, Isaac, Rebecca, Jacob, and Leah
(according to some imaginative commentators, of Adam and Eve as well).
So the cave might become a setting in which the ancestral spirits meet
and converse.

Similarly, the cave in which Jesus is entombed can become a theater
of constructed encounters.

But with equal effectiveness, the director can simply wonder aloud
what it would be like to have characters in the Bible who have never met
meet each other and talk.

"You can be any character in the Bible and meet and speak to any other character in the Bible. Come sit in this chair. Tell us who you are. And here is a chair for the person you want to encounter. Tell us who that is, and we'll see if someone will come to play that part."

There are, in addition to these three types of encounter—explicit, implicit, and constructed—two others that need to be mentioned: the encounter between parts of the self and the encounter between the human and the Divine. For these two types of encounter the story of the wrestling between Jacob and the adversary serves as a model.

The Encounter between Parts of the Self

JACOB WAS ALONE; AND A MAN WRESTLED WITH HIM UNTIL
DAYBREAK. WHEN THE MAN SAW THAT HE DID NOT PREVAIL
AGAINST JACOB, HE STRUCK HIM ON THE HIP SOCKET; AND
JACOB'S HIP WAS PUT OUT OF JOINT AS HE WRESTLED WITH
HIM. THEN HE SAID, "LET ME GO, FOR THE DAY IS BREAKING."
"I WILL NOT LET YOU GO UNLESS YOU BLESS ME." SO HE
SAID TO HIM, "WHAT IS YOUR NAME?" AND HE SAID,
"JACOB." THEN THE MAN SAID, "YOU SHALL NO LONGER BE
CALLED JACOB, BUT ISRAEL, FOR YOU HAVE STRIVEN WITH
GOD AND WITH HUMANS, AND HAVE PREVAILED."
"PLEASE TELL ME YOUR NAME."
BUT HE SAID, "WHY IS IT THAT YOU ASK MY NAME?"
AND THERE HE BLESSED HIM (Genesis 32:24-29).

Some people think that this wrestling takes place between Jacob and himself, that two parts of his own soul contend.

The encounter between two aspects or parts of the self is always a rich possibility for Bibliodrama.

For example, when Abram receives the call to leave his native land and his father's house, it is easy to imagine a struggle within him. In fact, the whole difficult ordeal of his vocation is full of inner battles, the climactic one being, of course, the three-day journey to Mt. Moriah. The dialogue between the good and evil energies in the soul, between higher and lower powers, between duty and selfishness, between head and heart, between faith and fear, between self and surrender: All these internal wrestlings may be given embodied form as encounters.

The introduction to such encounters can be simple. You need say only that you wonder whether a particular narrative moment might conceal a character's internal struggle. For example:

"Sarah is still unable to bear a child and starts to think about offering Abraham to her maidservant Hagar. What do you think the back-and-forth inside her in this moment might be?"

Or "Laban has come to Rachel and told her that she must let her sister Leah stand in her place the next day at the wedding. I wonder what this moment might have been like for Rachel. Not easy, I would imagine. Your father has left you with your orders, and you feel yourself struggling between two opposing feelings. Can someone be Rachel at this moment and tell me what is going on inside you? Or better yet, someone speak as one side of Rachel, and then someone else speak up as the opposing voice." (Here you might place two chairs with their backs to each other simply to concretize the inner conflict.)

The Encounter Between the Human and the Divine

The second encounter that we can find in Jacob's wrestling is the encounter between the human and the Divine.

The dark night of the soul dramatized in Jacob's solitary encounter with the Divine can be located in many places in the Bible. Though Jacob wrestles almost wordlessly, it is possible to imagine the wrestling as a dialogue in physical form between heaven and earth, spirit and flesh, God and the human soul. Each of the biblical figures who deals with a divine summons or mission has her and his experiences of questioning, doubt, or challenge. We find this debate rendered in words between Abram and God before Sodom; and between Moses and God before the burning bush in Exodus.

Many characters, however, are not given the chance to talk to God in the Bible, but we know they have something to say. What does Sarah say to God when Isaac is born? What is her prayer of thanksgiving, and what would God say to her? How might one conclude the Song of the Sea Miriam begins in Exodus 15:20-22? What does Joseph say to God during his years of imprisonment?

The Bible is full of unspoken prayers and agonized questionings. Imagine the last words of Adam and Eve to God as they leave the Garden of Eden. Imagine the last words of Moses to God before he dies. Prayer and supplication need not go unanswered. One of the challenges in directing an encounter between the human and the Divine is to imagine the response of God even when God is silent in the text.

In establishing such an encounter, you need a chair for the human and a chair for the Divine. The chair representing God may remain empty, or it may be inhabited by a representative of the Divine, an emissary or angel who has the authority to speak for God. Or God (Him/Herself) may come on stage.[13]

Encounters are the crucible for drama, and the Bible is full of them. This interplay of perspectives, this dialogue between opposing perspectives, need not demand the dominance of one position over the other but can lead to a sense of deeper understanding for both.

Armed now with a sense of how to handle the sculpting of a scene and the dynamics of an encounter, we are ready to put the elements together and walk through a Bibliodrama in its longer form.

---

[13] Bringing God on stage is a tricky business and may be quite offensive to some. I deal with this more fully in Part Ill, section 3.

Part II

The Longer Form

4

Text Selection
and Text Preparation

We now come to the selection of the bibliodramatic text and to your preparation of it—proportionately a task of greater importance given the longer and more complex requirements of a full length Bibliodrama. I have already talked about this in Part I, where our focus was on single scenes. I return to this subject again as we think about the longer form of a Bibliodrama: as a series of inter-linked scenes that will form a larger drama. Now text selection requires us not only to find a fertile starting point, but to have in mind a sense of a middle, and of an ending.

The task of selecting and preparing the story for enactment is your homework and part of your warm-up. In the course of thinking through a story, you will become increasingly aware of and excited by its dramatic possibilities, and that excitement primes you for sharing this work with a group. **Especially in your first ventures into the longer form, it is important to select a story that intrigues you, challenges you, and feels meaningful to you.** Your engagement in the story will communicate itself to the group and help to warm them up to their own engagement with it.

The selection of a text upon which to base a full-scale Bibliodrama is an important task and one that the director usually takes charge of. There are four principal reasons for my assigning the director this task:

1. Your having chosen the story beforehand heads off endless and fruit-less group-discussions-about-choices that can serve resistance rather than facilitating action.

2. It gives you, as the director, some measure of control over the kind of materials (emotions, issues, ideas) a text might elicit and, therefore, the affective depth a story might reach.

3. It allows you to prepare commentary and traditional sources for the group or class ahead of time.

4. It gives you a head start; it helps you be the most prepared member of the group. Preparation can lessen anxiety, if you do not hold too fast to what you have prepared.

Text Selection: Three Criteria

My selection of a story is guided by three things: first, by what I call ease of access and entry; second, by depth of field; third, by a sense of an ending.

1. Ease of Access and Entry: Despite the fact that the Bible is the most widely owned book in the western world, its contents are not well known. But because, in a Bibliodrama, people are facing the Bible, they feel they should know it, and when they are unsure about their knowl-edge, they feel embarrassed. That sense of ignorance and embarrassment can feed into the anxiety people may already have about role-playing. Therefore it is important, at least in the beginning, to select a text that is accessible to everyone, a story that people either know or can be helped to know relatively easily.

Sometimes a little storytelling is useful both to (re-) familiarize a group with the story you want to do with them and as part of their warm-up to play. For example, if I am going to do a Bibliodrama on Jacob's wrestling with the angel (Genesis 32:23-33:5), I need to back up and make sure the group understands the context. I must review Jacob's betrayals of Esau in their childhood, his flight, his life in Haran, the return, the four hundred armed men Esau appears to be marshaling against Jacob, etc. All these elements bear on the wrestling and its immediate aftermath.

Often this storytelling takes place as an interchange; I will tell some of the story and ask for details from the group, and then together we will build up the story: *"What happened next?"* This process of building up the story collaboratively has several virtues. In the first place, it engages people and therefore begins to form a group that is collaborative and participatory. Second, it gives me my first impressions of the participants: Who is ready to speak out? Who is quiet? And third, I can also begin to measure a whole series of variables that will be important to the way I pitch the Bibliodrama: such things as depth of knowledge, ignorance of the story, articulateness, brightness of affect, tendency to dominate, attentiveness, etc.

But you have to be careful; too much storytelling, too much narrative detail, and you can smother the warm-up rather than excite interest. You can make it feel like just another class where the teacher knows most and best and the students are trying to supply the right answers. Instead, aim for broad brushstrokes that lead toward a particular narrative moment, the line in the text where your Bibliodrama proper will begin.

Ease of access also means ease of entry. Not only do I want to take a story people know well or can know fairly quickly, I also want to begin the story in a place that is easy to enter. By this I mean a place of broad possibility, ideally with many characters who can be heard from in the opening scene, with chances for humor and playfulness in the setting or situation. I have found that maximizing the group's involvement requires warming them up to the process of role-playing; and that involves offering parts that at first do not require strong emotional commitment or penetration. It is not a good idea to attempt to plunge your group into the most dramatic part of a story; they will not be ready, and the Bibliodrama will not work. **Ease of access involves beginning at the periphery of the story and moving gradually toward the center.**

For example, in a Bibliodrama that wanted to explore Jacob's night of wrestling, it would be asking too much of the group to identify with

Jacob's thoughts and feelings at that highly charged moment when he encounters the adversary. The group would not be ready to step into his shoes at this point because we have had, as a group, no chance to develop the context out of which this moment comes. We have had no time to warm up together, to get a feel of the process, or to become imaginatively invested in the story.

In this case, I would back up a bit, beginning the actual Bibliodrama with the scene of Jacob sending his wives and children across the river. After sketching in the relevant details of the background to this moment, I might begin in the following way:

"You are Jacob. What motivates you to separate your family as you do? What are you feeling?" After that, I might then go on to interview the significant people in the scene: Rachel, Leah, Judah, Joseph, and the serving girls, Bilhah and Zilpah, who are also mothers. I might play out a number of the conversations Jacob could have with each of these figures, their questions and statements to him. All this work is peripheral to the main scene but prepares us for it.

Only then would I approach the scene I had chosen for the climactic focus of the drama. And even then I would start by warming the group up to Jacob after he has sent his family away, when, as the Bible tells us, "JACOB WAS LEFT ALONE" (Genesis 32:25). "Tell me, Jacob, what are some of the things that you are thinking of on this night."

In short, as I look for texts, I look not only for good dramatic moments, but also for entry points—nonthreatening, open-ended beginnings that can let people be gradually and variously drawn into the imaginative world of the scene. I think carefully, too, about my opening questions, and how best to lead the group from the periphery of the story toward the center and the climax.

2. Depth of Field: The second criterion I look for in selecting a text is what I am calling (borrowing the term from photography) depth of field. Used in the context of Bibliodrama, depth of field has to do with how the scenes in a biblical story might touch on our lives, what strings it might touch in our hearts.

Some of the best texts for a Bibliodrama contain life cycle

events—births, marriages, deaths, or moments of initiation and life change that can evoke similar moments in our own development: leaving home, getting work, resolving conflicts with siblings, discovering a sense of spiritual truth. A bibliodramatist soon learns to search stories for their archetypal dimension, for those qualities of drama and meaning that persist in a timeless way and figure in our own lives. Such scenes make excellent vignettes in and of themselves or climactic scenes in more extended dramas.

The fact is, of course, that almost every moment in the biblical narrative can be seen as having an archetypal status, since the Bible is a repository of what we have come to define as the archetypal. It is sometimes hard to remember just how deeply the patterns of biblical story—the kinds of tales about family and community and human development it contains—have shaped all subsequent narratives. They also shape our ways of thinking about ourselves. **To play out a significant moment in the biblical narrative is, almost inevitably, to play into significant moments in our own lives.**

Text selection, then, involves our thinking about what a certain biblical narrative may be about in the most generic, thematic sense. Is it about love, death, separation, reunion, loneliness, search, leadership, obedience, self-delusion, enmity? To identify these thematic levels helps the bibliodramatist to open those veins of feeling and association in the group that will bring the relevance of these passages alive.

It is my task as director to survey beforehand the kinds of emotional, theological, and moral ground that a story will, or may, ask us to explore. Where are the steep places that a group may struggle to climb— God-moments, moments of prayer or celebration? And where are the caverns where we may discover sorrow or rage? Many of the biblical stories are laced with pain, and though I do not want necessarily to avoid painful stories, I want to have some idea of what kind of pain I might be getting myself into. (And, too, as I shall discuss in a moment, I will be thinking about endings; I will need also to imagine some routes out of the pain a story may bring up for us.)

For example, I rarely do the story of the sacrifice of Isaac unless I know the group fairly well or have been asked specifically to undertake it. I think that it is one of the most painful stories in the Bible. It may be easy of access—it is surely well known, and there are ways of beginning to work with the story from the periphery. But its center is terrible and terrifying; the dramatic climax, though one of deliverance and reprieve, comes after enormous, almost unendurable agony.

Though that level of anguish may not be the whole story, it cannot, must not be overlooked by the director looking for a text.

There are other stories that I place in a category with the binding of Isaac. For me the depth of field is too deep. The rape of Dinah can bring up unbearable feelings for certain participants; the story of Job is almost out of reach for the naturalism of Bibliodrama; the story of Lot and Sodom cannot be easily approached in certain settings; the nakedness of Noah poses obvious problems. And the gospels furnish their own daunting stories: The crucifixion can be unendurable for many and probably ought to be done, if at all, at the appropriate time of the year; the various miracles of healing virtually defy enactment. These are some of the texts where I fear to tread bibliodramatically.

On the other hand, think of the possibilities in the story of Ruth or Esther; think of the Passover narrative bibliodramatically, or the story of Miriam's confrontation with Moses over the Cushite woman, and her punishment; think of Jonah, David, scenes from the life of Jeremiah. There are the parables in the Christian Testament; there are stories of ministry, brotherhood, betrayal, and healing that offer excellent opportunities for interpretive play. Here the field is vast and the depths are manageable.

3. A Sense of an Ending: My third criterion for text selection bears on closure. In thinking about a text and its bibliodramatic possibilities, it is critical to give thought to possible endings. How far might I get in my Bibliodrama? What is the sequence of scenes I am considering? How do they build? Where might I end? What kinds of emotions and images might have been stirred up by the Bibliodrama? How can my closure help settle things down? Does the story end in death or reunion? Does my anticipated final scene end my Bibliodrama in bleak loss or unspoken rage? If so, I need to find a place to conclude that will be more positive and affirming. Whenever possible, I wish to select a story that leaves a group with a feeling of hope and some sense not just of conclusion but of closure.

It's the understandable concern of every director to bring a drama to a satisfying, even an aesthetic close. If the drama has taken us into feelings like grief, anger, or the sense of loss or vexation, then as a director you want to bring people back "up," so to speak, and do so in a way that feels authentic to and integrated into the drama.

For more on this subject, see section 6 of Part III, "Some Conventions for Closure."

When all is said and done, however, the fact is that **you can't always plan your endings.** Or to put it another way, **you can't always get the endings you plan.** Because Bibliodrama is a spontaneous process, you never can be sure where you will come out of it. It is important to have a destination in mind, and with that, an idea of how, ideally, you would like to reach it and then to close the drama, but hold to your vision lightly. Do your best to go with the drama as it evolves. You want, as best you can, to respect and to follow the spontaneity of the group.

4. The Text You Select Is You: As I search for and select my story, I need to be aware that my selection may have more than a little to do with my own needs and preferences. **My warm-up to the text—my own relationship to the story I select—is an important part of my preparation. I need to explore a little of my own interest in and predilection for a certain story.** What does this story mean to *me*? If it is not drawn from the lectionary or the biblical portion assigned for the week, then why am I drawn to it at this moment? How do I connect to it? What are the emotions and interpretive ideas I think are important to elicit? And why? How is this story a mirror for me? Which character or characters speak to me? Which—if I can detect my resistance—do I seem to avoid? These questions help me to be clearer about agendas that might otherwise over-determine my reading of the story. Coming to terms with my own understanding and interest in the text is an important aspect of getting clear and ready to direct.

Text Preparation

Once you have selected a text, you start to map it out. **Mapping a text involves thinking of a story in terms of scenes.** As in conventional theater, a scene takes place in a particular setting and involves a certain number of characters. In Bibliodrama, the dramatic condition of a crucial character often provides the material for a scene, or a scene may be built around sculpting and/or encounters. Scenes may be brief or lengthy, and their duration is often determined by how much your players unearth in their enactments.

It is always hard to be sure beforehand how long a scene will last. Sometimes you see little in a biblical moment, but your group turns up unexpected possibilities. Often you see a certain depth or complexity, but you cannot sell it to the group. It is not easy to arrange a drama to conform to the time allotted to it. In this regard, you can always *tell* what you had planned to play; storytelling can serve to abbreviate a scene or replace it entirely, if time demands you to move on. Given this option, it is advisable, then, to **plan more scenes than you may actually have time to play; it will give you a sense of having reserves.** And in case one particular scene does not excite your group, you have others you can suggest.

Mapping can be easier if you think about a series of questions for each scene you are preparing. You can use the following eight questions to structure your preparation of a scene.

The Eight Questions

1. **What part of the story will I *tell*** (or have the group tell with me) in order to set the stage for the movement into action? You will see this amply illustrated in the account of the Bibliodrama that follows.

2. **What parts of the story will I *read*** in order to set the context for the scene we are about to play and—if this is the first scene in the

drama—for the drama as a whole telling? (For example, if I am going to "do" the Joseph story, what kind of *general* background does my group need for the story as a whole? And what kind of *specific* background in order to enter into the particular scene I have selected reading?)

3. **What is the *threshold moment* and the *threshold question*** that, when I put it to the group, will (I hope!) take the group into voicing and play? (This is the moment when you say to the group something like the following: "OK, let yourself imagine that you are Jacob or any member of his extended retinue just catching sight, from the rise of a hill, of the land of Canaan. Who are you? What do you see? What do you feel?" Those last questions launch the group into role and formally initiate the action phase of the Bibliodrama.)

4. **What do I want to make sure I cover in each scene?** (This has to do with the kinds of situations I would like to develop inside of a scene, the parts of the story I want the group to do in action.)

5. **Which characters do I want to hear from?**

6. **What opportunities do I see for encounters or sculptings?**

7. **Where will the scene end?**

8. **And, if this is not the last scene, then what kinds of transitions can I gracefully make to the next scene I want the group to play?**

A Bibliodrama is a skein of scenes woven together to form a whole. You prepare your Bibliodrama by plotting a master design. Create your own storyboard outline of scenes for your drama. Later, you can attach notes to it that will refer to certain commentaries you want to bring in either during or at the end of the action phase. For each scene, you need to ask yourself the same eight questions proposed above. In this way you build up a plot outline of your drama based on clearly imagined scene segments. These you plot toward what you hope will be your ending and closure.

In directing each fresh scene, remember you will need to refocus the group on this new phase of the story. The warm-up of the participants is usually cumulative, making it easier, as the drama progresses, for players to shift from role to role and scene to scene. You always need to be aware, however, that a new scene requires a warm-up, as do new characters. Generally, one good way to help participants get ready for a new scene is by doing an appropriate amount of telling and/or reading.

Preparing for the last scene:

As far as your ending is concerned, you want to think about these five questions.

1. **What will be your final scene?**

2. **What note or mood does the drama end on?** (You cannot be sure, of course; there are too many variables. But you can certainly imagine how your final scene might leave people feeling.)

3. **If that final mood might be distressful to your group**—a death, a loss, a leaving, an injustice, a wound—then what do you have to do to provide some sense of hope or positive closure?

4. **Who would you like to have as the last character you want to hear from?** Can that character help give you the lift you need or provide you with a prayer or wisdom that will bring some sense of harmony at the end?

5. **What else do you have in mind to harmonize the mood at the end:** music, a chant, a piece of poetry to read? Remember that your group will appreciate your having a closure of some kind for them to try.

As you prepare your drama you may want to consult critical writings and commentaries. Becoming a student of your passage does not require you to be a scholar of the Bible, but the commentaries of educated readers can certainly help you see more deeply into your chosen story. These commentaries can also be brought in, either during or after the drama, to connect your group's Bibliodrama to the traditions of scholarship. As I said above, in creating your storyboard you can note what resources you can bring in at various points. Often commentary can serve to ease a tense emotional scene, getting people out of their feelings and into their heads.

Developing a plot outline of this sort is demanding. As you become more skilled and confident, less preparation will be needed; you will be able to trust your ability to steer while your drama is in motion. Also, you will develop a repertoire. Directing a drama a second or third time is very different from directing it the first time. The first time takes the most preparation, but once that work is done, you can build on it, tinker, embellish, and develop your story line. There will be fewer surprises, though there will always be some.

And lest all this seem too unfamiliar, let me remind you of a few ways plotting a Bibliodrama draws on some familiar skills. In creating a lesson plan, teachers think through the topics or ideas they want to cover, often mapping out complicated educational strategies. Or we are asked by a friend how we prepared a particular dish for dinner; we know how to break it down into its ingredients and to communicate the steps we took in putting the meal together. Or when we travel we plan an itinerary, think about stops, rests, possible side-trips, and how to get from one place to another. Some of these skills—of foresight and design—can be transferred to the plotting of a drama.

Also, as you acquire bibliodramatic experience from directing small vignettes or single scenes you will be able to draw on that experience as you approach a larger piece of work. You will be able to weave the elements together—a sculpture here, an encounter there—that will provide variety to a longer drama. In the beginning, of course, it is natural to hold tight to your game plan, but as you gain confidence in your ability to shape what the group is producing you will be able to let go of your carefully devised drama and go with the flow.

Preparing and then letting go

But remember: Once you ask your opening question, the Bibliodrama will unfold as an interchange between your fantasy of the way it was supposed to go and what actually turns up in the living process of the work itself. All your preparation is invaluable, even though you may jettison parts of it as the Bibliodrama unfolds. You cannot anticipate everything, but your thorough study of your story—your ideas for tactics, possibilities, and endings—equips you to respond to the role-playing of group members with a sense of overview and dexterity. You may not be able to use all that you have planned, but you will feel readier to field your group's spontaneity because of it. There will be times when you feel you are swimming in chaos, but at just such moments you can return to your game plan and, even if the transition seems awkward to you, move to a new scene.

5

The Warm-Up

Antidote to Anxiety: The Director

As we approach the longer form of Bibliodrama—a session that might last as long as an hour or more—we return to square one: the warm-up. With a multi-scene drama ahead, the director's anxiety level may be higher, so inner preparation and text selection may require more time and thought. Also, in carving out a critical path through a set of scenes that involve several characters, the director needs to think about transitions, about the movement from one focal point to the next. It is like preparing for a game of chess: You can rehearse gambits, but once the game is in progress, you have to respond to the options as they arise from play. The director's overriding principle should be: **Respect and respond to the spontaneity of the group as it comes into contact with the text and your questions.** Or, conversely, the group's will should overrule a director's desire to play out too slavishly the drama plotted beforehand. But one would be foolish not to have a game plan, and in approaching a longer drama, the director is advised to have in mind a course of action, a set of scenes, transitions, and closures.

Stage fright: Yours

I have already broached the subject of the director's warm-up in Part I, but let me elaborate here, for the longer the projected Bibliodrama, the longer you may need to spend in preparation, study, and plotting. Also, it is likely that your own anxiety will be greater as you approach the greater assignment of a drama that may last an hour or more and be composed of a number of scenes and characters. So your warm-up, aside from addressing technical challenges, must attend to what may be your heightened anxiety level. That anxiety comes with the territory.

Most people who imagine themselves trying this method feel something like this:

> I can't do this. My class will see right away I don't really know what I'm doing. I haven't studied this enough. They won't take part. They won't give it a chance, and they'll miss the richness and interest in this method. I won't get a chance to get them going. But then again, suppose I do. Suppose they get going too much. What if someone gets too involved? What will I do if someone gets angry or starts to cry? I'm not a therapist. I'm not trained to handle emotions in groups. I could get into big trouble here....

This little soliloquy touches on the two predominant fears people face in doing this work, especially in the longer form. One is the fear that no one will say or do anything. The other fear, polar opposite and perhaps more daunting, is that you will lose control of the process, that emotional forces will be unleashed, that someone will have a psychotic episode! Go nuts! Once you move even a few steps beyond the bounds of expected and conventional behavior in the classroom or from the pulpit, once you invite in the maverick of spontaneity—well, where will it end?

The anxiety at work here is completely normal. It arises when we try something new, when we are playing a new role. The skills that make that role comfortable only come in time; the breaking-in period, with its jagged learning curve, is nerve-racking. And if that anxiety is exaggerated into fear, and that fear is given its head, it may in the end persuade you never to try at all. So some courage and some process of self-strengthening is required for most of us before we even begin.

Centering Exercise

The following exercise is one that I use often, even after many years of practice in directing Bibliodramas of all sizes and shapes. It may not work for you in its present form, but it might—or some variation of it might. In any event, it's worth trying.

1. Find a quiet, distraction-free place to sit; have a pen and paper near you for writing. Now place before you an empty chair.

2. Look at that empty chair and see sitting in it someone living or dead, real or imagined, whom you can take as a **source of wisdom and inspiration**. Give that figure his or her name.

3. Write a brief letter to that figure which you begin with, "Dear...," and in which you spell out *briefly and honestly* your anxieties about directing a Bibliodrama.

4. Now imagine that the figure to whom you have just written is writing back to you. Take down her/his words as if at dictation. Write without censoring or pause until you feel you have taken it all down.

5. Read back to yourself what you have written.

Before almost every session I conduct, I spend a few moments with my journal.

Here is a sample of a letter to my "friend," written before I began a weekend of work at a church in Baltimore several years ago.

> Dear E. . . ,
>
> Well, here I am again, jittery and feeling unfocused. Being here at J's is a big deal for me. I really respect J and want to do well here. He has been doing Bibliodrama with his congregation, and I think he's a tough act to follow. I want to wow everyone, and I am

feeling a lot of pressure. Help!

Here is what I "got back," so to speak, from my spiritual encourager:

Dear Peter,

You are anxious, and it is understandable. No matter how many times you do this, there is always the feeling of the first time. That is because every time is new and unpredictable. J loves and respects you; he is not competing with you or wanting anything but good things for his flock. Let yourself feel his warmth and support.

But also remember this is not about your looking good or coming off well; it's not about your ego. This is about working with people in a human way. You can always admit you are stuck or puzzled. Keep the process open and light. There is nothing to prove, no one to impress. There is no right or wrong here.

Let yourself explore this biblical story with people. **Exploring** is key. When you explore you are simply inviting an open process. You have no map; you have never been here before.

Enjoy the looking around with people, the discovering. There is always more going on than you can be aware of. Trust yourself and trust the process and trust those invisible forces that attend such work and support your eccentric form of ministry. Open your heart and breathe.

All will be well....Love, E

I feel a little foolish sharing these very private words. It is, after all, the personal—and perhaps, some might think, even childish—way that I soothe myself. But I have found that unless I take care of my jitters ahead of time, they will communicate themselves to the group. My ease puts others at ease. For me this kind of warm-up lessens my nervousness and releases my spontaneity, and I know I work best when my heart is open.

Articles of faith

In addition to this inner dialogue there are three factors that reassure me in the face of my anxieties: the voluntary and collaborative nature of

Bibliodrama; the self-monitoring of the participants; and the sacredness of the stories. A few words about each.

- In the first place, I remind myself and later the group that no one is to be compelled to take part. It is the obligation of the director to assure people that they are always free to sit back and observe. Remember that you can always stop the process, either for a moment or completely, or you can help participants step away from a role or a scene that is suddenly too loaded for them. Their knowing that they can say "No" is imperative before they can allow themselves to say "Yes."

- Along the same lines, you can also ask the group to share in the responsibility of watching out for the well-being of participants. A statement like the following can help people to feel they have control over the process and help you feel you have support in the group: **If you feel, in the course of our Bibliodrama, that I am not being sensitive to the discomfort of any member of the group, please let me know. Just raise your hand, and we'll check it out. Nothing is more important to me than the feeling of safety among us.**

- In the second place, as I've said before, I believe that people involved in the bibliodramatic process do not undertake more than they are ready to handle, and certainly not in groups that are, ultimately, "public places." There are, to be sure, people who can disturb any situation with their antics and their needs to be recognized. Courtesy, tact, firmness, and humor are the skills we draw on to manage such situations.

- The third article of faith that sustains me is the knowledge that Bibliodrama involves the Bible. Scripture is its soil and source. The emotions, passions, and meanings found in and stirred up by a bibliodramatic exploration are ultimately to be seen within the universe of the text, in its ultimate goodness and illumination. The Bible, in all Western traditions, has been the supreme book of hope. The immediate and terrible dramas of its protagonists are only part of a much larger cosmic myth of return, repair, redemption, and reconciliation. The Bible affirms that there is a mystery working in human experience that has divine origins and designs. As that design unfolds we may unknowingly prove to be God's agents. Moreover, even if we are mistrustful of ideas of providence or skeptical about a personal God, we can find in the Bible stories of dignity, faith, and perseverance in the face of ordeals and the unknown.

Participants in Bibliodrama have some sense of this odd double reality. Fully aware of their tears and fears as players, they are, at the same time, actors who retain an awareness that they are involved in something taking place inside a sacred tradition. That participation in tradition can give additional meaning, even sanctity, to our play.

Scripture is like a great canopy; in its shade hundreds of generations have been consoled, uplifted, challenged, and inspired. What that is human has not been felt or seen in the biblical tales, or considered by the commentators? Do we really need to be afraid or ashamed of the part we bring to it or find there? At any moment in our travails in Bibliodrama, as in life itself, can we not pray even to a hidden God or reach out to one another?

These are the supports that buttress me each time I conduct a Bibliodrama. The effect of doing Bibliodrama has been cumulative; each small success builds a greater confidence. I have come to see Bibliodrama as a form of liturgy, a living spiritual dynamic. Each time I step into the field of force it generates, I feel affirmed. I feel connected in a special and vital way to a community, to a text, and to an immemorial tradition.

Antidotes to Anxiety: The Group

Stage fright: Theirs

There is a direct connection between the director's warm-up and the warm-up of the group; the group's warm-up very much depends on how the director is feeling. If you are jittery or hesitant, the group will consciously or unconsciously know it, feel it, and believe that there must be something to be jittery or hesitant about. Conversely, **if you have dealt with your own anxiety and come before the group open, relaxed, humorous, and ready to try something new, you will communicate to the group a sense of ease and adventure.**

And, it must be said, it's almost impossible to fool a group. You may wish to appear relaxed while inwardly feeling tight, but the group on some level will feel what's really going on in you. It is far more advisable to say openly to the group that you are nervous about trying something new than to fake it and to have group members feel ill at ease for reasons they cannot understand.

Also, what you feel as you approach a Bibliodrama, your group may feel as well. Not just from you, but on their own. They, too, could be anxious about the new roles, new learning, new relationships with one another that this different way of studying together might evoke. Your having in some measure come to terms with your fears frees you to attend to theirs.

There is nothing wrong with making time at the beginning—as part of the group warm-up—for people to talk about concerns about starting something new. **In fact, one of the best and most appropriate ways of warming up a group is by making explicit the fact that you and the group are undertaking a new experiment. You can start by thinking together about what the concerns might be that we bring to such an undertaking.** Of course, too much of a focus on anxiety can heighten the very thing you are trying to lower.

Guidelines

During these preliminaries you will want to talk about guidelines and protocols, the rules of the game. People need to know the rules, not laid down as something rigid or burdensome, but as parameters within which to feel safe and free. These guidelines are few, but they are crucial.

The first has to do with permission not to play. You must make it clear at the outset that though you are proposing a form of participatory study, anyone is free at any time to be an observer. Concomitantly, anyone— even if they are in the middle of a sentence—is free at any point to call a halt to their participation and decline to continue. As director, **you must respect and keep alive the option of non-participation**. You need to be aware that a person may be saying that they do not want to go on with their playing of a part *even if they are telling you that in implicit rather than explicit ways*. Their tone, their body's hesitancy, a look you catch on their face, a certain tendency to break out of role: All these are indicators of a resistance that needs to be recognized and honored. As I said before, you can always check on it:

"Are you OK with this role? Do you want to keep going with this? Someone else may be quite willing to play the part from here."

Being sensitive to the limits of play among your participants is a key factor in keeping yourself out of the hot water you were anxious about in the first place. **Don't push**.

The second rule is that **playing involves taking a role**. Bibliodrama, you may explain, is a way of exploring a biblical story by speaking as the characters within it. You, as the director, will do your best to help people speak in role. Once the "play" or "playing" begins, then people take part by taking a part. The parts may initially be defined by the passage you have chosen, but people may discover voices in the text you had never imagined in your preparation.

In the Garden of Eden, for example, you thought of Adam, Eve, the Serpent, and God as characters, but someone suddenly wants to play Lilith, or one of the angels sent to guard the way to the Tree of Life after the expulsion of Adam and Eve.

Encourage the group to find parts beyond those you may propose; your only requirement is that when they speak as "I," it must be an "I" within the tale.

The rule of staying in role should be observed throughout the play of the Bibliodrama. Often, however, interruptions to the process come in the form of members of the group wanting to question or comment on what is going on. **Resistance to play takes the form of dropping out of role.** It is always my preference to ask people to stay in role, and so I may ask people to hold their comments until later, or I may help them find a way of commenting or questioning within the form of a role-play. (You will find examples of this later in the book.) Whenever possible, don't let members of the group break role. If they do, they can dilute or cool down the process of role-playing.

On the other hand, letting people question what you are doing or why may help to keep the process from getting too deep. Some give and take about the process can leaven the mood, and often other members of the group will be the first to tell those who constantly interrupt to "give the process a chance." There is no formula here to guide you exactly in moderating participation. Being flexible and open and relaxed—that is to say, not feeling bound to keep the Bibliodrama pure—will often send the more important message to your group: namely that you care and are interested in whatever comes up for them in the course of the session.

There is a kind of bibliodramatic law at work here: **The longer people stay in role, the deeper the affective level of the drama is likely to be.** This is because people draw, at least in part, on both their conscious and unconscious experience in playing a part. Spontaneity and imagination feed on deep sources. If the purpose of text-centered Bibliodrama is to tilt the balance of participation toward the text and not toward the self, then the director must be careful not to keep people in role too long. Some people will welcome the challenge of sustaining a part, of investing more deeply in it, but some people will be frightened by what it is calling out of them. By not being too rigid in conducting the role-play, by allowing people to interrupt the process and to step out of role, the director insures safety—even if it is at times a little too much safety.

It is far wiser to err on the side of safety. And remember: Anytime you as the director want to lighten things up, you, too, can interrupt the process with humor or by breaking people out of role. **Anytime you need to relieve the intensity of the process, you can shift from role-play to text and commentary.** This shift will allow people to move from the affective to the cognitive, to get some perspective on feelings, and to deal with the biblical materials in a safer, more distanced way.

Confidentiality

Some practitioners of Bibliodrama believe it is important to bring up the issue of confidentiality at the beginning, as part of the director's prologue. Personally, I do not raise it at this point. In the first place, the work of the group may not include material we feel is "sensitive." **To speak about confidentiality too early runs the danger of making people think there is a therapeutic agenda afoot; so don't bring it up prematurely or unnecessarily.** I reserve, and often exercise, the option of speaking about these matters at the end of the group when I can assess more accurately whether there has been personal and therefore sensitive information that needs the cloak and the contract of confidentiality.

The Director's Prologue: Sample Script

By way of concluding this first phase of the warming-up process, let me offer one kind of sample script: what I am calling the director's prologue, which prepares the group for the work you want to do with them.

The example that follows assumes that the group you are working with is familiar with you and with Bibliodrama, ideally a group that has been introduced to some "short form" of Bibliodrama before this longer one. (It is rare that you will do a long Bibliodrama cold.)

You might begin in the following way to warm them up.

"Good evening, class. We've been playing with the technique of

Bibliodrama off and on for some time now. This evening we're going to see what happens when we stay with it longer, do several scenes. Some of you have been asking that we give ourselves more time to get into a Bibliodrama together. So here we are.

"Frankly, I'm a little nervous about tackling a whole Bibliodrama, but I have been reminding myself that we are here to explore a story and learn together. It always feels like a first time. And remember, our usual ground rules are in place: You participate only insofar as you want; you can always step out of the part you're playing; and when or if you think I am not hearing someone who is telling me they are uncomfortable with a role, you not only can, you should check it out with me immediately. Just raise your hand, or if that doesn't get my attention, feel free to interrupt.

"What we're going to do together is look at a biblical story we're all pretty familiar with. We're going to refresh our familiarity with it by some storytelling and reading, and then we're going to step into the story and make it our own. I want you to feel free, as always, to question what we're doing, but maybe some of your questions you can save until after we've done our Bibliodrama. You can also just watch and listen. There is no need for you to take part unless you want to. What we're going to do is step into the shoes of the characters, step into some of the gaps and open spaces in the tale, and see what we find there. As much as possible, let's proceed as if the story is happening **now**."

The foregoing is a general introduction that can be used for almost any situation in which you are introducing people to Bibliodrama. Teaching styles vary a great deal in this matter of the opening. Some people always begin the Bibliodrama with a study session, where the text is in front of everyone. Others, like myself, like to get going more quickly with the Bibliodrama.

Prologue to the Bibliodrama of Joseph in Egypt

What follows now is the specific introduction tailored to a particular group and to the particular story about Joseph (Genesis 37ff, but particularly 40 and 41) I am going to be examining in the rest of this book. This prologue illustrates the relationship between telling, reading, and the threshold moment of play.

(Note: The entire Bibliodrama of Part II is based on a reconstruction of an actual drama I directed for an adult class in a synagogue where I had been invited to teach. It was the third session of the weekend, and participants knew one another and me pretty well. I had a little over an hour to work in, and there were about twenty adults in the group. We were using a classroom and were seated in a horseshoe with the open end of the horseshoe and its center available to become our playing area. I had brought into the class a number of metal folding chairs. These were stacked off to one side.)

"The passage I have chosen for us comes in the middle of the story of Joseph. It comes after Joseph has been favored by his father, Jacob, after he had dreamed his two dreams as a seventeen-year-old, dreams that give his father pause for thought and his brothers cause for anger. It comes after Jacob sends Joseph to find his brothers, after the brothers throw Joseph in the pit, after...well, what happens next?"

"They sell him into slavery."

"First they want to kill him."

"They all don't want to kill him."

"Reuben and Judah want to save him."

"OK," I say, "these details are important, but what happens next?"

"He gets thrown into prison."

"Before that?"

"Joseph is bought from slavery by a nobleman named Potiphar."

"Joseph does real well. He rises to a position of authority."

"It says in the Bible that 'God favors Joseph.'"

"I think Potiphar's a eunuch. Can't the Hebrew word that describes him also mean eunuch? I'm sure I read that somewhere."

(As often happens, I don't know the answer to this question.) "I don't know," I say, "but the question of Potiphar's sexuality is perhaps implied by what happens next. He has a wife, you recall."

"Yeah! She tries to seduce Joseph."

"Yeah, it's like the movie *Disclosure*. Did you see that movie?"

"No, but I read the book."

"Yeah, who wrote that?"

"And what"—trying to maintain control—"happens next?"

"Potiphar's wife takes a fancy to Joseph. She makes a pass at him."

"And he rejects her."

"And then she accuses Joseph of harassing her, and Joseph is thrown in jail."

"No due process."

"Well, he's a slave. A Jew."

"Good. Now we are getting close to the passage I want to explore with you. While he is in prison Joseph again distinguishes himself. It is said about him, as you've already mentioned, that 'God is with him,' whatever that means, and though he is still in jail, he rises to being the warden's assistant.

"While he's in jail two serving men from Pharaoh's court are also imprisoned. One is the chief baker, the other is Pharaoh's cup-bearer. And in the course of their confinement these two men each dream a dream. On the morning after their dreams Joseph notices each seems puzzled and downcast, and, asking after their welfare, Joseph learns that each is bothered by a dream. Joseph invites them to tell him their dreams; this they do, and he promises them that God will see to their interpretation.

"Joseph tells the baker that his dream foretells his impaling in three days' time. The cup-bearer's dream foretells his restoration to court, and Joseph asks the cup-bearer to remember him to Pharaoh and to intercede for his release from prison. But the Bible tells us that 'the cup-bearer forgot Joseph.' That's the exact quote. And two more years pass.

"Then we come to the momentous occasion when Pharaoh dreams his two dreams, and this is the text we shall begin with—not the dreams themselves, but the immediate consequences.

"Pharaoh, we are told, awakens from his dreams, and we read (Genesis 41:8 ff.) that Pharaoh's 'spirit was agitated.' Let me read you what follows:

AND HE SENT FOR ALL THE MAGICIANS OF EGYPT, AND ALL ITS WISE MEN; AND PHARAOH TOLD THEM HIS DREAMS, BUT NONE COULD INTERPRET THEM FOR PHARAOH.

THE CHIEF CUP-BEARER THEN SPOKE UP AND SAID TO PHARAOH, I MUST MENTION TODAY MY OFFENSES. ONCE PHARAOH WAS ANGRY WITH HIS SERVANTS, AND PLACED ME IN CUSTODY IN THE HOUSE OF THE CHIEF STEWARD TOGETHER WITH THE CHIEF BAKER. WE HAD DREAMS THE SAME NIGHT, HE AND I, EACH OF US A DREAM WITH A MEANING OF ITS OWN. A HEBREW YOUTH WAS THERE WITH US, A SERVANT TO THE CHIEF STEWARD; AND WHEN WE TOLD HIM OUR DREAMS. HE INTERPRETED THEM FOR US, TELLING EACH THE MEANING OF HIS DREAM. AND AS HE INTERPRETED, SO IT CAME TO PASS: I WAS RESTORED TO MY POST, THE OTHER WAS IMPALED.'

THEREUPON PHARAOH SENT FOR JOSEPH...

"And now let's begin our Bibliodrama. We are about to step into the story. Let yourself imagine that you are here in the court of Pharaoh. You have seen and heard of his agitation; you have seen him send for all the wise men and magicians of Egypt; perhaps you are one such wise man or magician; perhaps you are a member of court, male or female, noble or serving person, who has witnessed the unanimous, perhaps unprecedented, silence of Pharaoh's advisors; you may be Pharaoh himself, his wife, or the cup-bearer. You see the cup-bearer step forward and speak the words you heard him speak to Pharaoh about the Hebrew youth in prison who interpreted his own dream and that of the baker, and you are hearing Pharaoh send for the youth.

"Who are you? What are you thinking as this scene unfolds around you? Speak only as a character in the story...."

A Prologue Analyzed

I break off here because the actual warm-up ends at precisely this point. I am at the threshold, only a sentence or two away from moving the story into action and moving the group into role. The lines and the story I have just presented to you provide the warm-up; it draws the group toward the process of play. You will have noted that I have laid out the ground rules and then moved quickly to the story.

There are a number of comments I want to make about this prologue to action before we develop the action in the next chapters.

- In the first place, and as a matter of text selection, I have chosen the story of Joseph because it is familiar and because Joseph, the outsider/insider, is a perennially evocative figure for us to identity with. That is part of the story's ease of access. Moreover, Joseph's story is also a classic hero's tail full of mishap, ordeal, loneliness, and reconciliation; it has plenty of what I call "depth of field."

- As I tell this part of the story with the class and then for them, I begin to recast the tale from its biblical narration into something that we are seeing as a play unfolding before us. I shift the narrative into the present tense. I highlight a character (the cup-bearer, for example) who might be overlooked in the reading.

- Remember that the storytelling lays out the past; it allows people to shift from a passive to a more active kind of listening, from hearing a story whose ending they know to living a story through characters who do not know where their lives are taking them. Becoming active listeners, co-narrators, is part of the group's warm-up for the actual voicing of the roles. The virtue of telling the story, and of my telling the lion's share of it, is that it alerts and moves students who are full of intellectual questions ("Isn't Potiphar a eunuch? Who wrote *Disclosure?*") to a different agenda. Also, this collective storytelling, this insistence on a story unfolding rather than a story already accomplished, begins to generate a sense of expectancy that will help to undergird the role-playing we are about to do.

• The storytelling also provides a transition in your role as director. You shift from being the teacher to being the narrator; you are becoming the scene-setter, the dramaturge. You are inviting the group to see, to hear, to sense themselves within the story. All of that is also a necessary part of the warm-up.

• I am trying, too, through this kind of warm-up to the story, to allow and persuade the group to suspend their need to know where I am going, why I have chosen this passage, what I am going to do with it. This kind of storytelling frees people from their usual need to understand why something is happening; it changes students into imaginative auditors. And in a subtle way, listening to and feeling part of a story is evocative of childhood. We let go some of the analytical and skeptical edge of the grown-up mind; we allow the child's wondering openness, buried in us, to be stirred. The process is pleasurable; especially if we know the story, if not in detail, then in its major outlines.

• And finally—and this is the hook—most people in the group have never looked at this moment before. It seems unremarkable, innocent, and my choice of it arouses a certain unexpressed curiosity about why, of all things, I have chosen this passage.

The poet Samuel Taylor Coleridge spoke of the "willing suspension of disbelief" as being a prerequisite for the enjoyment of poetry. In part the function of the warm-up is to create this suspension, or at least to begin it. The "suspension of disbelief" is the climate necessary for the imagination to begin to work and see and sense.

6

Action Phase I:
Ease of Access

Trance

I want to inject a new term into the discussion of Bibliodrama, the word trance.[14]

Trance, as I use it here, means the experience of make-believe, of pretending, of letting ourselves enter an imagined world. Trance in some way brings about what I have already described as "the willing suspension of disbelief." The emphasis is on *willing*. The goal of this kind of entrancement is for the imaginative experience to take on a certain vividness, to become more real and present, and, finally, to assume a life of its own. The critical faculty is not suppressed, it is willingly *suspended*; and the participant can drop it back into place at any moment. **Part of**

---

[14] I use this word for lack of a better. The word trance has a number of heavy associations—of mesmerism, of deep and unconscious states of suspended volition, of psychedelic amazement or stupefaction—I wish to strip from my present usage. As my examples make clear, I mean the word to refer to the experience of sustained and voluntary concentration of the sort one experiences when one is "immersed in" creative work or play. It is not the state of being spellbound, but rather of being engrossed in a game.

the artistry of the bibliodramatic process is in knowing how to "set the trance," or how to "induce" it.

Looked at from this point of view, almost everything you do and say as the bibliodramatic director—how you shape the space, warm up the participants, speak to them, see them—should be part of the effort to create and then to sustain the trance, the dramatic illusion. **As the director, you must work hard, if subtly, to protect that fragile imagining, that make-believe, from the overbearing power of "critical disbelief."** At every step in the drama you must find ways to keep this disbelief at bay or, even more of a challenge, to channel disbelief into the drama rather than letting it break the spell. This channeling involves re-framing interruptions as unusual kinds of participatory acts. You need to pay close attention to how you speak to the group, how you move, how you respect the trance as it is being formed.

Let me give one simple example of how your manner of speaking influences the responses of your listeners.

Notice the difference between the phrase, "Now try to imagine you are here in Pharaoh's court;" and, "Now let yourself imagine that you are here in Pharaoh's court." In the first case you are asking people to strain, to "try," with the assumption of effort and actually of effort unfulfilled. In the second case the word "let" gives gentle permission to the active imagination to succeed in doing what it can, in fact, easily do: to be "here in Pharaoh's court." As elementary, even as trivial as this difference in phrasing may seem, it makes a big difference when it comes to shifting people into a trance. **People have a tendency to take invitations to their imaginations literally, so you need to be careful in what you say.**

Let me go back and provide a close reading of my words to the group with which I ended the last chapter. After the introduction I said the following (and here I will break it down step by step with the rationale provided):

(1) "Let yourself imagine that you are here in the court of Pharaoh": Here the verb form "let yourself imagine" is the gentlest way to invite the listener to participate in an internal creative act. The emphasis moves toward the "you." "You are here..." and I specify where, "in Pharaoh's court." The introduction is both specific and open. You are in Pharaoh's

court, but you can be anywhere or anyone. One thing I have learned about bibliodramatic introductions is how readily they can be followed if they are done well.

(2) "You have seen and heard of his agitation; you have seen him send for all the wise men and magicians of Egypt..." Now two things are going on. In the first place, I am opening up the senses; you have "seen" and "heard." I am inviting participants to activate these senses of sight and sound. In the second place, I am recalling the story, but this time asking group members to recall it *as if they were inside of it*, rather than outside of it.

(3) "Perhaps you are one such wise man or magician; perhaps you are a member of court, male or female, noble or serving person, who has witnessed the unanimous silence of Pharaoh's advisors; you may be Pharaoh himself, his wife, or the cup-bearer. You see the cup-bearer step forward and speak the words you heard him speak to Pharaoh, about the Hebrew youth in prison who interpreted his own dream and that of the baker, and you are hearing Pharaoh send for the youth."

These sentences conclude the preamble to the induction. They suggest possible roles; they flesh out the scene and give people permission to step into it. These words more deeply engage the participants' sense of adventuring into the story. They also emphatically shift us into the present tense, for trance takes place now. **Trance of the sort I am describing may be thought of as taking a *there* and making it a *here*, of taking a *then* and making it a *now*.**

(4) "Who are you? What are you thinking as this scene unfolds around you? Speak only as a character in the story."

With these words the induction concludes; we are on the threshold of action. The actual words "Who are you?" invite participants to make a choice, and the words "What are you thinking?" invite participants to read their own minds, but now as players.

Scene One: Opening Moves

So how now does the Bibliodrama unfold?

Initially, in answer to my leading questions, there may be silence in the group. There may be no one that wants to speak. After a few moments I may interpret the silence, try to give it a voice.

"We are all dumbfounded at first," I say, playing a part in the Bibliodrama, getting it started. "None of the wise men or magicians have anything to say, and Pharaoh is sending off for a prisoner! We hardly know at first what to think."

In this way I frame the silence of the group as a part of the drama rather than as a part of their resistance to making the drama. From this point on I will attempt to frame everything group members say as part of the drama and in that way keep the dramatic illusion alive.

Someone speaks up, joining me as a player now.

"Pharaoh must have lost his mind."

People begin to play roles from their seats, raising their hands to be recognized. They are voicing their parts, and as you will see from what follows, my task is to **echo** and to **interview.**

"I am a court physician," I say. In this way I supply a role for a person who has not perhaps thought of who he is. Also, I assume the role and in that way join the player in the play. "I am worried about Pharaoh's mental health. He must really be desperate to resort to this kind of tactic." *(Echoing)*

"I don't know who I am, but this looks like it's going to be very interesting."

"Yes," I say, **echoing,** "things can be pretty boring around here. The last time we had any fun was when the baker was impaled. This has the makings of something sensational."

Someone else says, "I can't believe there wasn't someone among those wise men who knew what these dreams mean."

"Who are you?" I ask, now wishing to begin to get people to take the step of seeing themselves in a role.

"I'm... I'm...I'm just a member of the court. You know, no one special."

"But it sounds like you're a little skeptical about these so-called wise men." (**Interviewing.**)

"Yeah, that's right. We have the greatest magicians in the world; we're the greatest country in the world. They've always got an interpretation.

What's going on here?"

"Either there's some kind of conspiracy of silence here," I **echo**, "or we're up against something really unusual. Either way I feel..." (And I leave the sentence hanging, so that the player thinks to fill the gap.)

"...scared."

"Yes," I say, "this is all very..." (Again the unfinished sentence.) "Unsettling. In fact, it's downright weird."

Someone says, "I'm one of the wisemen, and I'm not going to open my mouth. Pharaoh is very unpredictable. If he doesn't like your interpretation—well, you know what happened to the baker."

"Yes," I say, **echoing**, "part of being a wise man is knowing when to shut up. I'm not going to be the first person to tell Pharaoh the news. Even if I knew it."

Someone says, "I've heard this Joseph is a pretty cute guy."

"Who are you?" I ask.

"Oh, just one of the girls who hang around the court."

"Married?" I ask, **interviewing**.

"No... I'm sort of an ornament around here."

"Who told you he was cute?" I ask.

"Potiphar's wife, actually. Long time ago. She was really hot for him."

"Whatever happened to her?" I ask.

"Oh, she's right over there," she says, and she points to another woman in the group.

"Oh, no!" this other woman groans.

"Oh, no!" I say, "I didn't think I'd ever see this kid again."

Here is one of those moments when I translate a response back into the drama, for the "Oh, no!" was clearly to me and to others the expression of the dismay of a group member unexpectedly roped into being a participant.

"Yeah," says the woman now playing Potiphar's wife, "what if he's able to interpret the dream...what if Pharaoh likes him..."

"Then my goose may be cooked," I finish for her.

"Yeah. I'm going to hide in the back."

Here the person who has been pulled in finds a way of backing out, and even though her contribution showed a lot of spontaneity, I need to respect her desire to fade back into the woodwork.

"Is your husband here?" I ask her.

I hope that she can finger someone else and in that way let this casting from the group spread a little more. When group members pull one another into the game it's very different from when I do it. If I pull people in, they may feel unsafe; but if group members cast one another, then it becomes a kind of game of bibliodramatic tag or hot potato. "Can you hide behind him?"

"Yeah. He's here."

"Point him out to me," I ask.

"He's right here," she says, pointing to the man sitting next to her. He just nods.

"What's going on with you?" I ask this Potiphar. I have no idea what he will say.

"I always knew this kid was special. I never should have listened to my wife."

Echoing: "I'm in a damned uncomfortable position here, and it's not the first time my wife has done this to me."

Again, I am wanting to side with my player, to let him know I hear his discomfort at having been put on the spot.

"That's right," he says.

"So how are you feeling at this moment?" I ask.

"I'm all mixed up. I liked Joseph. He was a great worker. I trusted him. I felt torn apart when I had to report him to Pharaoh, because I know my wife, and I believed she was probably fabricating this."

"You never believe me!" Here Potiphar's wife jumps in, much to my surprise.

"And anyway, you're a eunuch," says the person who, back when we were retelling the story, had asked a question about this. "She probably needs someone who can make her feel like a woman."

Now for the first time I break a sweat. I fear that the man who has been pulled into the story may feel attacked. I can't tell whether this is something vicious or playful. I don't know who knows whom in the group and what they know, but I know I have to handle this somehow. I feel instantly protective of "Potiphar." I am faced with the dilemma of how to keep alive the trance, such as it is at this early point in our play, while easing the moment. Directing Bibliodrama is full of little challenges like this one.

"Well, whether this is true or not, Potiphar," I begin, turning back to the man, who is clearly uncomfortable in this moment, "the fact is that you saw something in this young man, Joseph, whatever it was your wife saw. You bought him from slavery; you gradually elevated him to a position of authority in your house. What was it you saw in him?"

"Well..."

Have I given the person playing Potiphar a way of building himself some dignity? I see him gamely staying in the role. In itself that tells me a lot.

"Joseph wasn't just a slave boy to me. He had something special about him. I sort of adopted him, taught him Egyptian, helped him to feel like he belonged. He cared about me."

"Yes," I say, **echoing** now and knowing I have just seen a brilliant interpretive move, like a chess move inspired by being cornered that turns into a whole new gambit. "Yes, seeing Joseph now reminds me of how much I have missed him. He was like a son to me, like the son maybe I could never have."

"Yes," says Potiphar, and there is some feeling rising in him that gives the drama a sudden sense of depth, "and I was like a father to him. He confided in me. He told me how he had been taken away from his father, and how special he had been to his father, and how special his father had been to him."

I let a certain silence gather around this moment. In the space of a few moments we have moved into the story, and the story has moved into us. This is text-centered Bibliodrama at its best, informed by the personal, but dedicated to the narrative. We are making surprising, touching interpretations, discovering a deeper level of emotional coherence in the story.

But while I am appreciating how a vanguard of the group has launched us into real bibliodramatic play, I feel that there are others who need to be drawn into the action. Too much participation too early from too few may keep potential participants in the role of observers. I need to return to my opening questions and include others who have not yet spoken.

"What about the rest of you?" I ask. "What are you thinking about when Joseph is sent for?"

"This is a great moment for me," says someone. "I was also sold into slavery, and I am only a slave here in court. I clean the messes of the so-called nobles. I am nothing in their eyes, but the thought of this Hebrew boy coming up here and doing something special, showing these Egyptians that we aren't dirt...that would be amazing."

Here I can feel the effect of the mini-drama we just enacted on the warm-up of the group. This response has a certain fullness. The player is able to identify himself in role and to amplify his state. There is nothing I need to add.

"Who else is here?"

"I am a court politician. This could be a tricky time. What if this Hebrew kid succeeds, pleases Pharaoh, says the right thing? There could be a whole new regime."

Echoing: "Yes, there could be a new alignment of power. I need to watch this one carefully."

"Right," affirms the man who just spoke. "Power is my game, and there may be a new game in town."

"I am a priest of this court. Pharaoh is not just our king; he is our god. The dreams of the god come from the gods. No Hebrew slave can meddle with the will of the gods. He can't be allowed to succeed."

Echoing: "I also have a lot to lose if this kid turns out to be right."

"No, you don't understand," says the priest, "Pharaoh is a god to me. This isn't about my position, my legitimacy; it's about my faith."

"So what do you think of a god who is willing to consult another's god?" I ask.

"Well...it's never happened before."

"Could be a real interfaith moment," I suggest, and this comment, upon the drama and at the same time within it, gets a laugh.

In the actual Bibliodrama, which I am only reconstructing and abbreviating here, this opening scene goes on much longer. I let it run in order to hear from as many people as possible. No small part of the energy that gathers in this process comes from the pleasure we all feel at how much we can find here. More and more boldly we flesh out a scene that is, in the Bible, hardly noticeable.

But my "interfaith" joke is a good example of how I will bring closure to a scene. My comment slightly jeopardizes the trance. The blatant anachronism shakes people just a bit, and something like that is my intention. To borrow a culinary image, it is like a dash of sherbet between courses of a rich meal: something to clear the palate.

So at some point, when many have been heard from, I am likely to conclude this first scene of the action. As a general rule, I prefer to shift my focus before a particular scene is too played out. I am mindful that people warm up at different speeds, and some of those who spoke first are likely always to speak first in a group. I need to keep the process going long enough to let the shyer but often more thoughtful people be heard. When enough of that has occurred, it's time to move on.

Further, the general rhythm of the Bibliodrama has been set in motion. The group has begun to sense how I will play with them (and I mean this in several senses of the word), what my role is as echoer, interviewer, challenger, story-shaper, deepener. They gain some trust that I am a good listener. Their basic fear that they will say something foolish or wrong has been relieved by my general interest in what each has had to say. They begin to believe that what is unfolding has no hidden doctrinal or moralistic agenda. They are discovering they are really free to play with the story. They begin to see the possibilities for invention. Their imaginations are stirring, and their spontaneity is increasing. They are beginning to have fun—fun with me, fun with one another, and fun with the text. Having held this single moment at this particular angle, I feel the need to turn the drama again, shift the focus, take them somewhere else, or deeper, but move on lest the energy stall.

A number of important things have already been accomplished. I feel that the group, at least for the most part, is really in the story, if not yet deeply in character. Certain relations have been suggested: the courtly lady, Potiphar's wife, and Potiphar, for example, form an interesting triad. There are a number of participants who have expressed an interest in the power struggle they feel may be imminent. There's the other slave, who watches with an entirely different perspective. He gives me a glimpse, if not a sense, of an ending. Might he and Joseph have a secret conversation at the drama's end? What would they say to each other? Might he be a kind of surrogate brother? I don't know. I may not remember him by the time the ending does come. We may be very far afield. But my own dramatic sense is quickened with these threads and themes. The group has suggested possible story lines, possible antagonists, possible materials out of which to make a drama. I can feel in myself a certain eagerness to find out what will happen next. At the same time, there are aspects of the method as yet undeployed, and before searching deeper into the emotional energies hidden in the text I want to make sure the group and I are playing with all the cards. Though we have at this point sketched in several characters, we have not yet explored one character in depth. I want to warm the group up to that kind of experience.

We are, to use our terminology, about to move from voicing, echoing, and interviewing to a scene of group characterization.

Scene Two

"Is the cup-bearer here?" I ask the group. "I need to speak to the cup-bearer." The briskness of my request snaps the group into a different focus. It is a measure of my confidence in the warm-up that I can speak in this way. I never fail to get at least one volunteer.

"I'm the cup-bearer," says a man in the group.

"I'm curious about something," I say, interviewing him. "The text tells us that Joseph did you an enormous service in prison, and that all he asked of you was to put in a good word for him at court. Yet it is said that you 'FORGOT HIM.' Is this so?"

"Yes," says the cup-bearer, "much to my shame it is true."

"Why did you forget him?" I ask.

"I... well...I don't know."

What is going on in this moment is that I have sprung a question on the player of the cup-bearer that he had not anticipated. I have, in effect, challenged his spontaneity, and his first answer—the answer of both the player and the character he plays—is to stall for time.

I become somewhat peevish: "You don't know? Did you think about him in all that time? Did you feel you owed him anything? Is this the kind of person you are?"

There are no rules for how one handles these moments in a Bibliodrama. What does not come off the written page is the expression of this man who has offered himself as the cup-bearer. I can see, in a way I can't show you here, that he is warmed up. He has been quick to volunteer; he is the same man who spoke as the politician earlier, so I have seen him in action already, and I have begun to feel a little concerned about his taking over too much. I have made a quick, intuitive decision to raise the stakes for his participation and by doing this either cool him down a little bit or really reap the benefit of his spontaneity.

"No... no... I mean yes, I thought about him, but you know, well, you see, I was just back in court. My position was by no means secure. I intended to say something to Pharaoh, but then when the baker was... impaled... God, what an ugly way to die. Pharaoh was in a foul mood. It wasn't the right time, and then... well, you know... the occasion passed."

"I see," I say, pleased that the person playing the cup-bearer has risen to the challenge and kept the play alive.

"I wonder," I say, "I wonder if there is another cup-bearer in the house. Is there someone else who, as cup-bearer, can answer this question as to why you forgot Joseph?"

Without making a big deal of it, I have introduced a key element of Bibliodrama, an opportunity for **group characterization**. The character of the cup-bearer, at this stage of its development, still belongs to the group. At a later point it may serve the drama for one person to inhabit the role and carry it along one of its possible lines of development. But at this point we are still excavating the character, searching into it, seeing him. So I ask who else can play the cup-bearer and portray him differently.

"I forgot Joseph," says another group member, "because he scared me. He didn't say he was going to interpret my dream; he said his 'God' would do it. I don't know about where he comes from, but in this country, Pharaoh's a god, and I was confused."

"I see," I say. "Something about Joseph and his relationship to his God left you feeling uneasy. Is that right?"

"Yeah. Scared. I mean he was so cool, so calm, and so right. It was like something came through him. I'd never seen anything like that. I was grateful, but he gave me the creeps."

"So you forgot him because you wanted to forget him."

"I suppose you could say that. I wasn't ready to pay the price."

"Yes," another participant interjects, catching the drift. "I mean, suppose this kid has a God? A powerful God. A God who is with him in Egypt, in prison even, a God who interprets dreams. Then who is this kid? A priest? A prophet? A seer? And what is my responsibility to him, to his God? I'm a simple man. The gods have never had anything to do with me."

"Except this time a God saved your life," I suggest.

"No," says another version of the cup-bearer. "God did not save my life. I would have been released whether this kid told me the meaning of my dream or not. The Baker would have died. I forgot Joseph because in the end he had nothing to do with it. He's in jail, probably deserves to be there, and I'm free."

"Well, then," I say to this latest cup-bearer, but also with my eyes including the others, "if all this is true, then why at this precarious moment in time, when all the magicians and wise men have apparently been stumped, with Pharaoh agitated and the court amazed, why do you choose this moment to lean over to your lord and master and bring up an incident that occurred two years ago? Why?"

It's a useful question. To notice this puzzling reversal of character challenges participants to reexamine their interpretations. It increases involvement, as good puzzles often do.

"Because this could be my moment. It's a gamble; sure, it's a risk. But there was something about this kid that did stay with me. I didn't forget him; I only didn't say anything to Pharaoh. I've got a hunch this kid will pull it off, and if he does—well, good-bye to cup-bearing. I'm on my way up."

"So," I *echo*, "life sometimes comes down to these moments where you gamble. At least if you're going to get anywhere. So I see my chance, and I've got the guts to go for it."

"Right. And you know, being a cup-bearer is obscure work. You long for your moment in the sun, your moment on stage. It's irresistible. Just the chance to step forward in front of all those smug bastards whose wine glasses I had to fill and show them they don't know it all—God, it's worth it."

"So, cup-bearer,"—I repeat my question, looking for more—"why do you step forward to remember Joseph?"

"You have to understand what kind of a cup-bearer I am."

The group member speaking now is a man who has been following our Bibliodrama with his Bible open on his lap. This is not unusual. I do not encourage people to read along, because it keeps them from fully imagining, but I recognize that reading along is a way of keeping distance and yet following and being part. Sometimes, too, it is a way of checking up on me. Often those who read along in this way are very knowledgeable about the Bible; others who do so may be wary of those who seem to be taking liberties with it. I have some trepidation as he speaks. Is a challenge coming?

"I am not a wine steward. I do not have a key to the cellars. That is not my job. I carry the cup of divination. If you read carefully, you see there is another kind of cup referred to in the story. Later Joseph has a cup of divination, and he puts it in—"

Here I interrupt. I am getting a form of role-playing I think of as mixed. The participant begins in role but then slides into narrative and interpretation. The man playing this part jumps ahead of the story and outside of it. The dramatic trance trembles like a scrim a stagehand has brushed past. We are reminded we are in make-believe. The director's task at this moment is complex. First, I must make sure that this participation is validated. Second, I must do what I can to bring this person into the fold of the drama. Third, I need to reestablish the parameters of our play lest we get into discussion rather than drama.

"Wait," I say, holding up my hand, "wait a moment, sir cup-bearer. You tell me something very important. I am a stranger to this court. I don't know who is here or what people do. So you are telling me that there is a kind of divination practiced here involving a cup?"

"Yes, to be sure. But I am not at liberty to tell you our secrets." Ahh, I think, the danger is averted. We are playing.

"And," I ask, prompting, "is there something in your divination process that led you to know that this was the time to speak up about Joseph?"

"Yes, most definitely. But I am not at liberty to tell you how."

"Of course. I won't ask, but what you are telling me is that you have been given some kind of sign?"

"That is right."

"...that, of course, you are not at liberty to tell us about, but by it you know that this is the moment. It is written."

"Yes. As we say, *'Beshert,'* fated, meant to be."

"Ahh," I say, "I didn't know *beshert* was an Egyptian word. Thank you," I say. "Is there any other cup-bearer here who wants to be heard?"

"Yes. I do," a woman speaks up, taking the part. "I love Pharaoh. I don't know about that fancy divination cup-bearer over there. I fill his golden cup from the pitcher. I taste the wine first. I stand by Pharaoh when he drinks, and I have seen him in all kinds of moods. I have seen him wild and, well, in his cups. But I have never seen him like this. He is truly agitated. These dreams are important. I wasn't thinking of Joseph at first. I had forgotten him. It was a long time ago. But then when no one could understand the dreams, suddenly I did think of Joseph. It was like he appeared in my mind, stood before me, looking at me. And then it was like I felt I didn't have a choice. I had to say something. I felt ashamed and scared, but I also felt calm and cool. Like suddenly I was being asked to play a part in something great and strange."

"So," I say, feeling the need to provide some coherence to this fractured portrait of the cup-bearer, summing up, checking back with the players, "on one level, some motive of self-interest seems to operate. The ego sees its moment for aggrandizement, but on another level, beyond the ego, you, as the cup-bearer, act in accordance with some vision, some hope. You risk something for a reason beyond self-interest. In your own way, though you are not a diviner, you have some sense of the divine."

"Yes," says yet another cup-bearer, "I was scared by Joseph's God, but I was moved as well. I felt creepy, but I felt in some way that I had been saved, and perhaps—I know this sounds strange—perhaps I had been saved so that I could step forward now, with my heart full of mixed motives and feelings, and serve that God."

A natural silence falls at this point. This obscure figure to whom no one in the group had ever given a passing thought, has, under our collective scrutiny and by means of our *group characterization*, become a figure of considerable depth and complexity. We have unearthed the possibilities of an internal struggle, of a moral and spiritual development, of a modest heroism.

I let this silence make a closure for this part of the scene. A fine dramatic insight is often a natural place of closure. It isn't so much that someone has made the right interpretation, but rather a rich one, one rich enough to nudge us into a state of appreciation, of savoring, and in this shifted state the players move for a moment into spectators. Their hold on their roles is loosed. Often a scene ends when a single interpretation or a polling and summarizing of them on my part seems to raise us to a different level of insight, and a natural reflective pause ensues. The skill-ful director will recognize this silence, give it the time it deserves, and then move on. In our unfolding drama, it is time now to shift the focus toward the protagonist, Joseph.

Also, let me say that scene endings can be a little messy and inconclu-sive; the group's interpretations are not always easy to sum up. Don't worry overmuch about these transitions within the drama. **What is most impor-tant in orchestrating a scene within a longer Bibliodrama is to watch the energy of the group and to end a scene before it feels completely played out.** I would rather disappoint some group members who still have their hands in the air, asking them to "Forgive me, but in the interests of time I have to move on," than to recognize everyone who wants to speak and in so doing beat a scene to death. **My agenda, especially early in the drama, is to stir up interest, involvement, diversity.** I was raised by a chess-playing father, and one of the things he taught me was to make sure I freed up my pieces early in the game so that I had mobility and choice as the game progressed. Something of this strategy underlies my opening moves in the early scenes of the Bibliodrama.

7

Action Phase 2: Depth of Field

Developing the Drama

We are now ready to initiate a deeper level of exploration. Various lines of possibility, leads and angles, extend from our first scenes, and the choice as to which to pursue is only partially determined from the themes, or interpretive ideas, or plotting possibilities already hinted at in the opening. The great shortcoming of writing about the bibliodramatic process, as opposed to witnessing it or participating in it, is that you cannot recreate on the page the energy of the participants as it is felt in the moment. Their liveliness, sometimes expressed verbally, sometimes by the animation in a face or the restlessness of a body, or by the insistent waving of a raised hand determines to a great extent where the drama will go next. *Where* we go is, at least in part, a matter of *who: Who* in the group has the spontaneity to lead us into the story, and in what ways?

The energy of unexpressed possibilities bubbles in a group where the text and the process are taking hold. Because you cannot know before calling on someone what will be produced or where it will take you, you, as director, must be ready with your spontaneity to move toward and not away from the most spontaneous elements of the group. At the same time, there are likely to be certain people who are too warmed up, whose needs to be actors can overwhelm the slower and more tentative involvement of other members in the group.

While it is important to honor the developing spontaneity of the participants, the director must also constantly steer a course between intuited variables. The director must seek to warm up some players and to cool down others, seek to homogenize the warm-up in the group, to spread and diffuse it so that it might reach some of those less quick to engage in our play. An experienced director will also recognize that there will be some who prefer to watch and remain silent, even as there is often a vanguard in a group who, by their engagement, can engage others. At this point, the director's task is somewhat like that of the chairman of a meeting. The director is to call upon certain members of the group who have not been heard from (and to respect, when stated, their preference to remain observers). The director is to moderate the enthusiasm of others by effective echoing and interviewing, to coach the tentative, challenge the engaged, and encourage the spontaneity and cohesion of the group. (While standing on one foot!)

Reading the energy of the group becomes one of the two ongoing tasks of the director; the other is keeping an eye on the development of the drama, an aesthetic and sometimes theatrical sense of possible shapes for the emerging story. That energy is expressed and made visible to the director and to the group by the quality of the participants' involvement in the roles.

This matter of quality deserves some elaboration. In a Bibliodrama, quality of role-playing touches on several things. There are certain aspects of excellence in role-playing that correspond to familiar theatrical values: voice, gesture, emotional presence. Ordinary people can have moments of astonishing authenticity in an improvised drama when their words and actions are infused by feeling. As a director, you seek to create moments in the Bibliodrama when the reality of the drama—the trance induced and sustained—is so strong that participants will act in ways that are persuasive and moving. But these qualities of excellence only go so far.

Actors in a Bibliodrama are also in the process of interpreting the text, and sometimes actorial values—presence, tone of voice, and power in action—are not as important as qualities of insight or originality of interpretation. As director, in my echoing, I can supply dramatic tone to comments rendered in a fairly flat, intellectualized way; but those comments, often the stuff of inspired insight, are themselves valuable. A novel response that opens a new vein of meaning in our collective interpretation has enormous power in the group; it is hugely stimulating. Suddenly participants feel a whole series of new variations become available. A certain single bibliodramatic insight can vastly extend the horizons of the interpretive game. By such a stroke participants, heretofore silent, are energized and engaged; a renewed sense of discovery infuses the group with focus and curiosity. Who knows what we might find between the lines of the biblical text? Who knows how wonderfully current the old story might be? **Excellence in role-playing is achieved when an empathic imagination plunges into traditional characters and stories and discovers new facets of possibility.**

There is also the matter of courage, a quality nearly undetectable, but nonetheless real, that often gives the bibliodramatic event an almost electric charge. Courage plays an enormous part in the drama, and it derives from players who are willing to reach into themselves to play a part and to draw up some emotional truth, some passionate insight, the full implications of which they might not understand themselves. It takes courage to represent that truth or insight in role in the group. As the drama progresses participants become increasingly aware that they are in some ways playing themselves as they are playing their parts. They become transparent to themselves, if not to others; and in that transparency participants see hidden aspects of their own psychological dynamics. To continue to play from that place of insight and transparency requires a certain bravery, but it is precisely the personal authenticity of the players, their willingness to draw on themselves, to stand on the ground of their own insights, that gives the Bibliodrama its aura of daring, risk, and excitement. I am impressed and moved again and again by how people rise to the challenge and opportunity of Bibliodrama.

The energy people put into a role-play will range from the understated to the hyperbolic. People can convey their distance from the process by ironic asides, little lapses in role, by such phrases as "If I were in court, I would say..." or using such terms as "I guess" or "I suppose." These are indicators to me that the participants are playing but keeping their distance as well.

But other people, even if brief, can speak with a certain vitality and emphasis, a certain emotional presence that alerts me immediately to their involvement. These players, regardless of the novelty of theme and idea they voice, will by their energy alone form the nucleus of whatever drama I develop in this second phase of the action. They will carry the story forward. For whatever reasons, their warm-up is the fullest, their spontaneity the brightest. Most often that is because something in the text and in their inner response to it (of which they may or may not be aware) is beginning to inspire them. And because this quickening is not always auditory, I cannot adequately convey it in writing. But in the room the clues are obvious in the animation of the participants, eyes eager to meet yours, a hand raised, a thoughtfulness of expression, a leaning forward to catch what others are saying, to see what others are showing by their own body language,

Given what I have recounted of the Bibliodrama up till now, I see several possible lines of development, some supplied by the group, some by the text. There is the hinted encounter between Joseph and Potiphar; there is the relationship with Pharaoh; and there is the marriage with Asenath, which comes as a climax to this phase of the Joseph story. But in any and all of these cases I cannot move forward without looking at Joseph and seeing what the group will make of him.

To mark the moving on of the drama I will in all likelihood read the words of the Bible. **A return to reading the biblical text can almost always be used to change the scene.** The written words bring us back from our multiple thematic diversions; our diffuse interpretations are confronted by the next given moment in the story. Certain lines of development close down; new ones open up. The group is challenged to keep shifting their attention, moving on, while at the same time various emerging ideas still simmer in the heart of group members. Hooked into certain favored readings, certain interpretations of character, participants will keep these alive and in development as the story line moves on.

Reading the text again reminds us of the shared structure upon which our elaborations rest. The voice of the Bible connects us back into the ancient myth that our work reanimates. Read aloud, the biblical words heard by us all reestablish the great framework within which all our individual differences, our varied interpretations, are held. Reading the Bible is reassuring. At the same time, reading a line or two from the Bible can remind us, sometimes with a certain amazement, of just how little we are working from, or, conversely, what latitudes we are taking for our inventions.

And so I read:

THEREUPON PHARAOH SENT FOR JOSEPH, AND HE WAS RUSHED FROM THE DUNGEON. HE HAD HIS HAIR CUT AND CHANGED HIS CLOTHES, AND HE APPEARED BEFORE PHARAOH (41:14).

The direction of each episode or scene recapitulates the overall movement of an entire Bibliodrama. Always one moves from the periphery to the center; each vignette or scene, each focal character, requires its own warm-up. If, in the scene we are about to do, the climactic moment is Joseph's entrance into Pharaoh's court, then the approach to that moment might begin with our imagining his condition during the final phase of his confinement. Each time I begin a new scene I will ask a simple question or two designed to invite participants to warm up to the part. I need to be sure to focus participants on the moment in the story when I want them to enter the character. Once again, the method employed in the following scene is *group characterization.*

"Joseph," I say (addressing the whole group, which by now fully understands that such an address is an invitation for each of them to step into role), "remember when the cup-bearer and baker were released from prison? Tell me, what was your state of mind at that time?"

"I was elated at the prospect of release."

"Word reached me that my predictions were accurate."

"God's predictions?" I ask, reminding our players of the text.

"Right, God's predictions, which I imparted. Anyway, I lived in constant expectation that I would be reprieved."

"So, Joseph, a week goes by. How are you feeling?"

"Impatient. My mind is full of all sorts of things. I want to go to Potiphar and see if I can clear my name."

"I want to find my way home."

"A month goes by," I say. "What happens to you? What are you feeling?"

"I have sunk into a depression deeper than any since the first year I was in prison."

"Why is that?" I ask.

"Because I have allowed myself to hope. I forgot that I was a Hebrew slave with no rights. There's no due process here."

"And your feelings about the cup-bearer?" I ask.

"Murderous."

"Six months go by." I suggest. "Now what's going on?"

"I can't seem to give up hoping. Each day I think maybe today... maybe today. But as time goes on I feel more despairing."

"I begin to resign myself again to spending the rest of my life here."

"Do you think of home?" I ask. "Of your father, your brothers, your sister?"

"I dream about them all the time. It's as if I can see their life going on without me. I can see my father still mourning. I can see little Benjamin growing to manhood. I can see my brothers in all their rivalries."

"A year passes," I say, moving us forward. "Tell me how you feel about God."

"I feel abandoned. I ask myself what I did to deserve this. I review my life. I see that I was perhaps an egotistical boy, but it was my father who favored me and set me up to be hated by my brothers. I didn't ask for that cloak, that burden."

"I question my dreams, the dreams I had as a boy that seemed to promise so much. I have never seen my father's God; I have never known that God. Perhaps this is all a dream."

"I vacillate between believing in God, in my life, in some eventual redemption from this place and a desire to give up, make an end to myself, or simply give in to bitterness. Each day tempts me to cynicism and despair. I feel at times I have a terminal and incurable disease, and that God is deaf to my prayers."

"So you pray?" I ask. "Tell me what you pray. Speak your prayer for me."

"I pray for release."

"I pray for patience."

"I pray to feel God's presence sustaining me."

"I pray to be kept from despair."

"I pray for a sign."

"I pray for my father and my brothers."

"I pray for the soul of my mother."

"I cannot pray. As the time goes on I find it more and more difficult to pray. Only deep in my heart I maintain a little ember of faith. It does not get extinguished."

"Twenty-three months go by," I offer. "Does anything change?"

"No, nothing has changed except that I have returned to living my life here as best I can. I have given up hope of release, but I have found I wish to live, to stay alive, and there is work to be done here. I have friends. I have a life."

"In recent weeks I feel a change has come over me. I have grown peaceful here. I feel God's presence even here in my prison. Small things please me. I have perhaps begun to go a little mad, for I laugh at little things; I watch the birds in the prison yard and discover I have a smile on my face. I dream at night, fantastical dreams."

"I have lately begun to feel something growing excited in me. I cannot predict the future, but I feel a change is coming."

"On the contrary, I feel more and more bitterness, I want release, and I want revenge. I have these dreams of power, and in these dreams I lord it over the whole world. I make others pay. I sit on a throne second only to Pharaoh's, and in my dream my brothers come begging, and I make them pay. I have become a torturer of souls in my dreams. I turn my back on God."

Note: I do not echo here. To do so would risk reducing the fullness of these responses rather than enriching them. Also, I need do no interviewing. I am quite pleased with the breadth and depth of these voicings. Further, I want to become less and less necessary to the production. As the level of involvement of the participants increases, my own level of participation can decrease. My goal in this work is for the players to take over the play in a controlled and yet dynamic way.

"So," I say, satisfied at how well we have warmed up to Joseph, how deep our searching of his soul has gone, "all of the above may be true. Two years is a long time after ten or eleven years of imprisonment before that. You were seventeen, Joseph, when you were sold into slavery, and you are close to thirty now. Almost half of your life has been spent in jail. During that time you go from youth to manhood, and the greenest years of your life are gone."

I can feel the group take this in; they are still in the role of Joseph; and my way of speaking to them ("you...you...you") keeps them in role. I know that few people have read this part of Joseph's life as slowly, as imaginatively as we have been reading it together; I know that the enormity of his ordeal is sinking in, and that in many cases group members are realizing how much of the familiar literature of the Bible might contain huge unexplored passages like this one, hidden between the lines. We have a sense, without necessarily putting our thoughts into words, of the unspoken depths of biblical narrative and the complex and wonderfully rich world of interpretation that can fill those depths. Silence such as the one that falls here is full of thought and feeling. I sustain the silence for a beat or two.

"And then the moment comes that is rendered in the following sequence:

'THEREUPON PHARAOH SENT FOR JOSEPH, AND HE WAS RUSHED FROM THE DUNGEON. HE HAD HIS HAIR CUT AND CHANGED HIS CLOTHES, AND HE APPEARED BEFORE PHARAOH.'

"So," I ask, "a moment ago, Joseph, you were seated in the barber's chair; a moment ago you were standing before the court tailor; a moment ago you were on your way up to the court; and now, in this instant, you stand before the closed doors of the throne room. Tell me, tell us: What is going on inside of you?"

"My mind is a whirl. I am overwhelmed and confused. Just when I had reconciled myself to a life in prison, am I to be set free?"

"I am ready. I am calm. I have been waiting for this moment all my life, and now it's here. I recognize it, and I am ready to seize it. I am a man made for opportunities."

"Pharaoh? Why Pharaoh? Has the cup-bearer finally remembered me? Or has something else happened?"

"I feel..."

I leave the sentence unfinished, using the gap to direct people out of the head and into the emotions.

"Afraid."

"Yes, I am afraid." Here another member of the group expands on the word, in effect echoing. "My life has this pattern in it of being exalted and then cast down. I was my father's favorite, then was thrown into a pit; I was elevated in the house of Potiphar, and was then thrown into another pit, this time a prison. So now what?"

"I feel afraid for another reason. I have this sense of my dreams coming true, of their beginning. I feel I am in a dream; this whole experience in Egypt is like a dream, and the dream is getting deeper."

"Dream, shmeem. This is politics. Something is going on. I don't know what, but things must be pretty bad or strange if they're asking for me to appear in court. I have to be careful. I remember what happened to the baker."

"I am again in prayer. I am praying for guidance, for clarity, for...I don't know what...presence of mind, maybe."

"Presence of God?" I prompt.

"Maybe."

"So," I say, "here is Joseph," and I place an empty chair to hold his imagined position on one side of our playing area. Also, by this movement to third person singular, I de-role the group. "At the very door of the court. Let's hold him there for a moment, and turn our attention to you, Pharaoh."

And here again I set out an empty chair. I place the chair at the other side of the open area before the group. In this single, simple act I concretize the theater of the imagination in which we have been playing out our scenes until this moment. These chairs, these props create a stage, establish a set, and bring the curtain up, so to speak, on a scene. I am preparing for an encounter.

"Pharaoh," I say, laying a hand on the back of the chair but looking out at the group, "let's run the story back a reel or two. I can only wonder at how you felt when all your wise men and magicians failed to interpret your dreams; I can only imagine your surprise when the cup-bearer came forward to tell you about the Hebrew prisoner who had interpreted his dreams and those of the baker (you remember the baker?) two years ago. Tell me, Pharaoh, why do you send for this youth, a Hebrew after all, a slave, a criminal? It seems, on the surface of it at least, a most unlikely move."

Director's Aside: Criteria for When to Get Players on Stage

The empty chairs for Joseph and Pharaoh mark a transition. Until this moment our playing area, though shared and co-created has been internal; the placing of the chairs externalizes it. One empty chair is for Joseph; it represents a person not yet on stage, but marked by the chair, for Joseph's presence. The other empty chair is the throne, and merely by placing this object before the group the space is now charged and prepared for actors. Now all the seated participants are more palpably in the world of the Bibliodrama; an inclusive theater-in-the-round has been evoked.

There are a number of factors that will bear upon my decision whether to fill these chairs or not, and though it is, at this moment in time, too early to decide, let me tell you the kinds of things I am weighing and considering as the drama unfolds.

In general, the larger the group, the less likely I am to cast people to play characters "on stage." Or, to put it the other way around, the larger the group, the more likely I am to keep people participating from their seats by voicing rather than by fully assuming parts. I may still use a chair or chairs to indicate characters, to create a ghostly scene, but I will keep the participants voicing the roles from their seats.

The reason for this is that once people come forward, either volunteering or selected to play a part—as, in this case, to take the part of Pharaoh or Joseph—there is a tendency for the rest of the group to ease back into the role of audience and to discontinue their own process of making bibliodramatic interpretations. As long as the entire group is involved, multiple possibilities for dramatic development keep opening up, and therefore group members are more likely to be on the edges of their seats, playing off one another while at the same time pursuing their own ideas. When no single line is selected for development, all lines remain available. The virtue of this, as I am indicating, is maximum participation.

On the other hand, this approach, while providing the greatest possible access to participation, makes for a very slow forward movement and sometimes a shallow dramatic event. To hear many voices is to cover a range of dramatic options, but no single one of them gets developed deeply.

The Bibliodrama I am recreating in this book is one that can be done with a very large group (I have done this story with 500 people) or only a dozen people. The description I am writing here derives from a group of about twenty. In that context, inviting people to play roles is desirable. In small groups, the access to the stage is more open; there is less danger of people falling into mere spectatorship; and the fear of self-exposure is less in a smaller group, for the trust level among participants grows stronger through the process of play. In small groups people feel the need to take the playing further, from voice to action, from their seats to the stage. At least this has been my experience. My sense is that people, recognizing the more theatrical possibilities in Bibliodrama, feel safe to try them out when the group is small.

Back to the Scene

As I launch now into the character of Pharaoh I bear in mind where the biblical narrative goes. One of the trickier aspects of conducting a Bibliodrama is balancing the emerging interpretations of characters—which are based on the premise that we do not know the future of their story—with what one knows to be the written and, in a sense, the destined future of those characters. One cannot, for example, play out this Pharaoh as one would play out the Pharaoh of Moses' Egypt. Most of us remember the Pharaoh of Exodus as a murderous tyrant who will not listen to reason or to the voice of God. This Pharaoh in Genesis, however, is a very different person; he will, in fact, listen to Joseph openly and respond favorably; he is able, through guile or greatness or both, to place full responsibility for the welfare of Egypt in Joseph's hands.

Bearing this in mind, I will listen to the responses my opening question evokes for a version of Pharaoh that is realistically skeptical—we want a worthy dramatic figure who can challenge Joseph—but also capable of recognizing an unlikely and gifted ally. Here, as elsewhere, my own view of the story influences my guiding of the drama, for I see in this man certain exemplary traits that distinguish him as a king. Certainly in this scene he seems to show a serious concern for his dreams and the welfare of his kingdom, and these concerns allow him to override politics, even religious interests, to seek out a remedy wherever he might find it, irrespective of class or condition.

As hands go up I look for those I have not heard from yet. I know by now who are the quick starters; I know who are the jokers and who, under their jokes, are serious; I know who the ironic distancers are in my group; I know who are the more spiritual or mystical among the players; I know who have taken risks and spoken unprompted from feelings; I know who possess an educated awareness of the Rabbinic commentaries. The voices of the players increasingly jell into a conversation within the group, a conversation about the Bible, its meaning and seriousness, about the moral and spiritual dimensions of its characters, the nature of God. My movement toward casting characters to play out parts is increasingly informed by what I am learning about my group. The Bible provides parameters that cannot be tampered with and which immutably define certain aspects of character. I steer between the fixed and the open, between the black fire and the white.

Now to return to the play. My last question was: "Tell me, Pharaoh, why do you send for this youth, a Hebrew, after all, a slave, a criminal? It seems, on the surface of it at least, a most unlikely move."

And the answers come.

"I have never had such dreams as I had. When I woke I was troubled as I had never been troubled. I had a sense of crisis, and when I turned to my court, to those who had always had the answers in the past, I was shocked at the answers they gave, their evasions, their silences. I did not know what I was looking for, but I know I did not hear anyone come forward and speak persuasively about what my dreams meant, or, perhaps even more to the point, what I should do about them."

"Sometimes," says another, "I am sick of politics. I heard many of my magicians talk, and everyone spoke from his or her own agenda. I realized that there was not a person around me who didn't have some self-interest that warped any counsel. My dreams were troubling enough, but when I went to my advisors and realized their partisanships, their rivalries, their pettiness, I felt deeply alone. It seemed that something I had always felt—how alone I was and how hard I had to work to balance various factions—now came crashing in on me. When the cup-bearer told me about Joseph, my heart went towards him in an intuitive leap. I don't know that I believed he could interpret my dreams, but it was a way of slapping my court in the face."

"Well," says a third, "the fact is I had another dream, though I told this one to no one. In this third dream I am standing in the presence of a child whose face is familiar, but I cannot place it. It is a face I have never seen before, and I am staring into the eyes of this strange being, and my own eyes are filling with tears."

Comments such as this one, which made a very deep impression on me personally, illustrate what it is I love about this work. Here a person in the group not only takes poetic license and adds a dream that is not in the Bible, but speaks in a deeply poetic way. She—for this was a woman's creative contribution—composes a dream that is poignant and utterly plausible. It is such interpretations as these that sometimes can give Bibliodrama the aura of an inspired event.

"I am," says another, "a desperate man. We take dreams seriously here in Egypt, and the foreboding I feel from these dreams really shakes me. When my courtiers are silent and my wise men and women are silent—and believe me, in this court no one is ever silent for long—I have the strangest sense that we have been put under a spell. The longer that silence lasted, the more desperate I felt. When the cup-bearer came forward I seized on his words. What had we to lose?"

I recognize one more upraised hand. "I don't know what I am doing, if you want to know the truth. I feel like I am still in a dream. You know how some dreams are so strong you can't shake them? Well, that's the way these dreams were. I felt as if I couldn't wake from them. Day and night their images persisted, and though I didn't know what they meant, exactly, I felt there was something premonitory about them. I needed to do something; something needed to happen that would wake me up, and the ridiculous idea of the cup-bearer seemed just the right thing to clear my head."

"So," I say to the group, "who here would like to come forward and play Pharaoh?"

Several hands are immediately raised. I select from among them. My criteria for selection are in part intuitive and in part the result of the past half hour of interplay. I begin to know my group. I look for someone who has a certain, for lack of a better word, presence. In this case I choose a woman to play Pharaoh; her earlier responses, her range of expression, something in her dignity prompt me to select her, and I have learned over time to trust these intuitions. It is one of the risks a director learns to tolerate: to call on a person to carry the action on stage without any guarantee that they can do it. At the same time I know that I have ways of replacing her if she seems to falter. I have recourse to other hands, to the process of doubling that keeps me in touch with alliterative players and versions of the play.

"You are Pharaoh," I say, seating this player on the chair-as-throne. "You are king of Egypt and regarded by your subjects, officially at least, as a god. You have dreamed troubling dreams; no one has been able to interpret them for you in a manner that satisfies you; you have a deep concern for your kingdom and a weariness with petty partisan politics. You are yourself a dreamer and have never felt more isolated and alone than you do at this moment, bearing the weight of your dream."

In this way I weave together many of the best strands of what I have heard and help the player assume the part.

"As you sit on that chair as upon a throne take a breath and breathe as a king. Imagine your crown, your robes, your place. Feel yourself into the role."

In this way I assist the player in deepening her experience of the role, helping her with a few suggestions to imagine the part more fully, to bring it into her body, and to engage her body, not just her mind, in the play.

Then I walk down the playing area to the far end, opposite the seated

Pharaoh, where the empty chair of Joseph waits to be filled. (I am follow-ing the steps outlined on page 91.) "I need a Joseph." And again hands are raised. I select a young man, and again my choice is educated intu-ition. He has an open face that hints at a certain inner candor and pluck; a brightness in his eyes, perhaps an inner brightness there as well. He gets out of his seat and comes forward, standing beside me. "The doors are yet to open before you," I tell him, both to delay the contact with Pharaoh and to establish the realism of our emerging staging. "You stand here after many years of prison, the last two years full of the deepest conflicts of faith and despair. Without being told why, you have been rushed from your confinement, bathed, shaved, and dressed. You now stand just outside the doors of the throne room. Are you ready?" This last question lives in both worlds, the world of the story and the world of the enactment. The player's answer, whether a "yes," a "no," or a "maybe," will fit our Joseph, for he, too, is a kind of player about to step onto the stage. "Joseph, the doors are opening," I say, and here I might mime the gesture of pulling them open. "In you go."

As Joseph begins his walk toward Pharaoh I address the group. "As we watch this interview between Pharaoh and Joseph, some of you may wish to add something as Joseph or as Pharaoh. You hear or imagine our characters saying something different from what these players say. There is a way for you to get those words into our story. Simply raise your hand, and I will know that you want to be heard. I will call on you; and then, either from your seat or going up and putting a hand on the shoulder of the character you wish to play, you can speak in role."

Director's Aside: Doubling on Stage

I spoke above about there being ways to bridge the poles between group characterization on the one hand and the potentially exclusionary process of having just a few group members take the stage as players, thus leaving everyone else as bystanders. **Doubling offers everyone in the audience a chance to be players.** With a simple signal any group member can let me know of his or her interest in providing a new facet of the character in play upon the stage. The doubling voice can be offered from the person's seat, or a group member can come forward, put a hand on the shoulder of the character to be doubled, and step into the role. Often I will place a second chair behind the chair in which the principal role-player is seated; the second chair is there to invite and to represent doubling.

By its very position that chair suggests that there are alternatives and variations for that role. There are things unspoken that may be voiced by group members coming up to offer their insights. Sometimes even the player occupying the first chair may get up and sit down behind herself, so to speak, in that way giving voice to her own unspoken thoughts and feelings.

Things that are said by the doubles are not overheard by the other characters. The convention here resembles the use of the aside in traditional drama. In order for the words of the double or the speech of the second chair to be heard by the other characters in the scene, the player who is being doubled must take the offerings of the group and speak them in his or her own voice on the stage.

The reason for this convention is to keep it clear what is the main action—i.e., that which the principal characters speak to and hear from one another, and what are the improvisations, the possible lines of development that embellish the main line of the story. To have the principals respond to the doubles would soon create an aesthetic as well as narrative confusion.

In some ways, of course, it already does create some confusion, and there is always the danger of clogging the forward movement of the story with too much of this kind of participation from the group. **Often the best way to use doubling is to help the principal players warm up to their parts by hearing from the doublers a few possibilities for interpretation. In other words, at the beginning of a scene or encounter, but not once it is underway.**

Doubling is also effective at any point when you sense a player is played out, or losing touch with the character, or maybe getting overheated in the role. **Then doubling offers the player and you a graceful way to substitute another actor into the drama.**

Sometimes the doubler will actually replace the character on stage when a particularly rich interpretive line is offered or when a scene seems played out and a new player, doubling into the story, opens up new possibilities. Sometimes the doubler will provide us with an internal soliloquy for a character; sometimes an expression of feeling that is not getting through in the dialogue as we are hearing it. If the enrichment the double provides seems to me closely in line with what the principal is already developing, then I tell the principal to take the double's words and say them in his own voice and in his own words. In that way the insights of the doubles may infuse the play of characters officially on stage. "Pick up on that," I will say to one of my actors. "Put what your double just said into your own words; let's see what kind of a response you get."

In sum, then, doubling is a way

- to engage more players in the development of the drama;

- to keep alive some if not all of the interpretive variations, thereby making it clear that the scene, as we are playing it out, represents only one possible line of development;

- to bring onto the stage a new player.

Joseph walks forward. To plant the idea of doubling I say to the group, "One word to say how you, as Joseph, feel as you take each step." "Scared."

"Excited."

"Quiet."

"Praying."

"Proud."

"Confident."

"Small."

"Ready."

"And now you stand before Pharaoh." Joseph, the actor, instinctively bows but does not kneel. "And," I prompt the group to draw people into the moment, "give me a few words for what might be going on inside of Pharaoh as he sees this young man walk toward him."

"He's young."

"He's handsome."

"He reminds me of my dream."

"He looks frightened."

"I need to test him."

"Could he be the one?"

Then, addressing Pharaoh, I say, "So in this dialogue, Pharaoh, you will begin. We know that in time you will tell this youth your dreams, but perhaps there is a feeling-out process before that happens. Begin."

I step back, literally and figuratively. Until now I have been very active and involved in arranging the drama. Now it leaves my hands, not completely to be sure, but the signal I need to send to the players and to the group is that the show is now theirs to shape as they wish. I need, in this moment particularly, to let go of my agendas and to see what comes from the two players and the group as doublers. I listen. I may act as a kind of gatekeeper for the doubling voices from the group, but I also want the two actors to enter the opportunities of improvisational play without being too conscious of me. When this kind of drama works best the players "get into it," play off one another's emerging characters, constantly challenged by the unexpected. The stage is set for an encounter.

The Encounter

P: How do they call you, young man? What is your name?

J: My name is Joseph, sir.

P: How old are you Joseph?

J: I am thirty, sir.

P: What is your country? Who is your father?

J: Sir, my father is Jacob, son of Isaac, son of Abraham. My father is also called Israel. We live in Hebron, in Canaan.

P: Nomads? Shepherds?

J: Yes, sir, but we have also settled in Hebron. We have been there for three generations.

P: And how is it that you came to be in Egypt, Joseph? You are a long way from your home.

J: I am, sir. It is a long story. My father—

P: Joseph, make a long story short. I have urgent business on my mind.

J: Sir, my brothers sold me into slavery.

P: Your brothers sold you into slavery. Why would they do that? Make it brief, Joseph.

J: In all honesty, sir, I don't fully understand why. There are times when I believe it was my own pride that caused my brothers to wish to be rid of me; at other times I think it was their pettiness and jealousy; at other times I think that my life is a dream, and I can't understand it.

P: Dreams...yes, dreams, to be sure. And you have been in prison?

J: Yes, sir. I have.

P: And your crime?

J: I was a serving man in a great house and was accused of improper conduct toward the lady of the house.

P: And was this charge true?

J: No, sir, it was not.

P: Well, that's too bad. But then again, everyone who goes to prison wishes us to believe he is innocent. While in prison you were, as I understand it, in a position of some authority. You remember two of my servants were once in prison, my baker and my cup-bearer, and they had dreams, and you interpreted them. You remember this.

J: I do, sir, but it wasn't me who did the interpreting; it was God through me. For God gives dreams, and only the spirit of God can discern the meaning.

P: Tell me about this God of yours, Joseph.

J: Sir, I only know stories of this God. My great-grandfather was called by this God to leave his native land and go to Canaan; this God promised my grandfather land in Canaan for his generations; my father once wrestled with this God and was told a great nation would be made of his children. I myself have never seen this God; this God has never spoken to me. But sometimes when I see or speak the truth I feel that it is not me but God who shows me the truth or speaks through me.

P: Joseph, you talk like a priest.

J: Among my people there are no priests.

P: Yet you have gods. Or...

J: One God who rules over all.

P: And no priests?

J: Perhaps we are all priests.

P: In Egypt I am a god, Joseph. What do you say to that?

J: Sir, you are a troubled god, for you wouldn't have called a servant and a stranger to come before you otherwise.

P: I am a god who has dreamed two strange dreams, Joseph. Shall I tell them to you?

Director's Aside: Strategies and Options

So far this encounter has surprised and pleased me. The feeling out of the two characters has been remarkably realistic. Most impressive is the ability of both players to adopt a kind of shared language, or level of language; there is a touch of formality, yet it is not stilted. Notably, no one in the group has raised a hand to make a doubling statement. The group, too, recognizes the delicacy of what the two players are trying to improvise, and there is enough originality and realism to keep the group's energy in abeyance. Yet the very realism and formality of the encounter between Pharaoh and Joseph lead me to want to invite the group to make some doubling statements now.

It seems to me we are at a transitional point. Joseph has acquitted himself well enough that Pharaoh is about to offer to tell him his dreams, and the story line we have been developing is about to resurface into the literal narrative of the Bible. The Bible tells us what Pharaoh is about to say to Joseph and what Joseph will say to Pharaoh. That script is in Scripture. But the drama, as we have played it out so far, tells us nothing about what the two men think of each other and what they are feeling as they play their scene. We do not have the emotional layer, the subtext. To get at that I invite members of the group to offer their doubling statements. I expect that some of these statements will shade and highlight different parts of the encounter. I put it to the group in this way:

"Let's stop the scene at this point, put it on pause. Let me ask you to come up and make some doubling statements for either Pharaoh or Joseph. What are things they might be feeling or thinking but do not say?"

Most participants come up out of their seats to speak, putting a hand on the shoulder of whichever player on stage they want to double. They say their piece, then sit back down.

"As Pharaoh, what surprises me before he even opens his mouth is what a beautiful-looking young man he is. He is not only physically handsome, but there is a glow about him, a kind of radiance. I have heard rumors about him, and I understand why Potiphar's wife might have been attracted to him." This person sits down.

Another comes up. "As Pharaoh, I wonder if it can be possible for me to listen to someone like this. First of all, he is young; he almost seems like a boy; he is uneducated by Egyptian standards. He is unused to the complexities of court political life. On top of that, he is a foreigner, a nomad, and the worshipper of an alien god. Can it be possible that the welfare of my country might depend on someone like him?"

A man from his seat: "As Pharaoh, I have to admire the young man's forthrightness. I am so used to sycophants, petitioners, and political insiders trying to gain some advantage that it is refreshing to meet someone who appears to have no agenda. What agenda could he have, except to be freed from prison?" And that will be easy enough to do. No, there is something about this Joseph that I like. A poise, a directness, even a kind of peacefulness."

Now I turn to Joseph. "Joseph," I ask the group, "what are some of the things going through your mind at this moment, things you might not be able to say aloud to Pharaoh?"

"As Joseph I am dazzled by this place and by this person. In my wildest dreams—and my dreams have been pretty wild—I never imagined something like this. Yet when I speak to him I see not a king, not a god, but a troubled man. I can see in his heart that he cares about his country and about his people. He is searching for the truth."

A woman stands to speak as Joseph. "Sometimes being an outsider gives you such a clear perspective. I see how this whole situation is ripe for manipulation. In telling Pharaoh the meaning of his dream I will plant the seeds in his mind for a role I might play. I will tell him he needs to find someone to manage the huge bureaucracy famine relief will require, and who better than me to run it? I am preparing him for a savior."

Another woman takes a very different tack. "As Joseph I feel that God is with me, and that God has been with me all along. I feel the door is opening. I believe this moment is part of my destiny. I am buoyed up by a strange exhilaration and confidence."

I am struck by this version of Joseph. It is rare to hear someone say that they feel God is with them, and I want to hear more from this player. Without releasing my first Joseph, for whom these doubling statements are being made, I invite this group member to come onto our playing area and put her hand on the shoulder of our primary Joseph (or simply stand beside him). I ask each, "Tell us what is it like to feel that 'GOD IS WITH ME.'"

"Well, in some way I suppose I have had this feeling all my life. It's not just that things have worked out for me. I have been high and low many times, and it's not a matter of egotism. I actually feel that I have very little to do with it—my personality, my talents—whatever they may be. It's more a feeling of trust, trusting that I will say or do the right thing, that there is something inside of me that guides me and that I can trust. Even when I spoke my dreams to my brothers I spoke from that place, though they thought I was boasting, and my father was displeased. Yet I felt that I had to speak my dreams, and the consequences of those dreams could never have been realized if I had not spoken them. Even when I rejected Potiphar's wife and got put into prison I felt bound by some sense of inner conviction to act in that way, and even during all these years in prison I have felt that God is with me. Men and women have been kind to me, spoken gently to me, and there have been many occasions when I felt that I was able to give strength or comfort to people who came to prison, to interpret dreams, to help people to pray, sometimes just to listen. I am no one special, but I feel that God has chosen me to be a player in His drama. I feel this because deep in my heart I am at peace."

Director's Aside: God-Talk

My inviting this Joseph to speak at length is motivated by a number of different factors, different allegiances I have in doing this work. To be sure, my conduct of Bibliodrama is always guided by my interest in the biblical narrative and the creation of interpretations. I want to encourage members of the group to exercise their imaginations and to open up new areas of meaning in the texts. I am also guided by the desire to see people work together in creative ways, to shape a drama together, albeit improvised and evanescent, that creates a shared sense of creative enterprise. I am animated also by a concern for individuals in the group who, in playing any character, might be touching on their own personal issues. If and when that occurs, I will make sure that person feels free to step out of a role and return to the safety and silence of an observer. And I have a fourth interest, and that is, wherever possible, to discover how people articulate their experiences of God.

Our experiences of God—our questions and epiphanies, our theological arguments, or our expressions of praise or gratitude—can rise naturally out of this work with biblical stories because those stories are so infused with a spiritual perspective. They are, after all, God-stories; the characters in them are all God-players. God may or may not be a character in our actual dramas (see Part III, section 2 for a discussion of the pros and cons of bringing God as a character into a Bibliodrama), but playing from biblical narratives always involves our thinking about God's role, about God's meaning, about divine will, about a providential plan, about feeling connected to God, to the feeling that God may be, has been "with us."

What I sense happening now is that a certain spontaneous spiritual energy is becoming manifest in the group. I hear a certain kind of God-talk, infused by a natural and spontaneous eloquence and not by dogma. Given my own predilections and values, I respond not only by giving it space, but also by seeing whether it catalyzes something kindred in other members of the group. Without breaking the trance of the drama and inviting people in the group to speak as themselves, I stress this particular moment by asking the group:

"Are there other Josephs here who remember times in your life when you knew the presence of God, felt that God was 'with you?' Raise your hands." I see a number of hands go up. I recognize them.

"I felt God's presence when I was a boy with my mother before she died."

"I felt God's presence when I was in the hills watching my father's sheep. At night. Alone under the stars."

"I felt God's presence when I almost died but was given a chance to live after my brothers sold me into slavery."

"I felt God's presence in prison, when I was able to serve others and feel love rather than despair in my heart."

"I felt God's presence when I have been able to see through the confusion of a dream to its simple truth."

Quite spontaneously the man playing the role of Pharaoh turns to me and says, "You know, I think I am having an experience of something unusual right now as I speak with this Joseph. I feel that the spirit of God is with him and extends to me also. It makes no sense, and yet I feel that everything is going to be all right. There is a feeling of peace emanating from this composed young man. I even feel from him a kind of love, as if he were sent—he a slave and a foreigner—to take care of me and of my people."

"There are people," I offer, "who unaccountably touch us with that sense of peace and security, who somehow seem to have God with them in their hearts. You often see it in their eyes." Pause. "And," I say to Pharaoh, recognizing a neat transition when I see one, "this is in fact what the text tells us you do feel. You will go on to invite Joseph to listen to your dreams. You will attend both to his interpretation and to his suggestion that someone be found to oversee the management of the fat and the lean years. You are so convinced by his interpretation and so impressed by the interpreter that you establish him as your chief minister, your second-in-command, and you speak to your court and your courtiers.

"I quote you: 'COULD WE FIND ANOTHER LIKE HIM, A MAN IN WHOM IS THE SPIRIT OF GOD?' This is an astonishing insight you have, Pharaoh, a deep revelation of the presence of God in this man, and so you turn over to him the keys of the kingdom, and you put him in charge of all the land of Egypt. You invest him with your ring; you robe and dress him in finery; you give him an Egyptian name; and in your last act of raising him to power you arrange to have him marry Asenath, the daughter of Potiphera, the priest of On. Why, Pharaoh, do you arrange this marriage for him?"

(On other occasions I have done this particular moment as a conversation between Pharaoh and the Priest of On. It has provided comic relief as well as a story within the story. But this evening I am keeping my eye on the clock, and there is not time to take this detour. I can get some of the same material by interviewing Pharaoh.)

While the group is refocusing on Pharaoh, I go over to my Joseph, thank him and invite him to resume his seat in the group. Now only Pharaoh remains onstage.

The Pharaoh onstage speaks. "I arrange this marriage because he is simply too handsome and now too powerful to be single. You know what happened to him in the house of Potiphar. Well, he is the most eligible bachelor in Egypt; I don't want him distracted. A marriage will keep him... you know... from entanglements." Taking these words as a kind of closure for the person who has played Pharaoh, I dismiss him from the stage with a sincere "thank you." I know where I am going in the drama, and in the next scene I will not need the king. But I also want to set the stage for this next scene, the marriage of Joseph, by spending a little more time with this question of why the marriage. So I ask the group as a whole, "Why do you arrange this marriage for Joseph?"

"As Pharaoh, I have married him not only to the daughter of a priest but, as the name implies, to a priest of the family of Potiphar; the priest's name is Potiphera. By this single stroke I have settled that unfortunate and scandalous aspect of Joseph's past. This marriage into the family of Potiphar lays the past to rest."

"As Pharaoh, I want to secure this Joseph not just from the snares of people who might use him for their own ends, but I want to secure him for Egypt. Unmarried and unattached, he might at any moment decide to cut himself free of his obligations to me. Though marriage is no guarantee of his loyalty, it is a powerful bond. It gives me some reassurance that he will be loyal to Egypt."

"As Pharaoh, I need to test him. I have arranged this marriage not with just anyone, but with the daughter of a priest. This will not only be a state wedding, but it will be a sacred union as well. I am glad to have this Joseph working for me, and with Joseph I have his God, and I want this God to be part of the Egyptian pantheon. This marriage with the priest's daughter will represent, if not a conversion to the religion of Egypt, then a joining of two sacred houses. I am testing Joseph. If he goes along with this marriage, then I believe he has in effect sworn his loyalty to Egypt."

"Yes, as Pharaoh, I arrange a marriage that is politically apolitical. He marries into the priestly caste. His children, if he has any, will not have any claim to temporal power; they will be part of the cult of the priests. Such a marriage quarantines Joseph even as it safeguards his loyalty."

"All this is too machiavellian. As Pharaoh, I want to make Joseph happy. Asenath is one of the most beautiful women in the kingdom, and the priest of On—unlike the priest of Het or Osiris or Ra—believes that all the many Gods are manifestations of the One, the On (punning). Of all our deities On is closest to this God of gods whom Joseph's tribe worships." This last interpretation, playful as well as just faintly plausible, provides one of those moments of transition a bibliodramatic director looks for. I join the humor of the moment with a phrase of my own. "Perhaps we should get on with our story." Groans from the group. "Right on!" someone says.. "Onhestly!" says another, and in such good humor, with the punning de-roling us without our even being aware of it, that we do in fact move on. I will prepare the group for what I imagine, given the time constraints, will be our final scene.

The Climactic Scene

I have had several possible climactic scenes in mind from my first reading of the text, but the one I am about to launch into is my favorite. The wedding of Joseph to Asenath is merely mentioned in the text:

> And pharaoh gave Joseph the name Zapeath-Paneah [in the footnotes we are told this is Egyptian for 'God speaks' or 'creator of life']; and he gave him for a wife Asenath daughter of Potiphera, priest of On. Thus Joseph emerged in charge of the land of Egypt (Genesis 41:45-46).

Yet this marriage, which is mentioned only in passing, must have been, if we think of the characters naturalistically, an event of enormous inner and outer consequence for the young Joseph and for Asenath. By their nature marriages are times of drama, comedy, and pathos; most life cycle events are. Many members of the group know this firsthand; so Joseph's marriage, the occasion that is only mentioned in passing in the text, becomes a *pièce de théâtre* that can be enlivened by a whole new set of experiences and associations.

Indeed, I am sure this marriage, arranged and apparently unromantic, will evoke comments and responses that bear on choice, matters of the heart, and the conflicts between personal gratification and duty. Add to this the fact that the union of Joseph and Asenath is a mixed marriage, an "interfaith marriage," and I think the right elements of moral complexity are present to charge our work. What kinds of conversations, internal and interpersonal, will we set going around this event?

I can begin to set the stage for a look at Joseph and Asenath by first imagining the community response to their impending marriage. It will be a way of moving from periphery to center. I can solicit this diversity of response by saying something like this to the group: "Pharaoh has announced the marriage of his regent to Asenath. Word goes out, gossip, comments, rumor. You are a reporter for the *Egyptian Times*. What are some of the things you hear people saying?" I let this sink in for a moment. I see some people start to smile. "So I hear some people saying that..."

"I hear people saying that this is not a marriage that can last."

"I hear people saying that the most eligible bachelor in Egypt is now off the market."

"I hear people saying that Joseph will have to undergo some kind of conversion ceremony."

"Yeah, they'll have to sew a foreskin back on."

"I hear people say that the Priest of On had to make major campaign contributions to get this match for his daughter."

"I hear Potiphar's wife has become a nun."

"I hear Potiphar is trying to get himself a position as Joseph's major domo."

"I hear the cup-bearer got a huge promotion."

"I hear he's going to be best man at the wedding."

And so it goes, a comic interlude of choric voices. After the humor—not without interesting insight—I regather the troops.

"There is one final scene I'd like to see us play out. I want to focus first on Joseph and then on Asenath. I imagine each of them in their private quarters."

And here I place an empty chair at one side of our playing space for the chamber of Joseph, and another chair across from it, for the chamber of Asenath. (In this way I establish the points of focus and concretize them.) I continue:

"Let it be the night *before* their wedding day. The preparations have been made, and the servants have retired. Each is alone. So, Joseph, let me begin with you. Tell me what is going through your mind tonight" (group characterization).

Once again, in order to set up a scene and to focus my group into the characters, I fix the time and the place. The role-playing requires an exact matrix of this kind, for the internal states we are so often at pains to evoke belong to a particular moment in the lives of the characters.

Different times, different places will always evoke a different set of words and images.

Hands go up. I recognize people one by one; I invite each speaker to stand in place.

"This is another of those times when I wonder where God is. The Lord does work in mysterious ways, but this marriage is not just about my own personal fate. Until now I have been the outcast of my father's house. But if I make this marriage, I feel that I will be actively turning my back on that house. Then again, what do I owe them? Egypt has been better to me than Canaan, and Pharaoh a better father than my own. A union with Asenath is beyond any marriage I could ever make at home. I wish my brothers could see me now."

"Do I have enough power here, enough security, to refuse Pharaoh's arrangement? There's a part of me that wants to refuse. When, I keep wondering, will my life begin, my choices, my will? I have been a pawn, first in my father's game of favorites, then on the seesaw of changes in my fate. I have been a slave or a prisoner for almost half my life, and now, even though it looks like I am a powerful man, in this most intimate part of my life, I will again have to do what I am told. I hate it. I want to say no. I want…I was going to say I want to go home, but I don't even know if that's true. Home scares me. I want my own life!"

"I don't know where I belong anymore. Here I am at a new height of power and influence. Everyone sucks up to me. The world is at my feet, yet I feel more alone than I have ever felt. I have a new name, and I wonder where Joseph is. No one knows me simply as Joseph. No one calls me 'Joseph,' and there is a part of me that would put that 'Joseph' behind me. Yet in some way I feel more like 'Joseph' than ever, more mysteriously involved with my own fate. And I miss my father. Tonight of all nights, preparing to marry, I want his blessing."

A hand is raised in the group. "Can I be Jacob?" I am asked.

"Certainly," I reply. "Do you have something to say to Joseph?" I ask, hoping to kindle yet another encounter.

"I do."

"What do you have to say to him?"

"Joseph, this is your father talking to you. Don't do it. You should marry a nice Jewish girl like your mother, or even your aunt. An Egyptian wife. Oy vey. What will you do on Friday night? Will your children be bar mitzvah'd? Your mother, may her name be for a blessing, would roll over in her grave."

Director's Aside:
Managing a Challenge

I have not until this point offered an example of the kind of thing that can, not infrequently, occur in Bibliodrama—namely, when someone offers an interpretation that is either anachronistic, as this one is, with its contemporary references to Jewish observance, or a kind of grandstanding, as this might be. I remember how, in response to this "Jacob," a flutter of laughter ran through certain quarters of the group. Such a moment as this presents a particular challenge to the director, for the make-believe of the drama is endangered.

Several things go through my mind.

It occurs to me that this comment and the laughter are an expression of a certain antagonism. I think in part the anger may be directed at me for having chosen a scene in which this issue of intermarriage—often so loaded for a Jewish group—rears its head. Though the humor feels a little hostile to the process, it is also an attempt to lighten a dramatic moment that for at least one participant might be threatening. The uneasy laughter lets me know that the player who is giving us this Jacob is not alone. Meanwhile other members of the group frown, feeling the mood shift. In the light of an interpretation like this one I feel anew the fragility of the bibliodramatic spell. Yet it is by no means uncommon for that spell to be tested, if not attacked, by a member of the group.

What is crucial in managing this moment is not to antagonize the antagonist by any sign of disapproval. Whatever my own displeasure might be at having my "show" interrupted, I am called to remember that this response comes from a place of legitimate concern in the speaker. I would do well to notice that he attempted to voice his reaction in role.

As director I need to respond in a way that respects the role player and preserves the drama. Here is an occasion when echoing as the director can accomplish two things at once. I can assure the participant that he is heard by accurately representing the content, and I can strip away the anachronistic quality of his words and return the discourse of our drama to that neutral terrain we have unconsciously created.[15]

So my echoing statement—my attempt to "get" what this participant is saying and in that way keep him engaged in positive ways in the making of our story—might sound something like this:

"Joseph, as your father I have a deep commitment to our traditions. It angers me, and more, it saddens me to see you willing to take such a course. How will you maintain the customs I instilled in you as a child if you marry a woman who is unfamiliar with those customs?" And I look immediately to the group member I am echoing to see whether I have tracked in on what he is saying. It isn't always easy to reengage such a person in the drama.

"No," says this Jacob, still nettled. "No, you don't understand; it's not for me that I am concerned. No, it's his mother I am speaking for."

Ahh, all sorts of little prickly difficulties and choices here. Now the man playing Jacob has told me what I missed and at the same time has directed his comments to me. The mask of role-playing is slipping; this

---

[15] This is a subtle matter, but worth noting. There is a certain language appropriate for Bibliodrama. On the one hand, it cannot be too stilted or stylized. The whole purpose of the interpretive endeavor in Bibliodrama is to connect our moral, emotional, and spiritual worlds with those of the characters in the Bible. We have to render our contemporary worlds in a language that is real to us. On the other hand, if that language is too flavored with our local idiom, then we run the risk of flattening the mythic dimension of biblical drama and the characters we are impersonating. Throughout much of the Bibliodrama rendered here the reader will note that at its best the style of language used by participant has a certain plausibility. We are not jarred by something that throws us into the twentieth century, nor are we distanced by ways of speaking that are artificially quaint. One of the principal tasks of the director, in echoing statements made by participants, is to establish this idiom of the drama, the tone and level of spoken style that can carry feeling and at the same time dignity. By the same means, however, the director can use his speaking style, his echoing style, to regulate the intensity of emotion or to undercut the overly or overtly dramatic and bring back a certain level of colloquial naturalism.

group member is almost speaking for himself. And I am being pulled on stage; I do not want to get roped into a dialogue with him. It's to Joseph that he must speak. I can, on the one hand, keep echoing this Jacob. I can say something like, "Joseph"—and here I remind my actor that he is to keep me out of it—"this is your father talking to you. I have had to represent your mother to you since she died. I have had to speak for her and to think for her and to act for her. I have done this out of loyalty and out of love. I am so worried that she would feel I had not done right by you as her husband, as your father; she would never forgive me for standing by silently at this moment in your life." Once again, saying this, I would check with Jacob. Perhaps now I will see him nod.

Or, if I find that I cannot get him right, I could say, "Is there someone here who can speak for Rachel?" My strategy now is to flow past him and also to provide some opportunity for this conflicted moment to be voiced in other ways. I go on, elaborating a possibility only now occurring to me, framing a story within the story, opening up new pathways for interpretation, thinking on my feet. "On this night when Joseph prepares himself for marriage, does he think about his mother? Does he wonder what she would feel and what she would say? Here we have heard one Jacob speaking for her, but let us have her speak for herself. Let us suppose Joseph falls asleep and has a dream—for he is a dreamer, and surely on this night of nights he dreams—and let's suppose further that you come, Rachel, and perhaps others with you. Who are you, any of you, who visit Joseph in his dream? What do you bring or come to tell him?" By this strategy I honor the contribution of the Jacob-player and use what is creative in it—namely, the spontaneity of introducing a character I had not thought of; but I expand it to allow a medley of voices into the scene, as visitations, as characters that appear to Joseph in a dream.

A Joseph speaks, supporting this move in the drama; I motion to him to stand up. "I am Joseph, and I am thinking of my mother. I have never loved a woman. I do not love this Asenath. Not yet, anyway. But my mother was loved. My father loved her enough to work as a hired hand for fourteen years. That is exactly how long I have been here in Egypt, in my own servitude. I do wonder what my mother would say to this marriage. It seems lifetimes ago that I saw her, and thinking about her makes me feel sad." I ask Joseph to remain standing. Who will talk to him?

"I am Jacob." A member of the group raises his hand, and I motion him to stand. I recognize this would-be Jacob as the man who played Potiphar several scenes back and who had talked of feeling adoptive toward the young man he bought out of slavery. We never did play out that thread of possibility.

"Yes, Jacob, what do you have to say to your son, and Joseph, what will you say in answer?" And here the Jacob walks toward Joseph, and the latter looks up expectantly.

"My son, I am so sorry not to be here at your wedding. My father and mother were not at mine, either. I, too, felt alone, but foolish and young as I was when I married, at least I married out of love. Your aunt Leah I married out of duty. I know the difference, and there is a difference. I fear you are losing your heart."

"So, what am I to do? I don't know this woman. You're right, it's a political marriage, not a marriage of love. Is this wrong?"

"I just don't know"—and here Jacob averts his eyes and sits down without conferring this blessing. Our Joseph remains standing, his head down. I say "Dreams can be so frustrating, the merest glimpses; a father whom you have not seen in many years comes and then vanishes again. Who else visits Joseph in his dream tonight?"

"I am Leah. Listen to Jacob," someone says, pointing to the man who had been a bit challenging earlier. "Perhaps God wants you to say no to Pharaoh, to reject this marriage, to keep separate from this pagan people. This is a test. Have faith that God will find a way for you if you stand by your principles."

"I am your mother, Rachel." Here a woman comes up and puts her hand on Joseph's shoulder. "My poor boy, I am sorry to find you here alone tonight. On such a night there should be celebrations and feasting. You should be surrounded by your family. I cannot give you any comfort. But I do not blame you for marrying. Good will come of this. Have faith." Joseph looks up and gives a wan smile as his mother, sitting down, fades back into the group.

"I am Rachel." Another figure rises in the group. "I have missed your life. Strange and terrible things have happened to you. This marriage is not what I would have wished for you. But you are my son. I waited so long for you. I love you. I see your distress. Do not add to it by imagining that I am displeased with you. Be a good husband. Honor your wife. Listen to her. In time you may find comfort in her, and may you be a comfort to her. This is not easy for her either."

"I am Sarah."

(Ahh, I think, the dream horizons have just been moved back two more generations. This kind of moment is exciting to all of us because it increases the possibilities of play, and it sends its quantum of energy into our process.)

"The inheritance will not pass through you because of this. Judah's line, not yours, will be seen as the true lineage from Abraham."

"I am Abraham," says another group member, standing up. "Joseph, let me remind you that after my wife Sarah died I took a wife from among the Canaanites. Her name was Keturah. God's dream for us is that ALL THE FAMILIES OF THE EARTH BE BLESSED. Clan marriages, tribal marriages, are not the end. The idea of pure marriage is a fiction. Who of us is pure? You are about to do a great work. In my time it was foretold that our people would become a slave people for four hundred years. You cannot know this clearly, but that great chapter is beginning. You are playing your indispensable part. You will have sons. You will be reunited with your family. There will be comfort and honor for you among your people."

"Father Abraham," says Joseph, "you at least heard God speaking to you. But I have never heard God speak to me. God may be with me, but sometimes I cannot see or feel it. I feel I am a stranger in this strange land."

"It is a feeling every man feels, Joseph. We can feel alone."

Director's Aside: Limitless Possibilities

Many hands are now raised. There is no need to include all of them here. We have hit one of those veins of spontaneity for which the bibliodramatic director looks. It is not surprising to find such a wealth of material here, though the first time I directed this particular story I was amazed because I had been grasping for something simply to smooth over a difficulty, something with which to handle a challenging participant, and it turned into a treasure of bibliodramatic play. This is not uncommon; the apparent dead end often opens up into a broad landscape of new prospects and possibilities.

When Bibliodrama enters this zone, this landscape—and by no means does it always do so—a number of things are going on. Clearly the fiction of Joseph's dream here is narratively solid, satisfyingly so. We have given the dreamer a dream. Also, it is an open dream; people can find all sorts of ways now to speak to him and to one another. And then the themes this gambit allows us to entertain are significant: marriage, intermarriage, the dead mother, the absent father, the foreign life, the lonely son, the distant kin, the silent God, the questions we all have about choice and purpose and meaning. The existential vitality of this particular narrative moment in the Bible intersects with our own experience. The realms of the Bible and our lived lives fuse and counterpoint. Our little stories pop open inside the big story; threads of connection cross from us to the biblical narrative and from the biblical narrative back to us.

Sometimes God wants to make an entrance here. I have heard Esau and Ishmael come forward and console Joseph with their own outcast stories, inviting him to think of them as his kin and asking him to remember them when it comes time to pay tribute to those who stood beside him when he felt alone. And the women have come. Not just Rachel and Leah, but Sarah and Rebecca. I do not prompt the group to supply figures for this dream. Groups know the biblical material more or less well. When, in subsequent groups, I tried this dream-story, it sometimes produced relatively little, sometimes much. But even when it was not taken up in a lively way, it suggested how we can create "dramas within dramas, innumerable points of view."[16]

---

[16] There is a certain danger for me in doing the same story repeatedly. When one has conducted a story many times, it is hard to regain what the Zen Buddhists call "beginner's mind." There are many kinds of agendas of which the bibliodramatist must be wary, for agendas will curtail the spontaneity of the group. For me the most perilous and subtle agenda is that of repeating or looking to repeat the plot line or push for the interpretive variations that once were original and

There can be many permutations and combinations in a scene of this sort, and what I have recorded here is meant only to suggest the kinds of participation possible. At a certain point I close down the scene. I may say something like this: "So it is a night full of disturbances for you, Joseph. Thank you." Then "Do you need to say anything before you leave our stage?" I want some moment of closure for the player(s) so that energy may be freed to take new parts in a new phase of the drama. At the same time, I do not want to break the spell or the momentum too much. In this case Joseph lets me know nothing is needed and sits down. I know I am asking some group members to bracket their feelings for the sake of moving on. Most can. Sometimes those who cannot will pull quietly out of the drama for a time and think their own thoughts; at other times a person might want to do a little more in role and in this way find his or her way to bring closure to a moment of identification.

Then addressing the group, I say by way of closure, "His dreams have been full of visitations. Finally he falls into a dreamless sleep, and all the shades depart." I let some silence fall during which I let people come back to a bibliodramatic neutral where they are no longer in a previous role or a previous scene, but in readiness to play new ones. "Take a breath," I say to the company.

"Meanwhile his bride-to-be has her own night to live through. Let the light come up on her here." I say and I move now to different place on our "stage" to indicate Asenath's chamber, where I have placed an empty chair for her.

"Tell me, Asenath, what goes through your mind on this night?"

Hands go up. I recognize speakers; they stand, speak, sit down again. I record here only a few of their comments.

"What does a woman have to say? Who listens? In this age I am merely a piece of property passed from my father's control to that of a husband."

"I am not only a woman, I am a priestess. This is not just a political marriage, it is a sacred one as well. Joseph...I have seen him...we have

---

full of life, but which on a later occasion, if I force them, will lack true spontaneity. Previous bibliodramatic insights, like biblical commentaries, should be available as gambits or glosses, but if one imports them to regain some previous bibliodramatic high, then you can miss the interpretations that might emerge in this moment and for the first time.

spoken; I feel that he is a man of God. His God, my god, one God, many gods: what does it really matter? There is a world beyond this world. Joseph and I serve that world. We'll find a way of serving together."

"If we have children, how shall we bring them up? Will he want them to know the ways of his father, or will they be brought up in the religion of my house?"

"I am just a girl. I am terrified of this great man, this eminent man. What will he want of me? Will he have other wives, concubines? Am I a mere decoration for him, like the signet ring Pharaoh puts on his finger? Am I merely part of his new identity? Part of his disguise? Will I ever know this man? Do I want to? Does it matter?"

"I will be forgotten in this story. I am only a name. My history will not be recorded. No one will think about me. I feel I am infinitely small, a name without a life, a speck of sand."

"Do I get to have a dream?" asks one Asenath. Then, turning to the group with a certain anger, she asks, "Who comes to me?" Here a member of the group becomes so fired up that she, in effect, becomes the director as well as protagonist.

Quick to respond, members of the group offer a variety of possibilities. Potiphar's wife comes, jealous and, after a dialogue with Asenath, repentant. It matters to the bride-to-be that her husband's reputation be cleared. Tamar, another of those important mothers whose inner life is left in shadows, brings a sister's support to a woman marrying into the family of Jacob.

"Be warned," she tells Asenath. "They serve a destiny that has a place for us only as mothers to their sons."

These sentiments inspire someone to speak as Hagar, the mother of Ishmael, who shares some of her story with Asenath. In one drama Dinah, Joseph's half-sister, found a voice. In a traditional rabbinic commentary Asenath is seen as the daughter Dinah bore from her rape in Canaan, and in this way the issue of intermarriage is sidestepped. But the Dinah I heard in that group spoke as a woman wounded by patriarchy.[17]

---

[17] Doing Bibliodrama in contemporary religious communities, organizations, and seminaries, I have appreciated the opportunities it afforded women to be heard, to develop voices within the drama that are not there in the canonized text. For me personally this work has been one way I have seen some of the challenging

Again my task here is to moderate the bubbling flow, and in particular now to watch the clock and gauge the energy of the group. I need to leave time at the end for closure and reflection, and even the liveliest scene begins at some point to lose steam. It is better to end a scene a little too early than a little too late.

Recognizing the need to draw this work toward closure, I speak to Asenath: "So for you, Asenath, there are many moods and feelings, many visitors that are part of the night before your wedding. Thank you for sharing some of them with us. You, too, fall at last into a dreamless sleep."

As the director, who is also the arranger of scenes, I have one last suggestion to make to the group before looking for an ending for our Bibliodrama. I am motivated by a desire to reach out to include as many people now as possible in a kind of finale, and also by the desire to bring this entire phase of the Joseph narrative to a conclusion.

"We know," I say, "that the wedding occurs. Joseph and Asenath marry. Joseph, you go off to organize the prosperous land and lay in the provisions necessary for the famine you believe will come. Asenath, you live your life. Perhaps you accompany your husband; perhaps you pursue your studies. But of you both as a married couple the biblical narrative has only one further thing to tell us. You, Asenath, will be mother to two sons. I would like to invite you both to play out one final scene. I'd like to divide our large group into groups of four. In each group there should be someone willing to speak as Asenath and someone who can be a double for her, and in each group there should be a Joseph and his double also. Those of you who do not want to play could join a group and watch."

---

feminist perspectives—and by no means articulated only by women—brought into a vital relationship with the biblical narrative. What is more, of course, women speaking up in congregational and educational communities continue to establish and expand their role in areas of study as well as in the more traditionally sanctioned areas of service. As I have seen repeatedly, Bibliodrama establishes a playing field in which not knowing as much as you think you should know doesn't keep people from participating. As a result, constituencies sometimes marginalized in worship communities from a full-voiced participation in acts of study—women, children, converts, and more recently intermarried spouses, gays, and lesbians—can in the Bibliodrama be heard and recognized. Theirs are often the most stunning insights because they seem to enter parts of the biblical narrative hitherto silent and dark.

As people get up I say, "Please don't talk as you do this so we can keep up the dramatic illusion. We'll have time to discuss things in a little while, but for now let's stay in role." I help the participants form groups of four or more. When they settle I ask "Asenaths, please raise your hands; now Josephs, raise yours. And doubles? And observers? OK. Good. Now stay in role through the following exercise. Here is where we are in the story, and when I finish orienting you I want you to have a conversation, Asenath and Joseph, with the doubles chiming in whenever they wish. The only requirement is to stay in role. Observers, you can help the players to do that if you see them slipping out of their parts. OK? OK.

"So the years of plenty have ended, and the years of famine are about to begin. During the years of plenty you two, Asenath and Joseph, have had two sons. Let me read to you this part of your story:

> BEFORE THE YEARS OF FAMINE CAME, JOSEPH BECAME THE FATHER OF TWO SONS, WHOM ASENATH, DAUGHTER OF THE POTIPHERA, PRIEST OF ON, BORE HIM. JOSEPH NAMED THE FIRST-BORN MANASSEH, MEANING, "GOD HAS MADE ME FORGET COMPLETELY MY HARDSHIP AND MY PARENTAL HOME." AND THE SECOND HE NAMED EPHRAIM, MEANING, "GOD HAS MADE ME FERTILE IN THE LAND OF MY AFFLICTION" (Genesis 41:50-52).

I repeat the names of the sons a second time. If I have a blackboard, I will actually write the sons' names on it with the extended meanings given in the Bible. "The meaning of these sons' names, 'God has made me forget completely my hardship and my parental home' and 'God has made me fertile in the land of my affliction,' suggest something of the inner life of Joseph through these years. Let us imagine that you, Joseph, and you, Asenath, have that kind of marriage where much can be shared and few secrets are kept. You are friends. Talk. Talk together about what your marriage has been like, what life has been like for you, and in particular what in the naming of your sons you are saying, Joseph, about what your inner life here in Egypt has been like. OK, begin."

Director's Aside:
Letting Go

While the small groups pursue their task I circulate unobtrusively, listening, and every now and then, if necessary, I may remind people to stay in role. To let the Bibliodrama proceed without my overall supervision always runs the risk of allowing those people who have been resistant to the process all along—uncomfortable with the play or with the content of the story—to talk as themselves rather than in role and so undo the illusion of the play. There are also those for whom the process has been so stimulating that they can hardly keep from sharing their insights; they, too, must be restrained a little longer. At the same time I cannot, nor do I wish to, compel a uniform participation. If people feel too locked into the role-play, they will express their reaction to this over-regimentation either by shutting down (and therefore pulling their energy, often noticeably, out of the group) or by being disruptive, challenging me, slipping out of role, whispering to their neighbor. Many times I need to remind myself what the point of this work is.

The point is not to sustain a performance. That cannot occur by my will alone anyway. The story and our passage through it must have a certain concerted integrity in order for people to enjoy staying in role. Matters of timing, depth, and the spontaneous originality of the group all determine how invested we become in our creation. But the purpose, finally, is a certain kind of fun. If the play is not playful—though it may also be deeply serious—then the Bibliodrama turns into something compelled, didactic, or driven by the director's need for a certain outcome. (Even the drive to produce a good Bibliodrama can be felt as an agenda.) In short, the reins need to be loosely held, and the horses of invention must feel free to range. From the outset I have had to make sure that no statement is off limits. In that same spirit, when I see the energy of the group begin to wane and dissipate, no matter how attached I may be to "one more scene," I need to be very careful not to run the play on too long. Even a touch of tedium at the end can contaminate what has come before.

Again the maxim is: **Better to end a scene too early than too late.**

So with one eye on the clock and the other on the group, its animation and silences, I measure out the time for this scene. Then I will call things to a halt.

"Thank you all, and just before we step out of role, tell me, any one of you who played Asenath, what is one thing you did not say to Joseph in your dialogue with him? And any Joseph, what is one thing you did not say to Asenath?"

"I did not thank her. She stayed with me. She helped me feel less alone."

"I did not tell him how much I felt like him, an outsider, someone with a life no one could really understand. I didn't say to him, 'Joseph, I, too, feel like I live in the land of my affliction.' I also..." And here the speaker, a woman, begins to weep.

Director's Aside: Handling Emotion

In this moment I realize that my invitation for people to say what they did not say has opened up this well of emotion. The characters have said to one another what they felt ready to say; I have asked them to go one step further. The already charged scene spills over. I am not distressed by these tears. I take them as a sign of trust in the group, in the process, and in me. They would not be there if the player felt unsafe. Further, I recognize how deeply appropriate they are to the context, whatever meaning they may have in the private life of the player.

Those who approach Bibliodrama without training in counseling or without experience in affective education may be alarmed when, as here, feelings overtake a player to the point where tears come. But let me remind you that the Bible is full of grief, of loss, death, separations, exile, and wandering. The Bible has in it more outcasts than inheritors, more sinners than saints, and even its exemplary figures suffer from their own frailties as well as from an inscrutable fate. So, too, do our lives. When our personal stories resonate inside the mythic stories, deep calls out to deep, and the hidden wells of feeling in us are opened through our giving voice to what is lying just below the surface of the narrative.

It has always seemed to me that emotion, such as the tears of Asenath, lives in two worlds, the world of the drama and the world of the player in his or her own personal life. As director I do whatever I can both to appreciate the emotion being expressed in a Bibliodrama and to make sure it is framed as the emotion of the character in the Bible and not seen as the sudden, disruptive feeling of the player who just can't control himself or herself. **Help the player keep the mask of the biblical character securely on is a guiding maxim.** I do this by addressing participants by their biblical names and by telling them that I understand how appropriate their feelings are to the characters they are portraying.

It is important that the director not be uncomfortable with feeling, for that discomfort will be communicated in many ways, consciously and unconsciously, to the group. To the extent that one of the sources of spontaneity, as well as one result of it, is the increasingly free flow of our emotional states, our lessening of our shame, and the slackening of our usual and often excessive inhibitions, then any shutting down of our feelings will shut down the drama. At the same time, **Bibliodrama is not a therapy session—and it should not become one. The director need not push for feeling to come.** When feeling does arise, it arises naturally out of the warming-up of the process. The director needs to remember that there are all sorts of unspoken agreements in a group, the natural restraints relatively sane people maintain with one another that keep things from getting out of hand. When, as is happening here, emotion deepens and words are replaced with direct emotional expression, the appropriate response is for the director to move physically closer to the person who is feeling strongly, offer a hand on the shoulder for support, and step in to echo the state, thereby locating it within the drama. This is what I mean by keeping the mask on.

So I say, moving toward this player and echoing her as Asenath,

"I realize that Joseph and I have shared some real pain, past and present. We know what it feels like to be alone, to be an outsider. I am glad we have each other."

Sniffing, the player nods. It is not so important that I get her right in my echoing, only that I provide a cloak to cover her sense of being suddenly exposed.

Sometimes this will be enough to allow the player to retire back into the role of observer. In some cases, as will happen here, these emotionally charged moments continue; the player goes on bravely in the role, using it both within the Bibliodrama and for his or her own sake. The person playing Asenath retains her awareness of the role and, keeping the mask on, will use it more consciously now, to say more:

"Yes. It's true. My father has disowned me, for I have brought up our children in my husband's ways. Yet I love my father and the faith of my childhood. I am angry at how small people can be, at how they put their religions before their hearts. It makes me sick. My husband and I often feel alone, but we have each other."

I don't know whether this player will revisit these moments after the drama is over in the reviewing time. But moments like this—and many that are unexpressed but no less powerful for players and participants alike—require the debriefing process that comes when we review the drama, if only for the decompression it allows us to have between the end of the drama and our return to our own busy lives.

I play the role with her, not so much echoing as making a duet with her. "I thank God for you, Joseph, whatever God that may be."

"Yes," says my player, blowing her nose, "it's true." We have a moment of silence. Some sighs are drawn. Some members of the group seem to be a bit moist around the eyes. Someone blows his nose. I may take the liberty of making a kind of framing comment here, such as:

"It's amazing, isn't it, what these biblical characters have been keeping pent up inside them all these years."

Or "I can almost feel Asenath sigh in relief that someone has actually discovered what she has been feeling."

Or "It seems right to me that we would, toward the end of our work together, come to feel the grief and the pain in this story. Whatever their successes, Joseph and Asenath still suffer from their sense of not fully belonging anywhere."

Such comments dilute the moment with a little distance and set the emotion in the context of our text-centered interpretation.

Then I will resume the drama: "Is there anyone else who wants to share with us the unspoken?"

"As Joseph I did not say to you, Asenath, how much I respect you. When I realize what it has been like for you, I realize I have too often taken you for granted. I feel lucky to have you as my partner."

"As Joseph I feel incomplete. We talked about how we had each other. We talked about how hard it was. We talked about our sons. But I still feel—and I know Asenath gets tired of hearing this—I still feel that I am not Joseph, that I cannot be Joseph until I live with my family again, until I see my brother Benjamin again."

"As Asenath I just want to say to this other Asenath"—pointing to the woman who has been crying—"that I know how you feel and we'll talk later." In just such ways do group members respect the role-play and stretch it.

Other hands go up. Other voices are heard. Silence settles. We have come far. We are ready to conclude. We have elaborated together a complex story. I look around the group, catch some people's eyes, smile, nod, shake my head as if to say "It's been quite a trip."

Then I take two chairs and place them in the middle of the group. "Here is Joseph." I point to one. "And here is Asenath." I point to the other. "And you," I say, sweeping the group with my arm, "are you. No one biblical, just you. Let's have a round of saying our full names, first, middle and last." The group complies; some are a little groggy, others impatient to get on to a discussion. I know the dramatic illusion—the "trance"—lifts unequally. We are in a certain limbo between the reality of our make-believe and the reality of our ordinary lives. "Before we completely dispel our drama, I wonder if anyone has anything they want to say to Joseph or Asenath or"—and here as an afterthought I place a third empty chair—"to any other biblical figure who has been part of our drama."

8

The Sense of an Ending

"Our Revels Now Are Ended"

Finding an ending and a graceful way to close a Bibliodrama is one of the hardest things to prescribe. The ending grows out of the specific drama. Sometimes a gentle and harmonious closing chord is found; other times the curtain seems to fall like an ax because we have run out of time. As director you need to remember that the Bibliodrama has been a long, sometimes deep, sometimes shallow trance. Again and again by your words you have induced and sustained it, repaired and intensified it, broken and resumed it. Now, as the drama is ending, your task is to lift the spell.

My own internal metaphor comes from diving. You have taken the players down below the surface, and you must bring them back up. Deep-sea divers know that if they come up too fast, they get "the bends," cramps that come because the blood has not cleared itself of the nitrogen of the dive. Depending on the depth, it can take a diver quite a while to be ready to climb back in the boat. So, too, with Bibliodrama. Often by the end, however, the trance is becoming shallow. Sometimes I even let it break itself; I do not preserve the same vigilance of keeping people in role, or I will make various comments that have a cognitive and distancing effect toward the end. But sometimes and for some people the trance is still deep, or has even deepened, and I become aware of the need to bring people out slowly and gently.

Gentleness is the key, gentleness of voice and tone. Some Bibliodrama directors begin to hum some repeatable tune or to start a familiar chant, and by that musical means they bring the group to another kind of consciousness. Some directors who have musical skills can pick up a guitar and use it to bring the group back to the here and now. The reading of the Bible can serve a similar end. But the key is gentleness, for often there has been a kind of psychic birthing, a kind of dawning of a new awareness about the Bible, about certain characters one has played, about something one has seen or heard—something vulnerable or spiritual—or one has felt something loosen and shift in oneself. All these motions may be hidden from view, but the director may feel them in the air, in the rustling of the group back to the present, in shy glances, in quiet voices. A gentle return is important.[18]

Here, as part of the process of de-roling and without wanting too quickly to dismiss our biblical prototypes, I again make use of the empty chairs. The chairs allow us to retain the ghostly presence of the biblical figures, but by letting the group speak in their own voices I allow them to relate *to* rather than *as* these figures.

"Here," I say, placing the chairs before the group, "here are the vacated spaces that Biblical figures just filled. Imagine seated here anyone from our drama to whom you would like to say a few words. After that we will clear the stage and reflect on our work."

"I want to say to you, Joseph, that I never realized what was going on with you. I mean, I read your story without ever thinking...well...anything, I suppose. I'm amazed."

"I want to say to you, Asenath, that my son married you. I mean my son is Jewish, and he married a non-Jewish girl, and it wasn't until I actually played you that I understood for the first time what it is... what it has been like for her. I feel... I feel I owe her some apologies."

"I want to say to you, Joseph, that I know what it's like to marry without your family's presence or approval. I won't say more than that.

---

[18] See Part III, section 6 for more discussion of closure.

I just know."

"I want to say something about Potiphar. I have never had children. I never had a son, and when I was talking about Joseph—you know, about feeling fatherly toward him—I was talking about myself, I guess. My wife and I are trying to adopt a child now."

"I want to say something to God. You know, God, you give us some pretty mixed messages. We are not supposed to marry non-Jewish people, but then Abraham marries...what was her name?"

"Keturah," I supply.

"Yeah, Keturah. I never knew about that. Is that really in the Bible?"

"Yes, it is. I'll show you later if you want."

"No, that's all right. I believe you. But here is Abraham marrying a non-Jewish woman. Abraham! And here's Joseph marrying Asenath, another non-Jewish person. I mean these are our ancestors. I don't get it."

"I want to talk about Pharaoh. I guess I'm guilty of prejudice. I thought all Pharaohs were bad guys. I lump everyone in with the Pharaoh of Moses, but I have to see that you were a pretty special king. I get down on everyone in public office in this country. I get pretty cynical, but I guess there are some good apples in the barrel."

You will note that in this closure process some people talk to and some people talk about the biblical characters. This is perfectly acceptable, and I don't push people into the direct method, because I am interested in loosening the bibliodramatic trance, of letting it come undone.

"I want to talk to Joseph. Joe, I know what it's like to be very successful, run the show, have a lot of people think you're a big deal—even think you're a big deal yourself sometimes—and feel lonely. It isn't all peaches and cream to be powerful."

Again, for the sake of keeping my account short, I will let this suffice for a sample of the kinds of things you might hear when you give the group a chance to address the characters in the drama.

"So, my friends, we are done. Stand up, take a deep breath, stretch a little as if you were waking up from a nap. Rub your eyes like children do when they are wondering whether what they see in front of them is real. Yawn if you can. And listen. Listen to how the great story continues:

THE SEVEN YEARS OF ABUNDANCE THAT THE LAND OF EGYPT
ENJOYED CAME TO AN END, AND THE SEVEN YEARS OF FAMINE
SET IN. BUT THROUGHOUT THE LAND OF EGYPT THERE WAS
BREAD. AND JOSEPH RATIONED OUT GRAIN TO THE EGYPTIANS.
BUT THE FAMINE SPREAD OVER THE WHOLE WORLD. SO
ALL THE WORLD CAME TO JOSEPH IN EGYPT TO PROCURE
RATIONS. AND IN TIME THE SONS OF ISRAEL WERE AMONG
THOSE THAT CAME TO PROCURE RATIONS, FOR THE FAMINE
EXTENDED TO THE LAND OF CANAAN" (GENESIS 41:53-42:1).

"And so it comes to pass that the next stage of the drama is ready
to unfold. We may look together at that another time. For now let's sit
back down, re-form our circle, and talk about what it has been like to
make this play."

It is at this point that I am likely to say something about confidentiality. "And as we do, let me say something about what we have shared
here today. Sometimes," I continue as theater gives way to education,
"Bibliodrama can touch on personal feelings and issues either in the enactment phase or in the reviewing. We have not only been learning about
the Bible, we have also been learning about one another. What we have
learned about the stories is ours to talk about with whomever we wish;
interpretations are always fun to share. But what we have learned about
one another is not for public consumption. Can we agree to that?" And
I wait until I get assenting nods from everyone. "Good. Thank you. Now
let's talk together about what we learned."

9

Reviewing

Reviewing, you will recall, designates the block of time reserved at the end of a bibliodramatic session for looking back and reflecting on what has occurred during the role-play. It is the time for you to help participants

- shed the entrancing effects of the work: **de-roling**;

- talk about the significance of the work for them: **sharing**;

- notice the ways the biblical text is more alive with meaning: **exegesis**;

- learn how others have approached the same passage: **consulting other sources**; and

- reflect on the craft of Bibliodrama: **processing**.

Of these five parts of reviewing, only de-roling must occur, and it must occur first.

De-Roling

There are any number of ways to shift people out of the role-play, both during it—when you are asking them to change from one scene to another, from one character to another—and when it is done at the end of the drama. **Being able to provide a clean ritual of de-roling is a necessary skill for the bibliodramatist.**

It is important to remember that roles find a way into our bodies. Often during a role-play, even without getting up from our chairs, we can shift into some pose or posture that is inspired by the role we are assuming; our breathing may alter slightly, and without being aware of it certain muscles may tighten. For this reason it is always a good idea to invite de-roling first of all by having people get up, breathe deeply, and move their bodies in free and spontaneous ways. "Shake it out" is often the simplest command. Then I will have people say their names, in effect reintroducing themselves to the group.

Another way of gently bidding farewell to characters who have been very real and present is for you to say something like this to your group after having had them breathe and move freely for a while, after having said their names, say:

"Now close your eyes and imagine that all the characters we have brought here are returning home—that is, to their places in the Bible. Imagine them taking their place in the Bible, where we found them first and can find them again." I give them a moment to imagine this.

"Now open your eyes, and imagine them here..." Here I will pick up and hold the Bible in my hand and wait until all eyes are open and looking at the Bible from which I have been reading during the session. I will lift it for all to see. I may riffle its pages, as if to say, "See, they are all nestled safely back in these pages."

"Now," I will conclude, "let's go around and have each person say his or her name, including, if you have one, your middle name or a nickname you had as a kid." This request often breaks any lingering connection to the biblical roles by forcing a higher degree of self-awareness than is usual.

Finally, if I am doing a Bibliodrama in a very large group (thirty or more), I sometimes request that each person turn to the person sitting next to him and take a moment to talk a little about something in the Bibliodrama that seemed interesting. Shifting people into a cognitive and reflective process in this way helps to disengage them from the drama. This last request—to talk about something interesting that occurred in the drama—is a way of inviting some sharing, though not in front of the whole assembly.

Sharing

Sharing should occur after the de-roling is completed and in a small group of twenty or less can be done by people taking turns to speak to the whole group, though often, it must be said, they will look at you. By now group members are securely back in their own identities; the go-round of names has anchored the fact. At this point, as all through the drama, the director needs to be conscious of how much time remains and to let the group know it is time to share.

There are parameters for sharing, and they need to be stated explicitly. One might say the following:

"Thank you. That was a wonderful piece of work you did. Even those of you who were quiet helped by your concentration. I am sure everyone, whether you took part or not, felt the reality of the drama at least at moments, felt it talk to you and talk from you in ways that may have surprised you.

"We have about fifteen minutes left before we need to end for today (this represents about a quarter of the overall time I have with this group). I'd like to invite anyone who wants to, to say anything you'd like about what it was like to play this story out. This part of the Bibliodrama is called sharing. It is a time for you to talk about yourself, if you want to. In sharing we do not analyze other people, how they played a role, what we think it tells us about them. And sharing is not really the best place for us to talk about our insights into the Bible. Sharing is the time for us to take the risk of letting other people know how we were affected personally, emotionally, spiritually by the Bibliodrama, either by our part in it or by what someone else's part brought up for us. You don't have to share; some of you may prefer to keep your experience to yourself. That's fine, too.

"I know for me..." Often I will speak first to break the ice and to model the kind of participation I am looking for.

"I know for me the whole issue of intermarriage is very relevant. When my wife Susan and I married I had very little sense of allegiance to a Jewish identity, and Susan was at least a nominal Christian. Susan insisted we have some part of our wedding ceremony drawn from the Jewish marriage service. I think she knew that being Jewish was a part of me, and she wanted that part in our marriage."

Often this is enough to set running a stream of appropriate self-disclosures. People will talk about their fathers and mothers, issues of feeling alienated, struggles with power, quarrels with God, bouts of despair, the trials of intermarriage, the experiences of making up with someone in their family they were estranged from, the unsettled ruptures, the lure of assimilation. All these personal stories will resonate inside the embracing biblical myth we have just explored.

It is in the sharing phase that I often feel—though do not necessarily address explicitly—a sense of the healing power of a commonly held story. As various group members speak about their association with the tale we have just told and enacted together, I feel us gathered under the canopy of biblical myth. We may feel again the power of a "master story," to give shape and depth to our personal stories.[19] Our dilemmas have been in no way resolved by our bibliodramatic enactment, but we are likely to feel less alone in two ways. On the one hand, we have had the chance to hear how others are going through or have gone through struggles similar to ours. We are less alone for knowing that. On the other hand, we have had the opportunity to recognize how all our stories are held within the framework of an overarching human story articulated thousands of years ago in a tale preserved and handed down to us through the generations.

---

[19] For a fuller development of the idea of a master story, see Joseph Lukinsky's "The Joseph Story as a Master Story," *Conservative Judaism*, Winter 1996.

Subliminally, there may be a subtle sense of ancestral presence, of archetypal dimension, of our common fate as story-beings living out in time our timeless tales. We are less alone for knowing this as well.

Exegesis

In many groups the kind of sharing I have been describing is not appropriate. In classrooms, where the mandate is the study of biblical texts, students should not be asked to bring forward materials from their own lives. In such contexts Bibliodrama can and should serve only as a form of literary criticism and biblical commentary.

However, you would be mistaken to think that the role-playing has not set off at least some personal resonances for your class. Some people may have been moved, touched, or troubled, and just because you are deciding, rightly, to skip sharing does not mean that people do not feel the need for it. Therefore some time needs to be made for it. **Unless people know they have someplace they can process their experience of the Bibliodrama in a more personal way, they will not be able to pay full attention to the exegesis, the literary analysis you are about to engage in.** And if people know that you will be available to them, then they will be able to wait and to think and study in class.

One way to inform your class of this option to talk to you later is to say something like the following:

"Perhaps for some of you this unusual way of studying a story has brought up things that surprised you a little. We are not going to take up time in the class for those things now, but I will be here after class and will be glad to make time for anyone who wants to talk to me. Or if you have to rush off somewhere, just give me a call if there's something you want to think about with me. I'm definitely available."

The sharing phase of the review has now been handled, if only symbolically. You have not left out a crucial dimension of your group's experience. You have let them know that you know there might be issues they need to take up in a more private context. Another way of saying this same thing is: **Don't do a Bibliodrama if you don't have time to make yourself**

available afterward for people to talk to you about their experience.

Now you are ready to move people into the exegesis stage of the review, and you need to alert them to what you are doing. One way is for you to make it clear that *your role* is changing back into being the teacher. That change might be signaled by your going to the blackboard and writing something on it, or assuming your place by your desk, or in some physical way letting people see that you are "teacher" again. This shift in your role occurs after the de-roling and after the nod you have given to a place and time for sharing.

At this juncture there are any number of things you can say that will mark this transition from director to teacher. Here is an example:

"We have used an unusual method to open up and to explore a complex and interesting biblical story. Many of us may be seeing things in the story we had never seen before, narrative details and dimensions of significance this method brings to the fore. In the ten minutes we have left I'd be interested in hearing some of the things that you have learned about the Joseph story through this method of study."

During such a discussion you are likely to hear students talk about such details as the divination thesis, which came about when one student connected the cup-bearer to Joseph's later use of his cup of divination. There may be talk about marriage practices in ancient Canaan based on Abraham's marriage to Keturah. Joseph's sacrifice of his own identity for the sake of power may become a topic of discussion; or, how frequently biblical characters take on some kind of disguise, or impersonation. The whole idea of intermarriage itself, the question of when and how it became consequential in the Judeo-Christian tradition, may be sparked by the exploration of Joseph.

In terms of narrative style, students may understand afresh the compressed and apparently unemotional manner of biblical storytelling. The effects of condensation, the power of single details to suggest immense possibilities, are likely to be more vividly felt in the light of the Bibliodrama. Issues of indeterminacy of meaning, of compelling yet conflicting interpretations, can raise questions that quickly become theological. In these and other ways Bibliodrama can be seen as a useful supplement to other kinds of interpretive enterprises.

Other Sources

I am not a scholar of The Midrash (here used with capital letters to indicate the collected body of classical rabbinic commentary that goes by that name), and I am only modestly familiar with midrash in its more contemporary forms. Readers of this book who know The Midrash will immediately recognize the ways that Bibliodrama can repeat or enlarge upon traditional commentaries. Bibliodramatists who work with the Christian Testament know interpretive sources they can turn to that will illuminate Christian stories. As I become more educated in these traditions I am more likely to reserve time at the end of a bibliodramatic session to read students some time-honored or contemporary commentary and to show how our work is, perhaps without our knowing it, in dialogue with the past and with our own time.

When I know other interesting interpretations I tend to keep them out of the drama, however, and save them for the end. My reason for this is that I want as much as possible for the player-participants to feel unintimidated by the great commentators of the past—even if, temporarily, it means being uninformed about them. In my view, students of biblical texts are sometimes too encumbered by the greatness of past interpretations; students too often feel they must be thoroughly acquainted with the wisdom of their predecessors before they can open their mouths. Or in the Christian community, where issues of doctrine and dogma are often primary, participants can feel hesitant about their own imaginative contributions. The respect many people have for biblical scholarship or for the authority of the pulpit can have the damaging effect of making people believe they have nothing to say. We have let the scholars and the clergy be our interpreters for so long that we have almost lost our voice, our conviction that the Bible is ours, too. The layperson's fear is that his or her ignorance will be immediately revealed and perhaps ridiculed.

I see Bibliodrama as a method of empowerment. It puts back in the hands of the layperson the means for making meaningful, relevant interpretations of biblical materials. To help that empowerment to occur, the director, when he or she is learned in the tradition, does well to withhold that knowledge initially so that participants can spread the wings of their own imaginative engagement. Once participants know what they have to say and they have heard their contemporaries wrestle with the same text and issues, then they can listen both with more interest—and, I think, with more profit—to the insights of the past. Furthermore, for all of us—participants and director alike—realizing the ways our own insights are conditioned by our culture, personality, bias, and experience makes us better able to recognize the conditioned quality—as well as the genius—of interpreters from former times.

Processing

This entire book may been seen as an attempt to *process* Bibliodrama, though mostly from the director's point of view. (Very little has been said in this book, for example, about how to act in a Bibliodrama, how to improve one's abilities to step into a biblical character and improvise, what kinds of study, training in voice and movement could help a person become a master performer.)

Bibliodrama is a craft, an art, and, like any of its kin, has its formal dimensions, its techniques, vocabulary, moves, and strategies. After the drama is done and you have guided the group through the various stages of review, you may see the value of discussing how your work as a director went, what succeeded, what did not, why you made certain choices, did not make others. This kind of discussion is particularly valuable in training groups where people are gathered to learn how to direct Bibliodrama themselves, and it is usually appropriate for the director to speak first and to let the group in on his or her thinking.

Sometimes in a non-training group there are one or two participants who saw what you were doing with a theatrical or artistic eye. They saw *your* performance, so to speak, and want to say something about it. You should hold off that kind of assessing comment until you are comfortable that the group's needs have been met through the other stages of review.

People may also have a need to object to things you did, and that is never easy to hear. But you need to allow such feelings to get communicated to you, though again it may be appropriate to invite people to talk to you after the session is over. Remember as you listen to such criticism that it may be the only way people know how to tell you that something you did or that happened in the drama made them uncomfortable. Criticism of you, in other words, may be one way a person is talking about his or her feelings. But it is very hard to hear this when such feelings are expressed as blame or anger or, as is sometimes the case, in a tone of intellectual superiority. Be careful not to get sucked into a discussion about you and your work until you have given people a chance to de-role, share, learn together, and recognize the connection of this work to the work of the past. A premature processing of your work can deflect people from their own experience.

But if, after those stages have been observed, people want to give you a hard time for something you did or did not do, then do your best to listen to them. It is your job even to learn from them, and to reflect either with them or later with yourself about what might have been stirring in you that led you to some places where certain people felt uncomfortable. Also, reserve the right to notice that this work does trouble individuals as well as the biblical waters. It takes a certain amount of courage to take people into the affective, imaginative world of Bibliodrama, and not everyone is going to like it. Give yourself credit, and don't expect perfection. And be cheered by my experience: I have found that some of the people who made the crankiest responses after a Bibliodrama let me know, at some later point, that they had come to see the experience as unforgettable and valuable.

All you can do is your best, and always be ready to admit you still have a lot to learn.

10

Curtain Call

Intelligent men and women—the spiritually awakening, the spiritually hungry—do not, by and large, turn to the Bible for nourishment or direction. The popular culture, in spite of all its talk about soul and myth, does not encourage us to seek in our inherited traditions the soul-myths we so deeply need. Few of our contemporaries, not professionally associated with the pulpit, any longer locate in the Bible those exemplars and paradigms, those archetypes of human experience and feeling that might connect our struggles for meaning with the quests of our ancestors.

Modern psychology has utterly divorced itself from the psyche of the tribe. Individualistic and demythologized in the extreme, our postmodern sense of self has lost all connection with the narratives of our religious traditions. We are all isolated in our own little stories; we have no sense that our little stories belong to larger ones. The Bible, for so long the instrument of community—though admittedly too often the instrument of exclusion and persecution—no longer provides a sense of center, a place of connection.

I see the work of creating bibliodramatic interpretations as an attempt to connect our individual lives with the biblical myths, to connect our personal histories to a communal and transpersonal history. I believe that engaging in this process of connecting is healing in a number of ways.

In the first place, it is healing because part of the disease of postmodern life is our sense of personal isolation from the capacious and consoling patterns of the past. The idiosyncratic, taken to its extreme, is idiocy. In Greek, the word *idiotes,* from which our word "idiot" is derived, means a private person. The idiot is a person so private, so unusual as to be incomprehensible to his or her fellow human beings. The idiosyncratic or private features of our self-images are now so predominant that we fail to recognize the common or homeosyncratic elements of our souls. When in the course of a Bibliodrama we forge a connection to the characters of biblical myth—when we speak as Eve or Adam, as Joseph or Miriam—we move from idiocy into relation; we discover ourselves within the traditions of the tribe. In that discovery we are repatriated from our estrangement in an inanimate material world to one in which our mythic ancestors may still speak to and through us. The past becomes present as it does in ritual and dream. Imagination extends its boundaries, and we are more alive.

Second, there is a healing that occurs simply in play. In our manic search for recreation we forget that "create" is the heart of the word as well as the heart of the matter. True recreation is creative play. As I see it, Bibliodrama is kind of group game of shared and sparking interpretation and insight; it is a kind of liturgical play. In fact, before liturgy became the province of the priestly caste, perhaps it was a participatory, group-generated form of mythic re-creation. I believe that our hunger today is as much for vital liturgy, for living and liberating ritual, and for truly replenishing recreation as it may be for private spiritual experience. God may be found when we close our eyes and breathe or pray ourselves into a state of ecstasy or to a place of profound peace. But God may also be found when we open our eyes and inter-act with other people in ways that release our spontaneity and allow us to experience fresh and noncompetitive forms of community.

Third, Bibliodrama heals the Bible itself. Bibliodrama has often been described as a kind of *living midrash.* I see midrash as a way of healing the Bible, not only of suturing its gaps and transforming its apparent inconsistencies into some larger coherence, not only of solving textual difficulties and threshing for meaning; it is also a way of easing its harshness by reinterpretation and of restoring its relevance to our lives. Bibliodrama, as a form of living midrash, becomes a way to liberate the Bible from its imprisonment in literalism or in coterie discourse and to bring it back to where it belongs, as part of the center, as a resource of imaginative energy for our quests and perplexities.

When we ask people to become Joseph and to tell us what he might *feel* as he stands on the verge of his new life, we give ourselves permission to revive his spirit. We give ourselves over to him, and paradoxically, he gives himself to us. In using our imaginations we reanimate (literally, *re-soul)* the old letters with a living energy. Bibliodrama's simple, radical questions and elementary steps free the biblical stories from the chains of dogma and moralism. The wildness of biblical myths, the multiplicity of biblical meanings suddenly open before us as a vista of fresh exploration. In Bibliodrama the Bible—once the living issue of a supreme imagination—can, in some small way, be returned to our imaginations where it belongs.

I think, too, that Bibliodrama has a role in repairing a world in which holy wars and fanatical acts demolish the delicate bridges of religious tolerance. The barriers between Christian, Jew, and Moslem are increasingly barbed and armed. Those barriers between the faiths, like the sectors of the city of Jerusalem, seem now increasingly dangerous to cross.

But Bibliodrama can remind us in a vital way that the stories and figures of the Western religious traditions belong to the same mythic human family. Abraham is the father of Ishmael and Isaac. Ishmael, first-born, is the sire of the Moslem faith; Isaac is the progenitor of the Jewish tradition; and Christianity, too, traces its origins to Abraham and his second son. The experience of call, wandering, prophesy, and the various dreams of deliverance and redemption are the family inheritance of all the western faith traditions and are deeply embedded in the culture and therefore in the psyche of every individual born in the West and Middle East. When we play into these figures and tales, giving them our voices, we understand the human dimension of our sacred stories, the common, mortal, even humble qualities that characterize our sages, heroes, and icons. In this context I have seen Bibliodrama create a kind of inter-faith arena in which we can explore one another's traditions, readings, cherished images without issues of creed or chosenness, triumphalism or salvific privilege being uppermost.

Finally, beyond needing some healing of the painful history of warring faiths, we need to find ways of having stories in common again. If as members of society we are going to be able to talk to one another, then we need to have common references and inhabit, however diversely, a shared order.[20]

Stories are what hold a society together. We call them "myths" when we look at the sacred stories of other cultures, and often we speak of these "myths" with a touch of condescension or skepticism. But our society, too, hungers for myth. The Bible was once our sourcebook for identity, for moral and spiritual illumination, for the myths of soul. It no longer can be, nor perhaps should it be, our exclusive anthology, but its stories still have the potential to connect us to ourselves and to one another and to the past. Without such connections we are prey to the terrible forms of idiocy already loosed in our world.

Bibliodrama, though by no means the only instrument useful for this cause, certainly has its place among the resources we can employ for the re-imagining of our religious lives. In this book I have brought only a handful of characters onstage; myriad figures are still waiting for us to embody them in holy play. Or perhaps they are waiting to embody us.

I spoke in the Preface about how Bibliodrama is a way of engaging people who have no particular scholarly education, no necessarily passionate belief, in a relationship with the Bible. Implicit in all that I have said is my belief that the Bible is worth having a relationship *with*. It may fairly be asked of me here at the end to say a few words about what I think the Bible is.

I do not dispute the findings of historical criticism, which point to the constructed nature of the book, the various strands and traditions that are woven into its fabric. At the same time, the biblical critics I most admire—Aviva Zornberg, Phyllis Tribble, Uri Simon, John Dominic Crossan, Robert Alter, Alicia Ostriker—treat the Bible's apparent inconsistencies, odd locutions, evident duplications as challenges to our interpretive abilities, as signs, rather than lapses, of sense and intention. Sometimes the

---

[20] Some readers may remember a Public Television series in 1996 hosted by Bill Moyers on the Book of Genesis. No small part of Moyers' goal in that series was to do just this: to remind us that we have common stories, that we need them, and that they are still capable of stirring us and surprising us with their immediacy.

intelligence required to find that sense rises to the level of wisdom and gives us a glimpse of a depth in the narrative design that can astonish us. Such writers have convinced me again and again that the Bible is a supreme poem, a superlative work of a timeless imagination.

And it is not the imagination of just a single artist, but of nameless and countless men and women: storytellers, legalists, poets, ritualists, singers, dreamers, historians, liturgists, prophets, and visionaries whose legacies were preserved by word of mouth, in stone, on parchment scrolls, on paper, in folktale and song until a time came for an anthology, for a record to be made. By whom and why that anthology was composed we will never know. But a great composite chronicle was set down of a mythic story, and it was set down so fiercely well that people said the Bible had been written in fire.

That fire is in the letters still, as heat may be said to be in coal. But like coal's heat, the fire in the Bible cannot be released without some labor, some catalyst, and that catalyst is reading, study, thought, the application of the imagination to the letters on the page. The black fire needs the blue fire of our own interest and attention. What is kindled from the mingling of these two flames is nothing less than sacred literature, and the sacred—whether in words or in places—is a vanishing category of human experience.

A final image:

I think of the Bible as a strange and holy city. You arrive at the imposing outer wall that girds the city all the way around, and you look for an entrance. You discover this city has gates, many gates. One, for example, is called the Gate of Faith; here people enter because they believe that the city was fashioned by God. There is a Gate of Mind where the scholars and the critics and the historians enter; they believe the city is endlessly fascinating to study. And there is the Gate of the Heart through which the poets and the converts pass; and next to it, just here, is a broad, low door over which the word *Bibliodrama* is inscribed.

Part III: Appendices

Appendix 1:
A Code of Bibliodrama Ethics

1. The bibliodramatist is, like anyone seen as a teacher or leader, in a position of power and authority *vis-à-vis* students or trainees. Therefore the first ethical requirement is a respect for the inequalities of power that are part of such a relationship. The bibliodramatist shall maintain appropriate personal and sexual boundaries in the conduct of this work. If a bibliodramatist charges a fee for this work, that fee should permit a sliding scale of payment so that this work can be accessible to as many people as possible.

2. The bibliodramatist is seen as someone who is teaching and interpreting religious texts. S/he shall make people aware of his/her level of knowledge, biases, and beliefs as they might inform the conduct of this work. Bibliodrama is not a tool for indoctrination; it is a method of exploration. The essentially inclusive and pluralistic orientation of the work should be maintained.

3. The bibliodramatist is not a therapist, unless, of course, s/he is credentialed as one. The nature of the work often gives rise to personal issues, and it is the responsibility of the bibliodramatist to contain the work

in ways that will do no harm to the participants and to refer troubled participants to appropriate credentialed resources. Training and practice in the management of the personal dimensions of this work are essential for a practitioner but do not qualify the bibliodramatist to practice as a therapist. Clergy who conduct Bibliodrama can, up to a point, rely on their pastoral skills, but they should be aware of their professional limitations, as they would be in any counseling context.

Appendix 2:
God In The Drama

There are times when a bibliodramatic scene cries out for the presence of God. This is not surprising, since God is a significant character in many biblical stories. Directors should be guided by their own theological scruples as to whether they will or will not bring God onto the stage. Some may rightly fear the reduction of the *mysterium tremendum* to the scale of play; others may feel that the personification of the Divine offends their own sense of religious decorum or may offend members of the group. Others may feel that God needs to be brought into the drama so that people can find ways of being in dialogue with the Divine.

In general, I have found that if God is brought into the drama, there is always some debate during the reviewing stage as to the appropriateness of this move. I know that I am guided in making a choice about God in the drama by my immediate sense of the context and of the tone and seriousness of the players engaged in the story. I carry enough of my own respect for the biblical God to want to make sure God-talk is not trivialized; on the other hand, the Bible is full of encounters between man and God, of God's voice in counterpoint to human voices, so you are certainly not doing the unprecedented by bringing God onstage. Furthermore, the tradition of classical Midrash offers many precedents for treating God as a character who speaks and acts beyond the black-lettered confines of the canon.

With this said, I offer one unusual and particular gambit in working with God in Bibliodrama: the use of **role-reversal**.

Role-reversal, as the name implies, takes place when characters exchange their parts. It is often a feature of the psychodramatic encounter when two people, expressing differing views and feelings, might at a certain point be invited to "role reverse." A then becomes B, B becomes A, and each speaks the words of the other, trying them on, seeing if they have gotten them right, experiencing the truth of the opposing view. There are times when a role-reversal works very well in Bibliodrama, but to do this successfully requires, I believe, some training in Psychodrama. I have not illustrated bibliodramatic role-reversals in this book; they really have no place in text-centered Bibliodrama. However, in the case of bringing God onto the bibliodramatic stage, role-reversal is often not only a good idea but a necessary one. I'll say why in a moment.

Take, for example, a scene in which we are exploring Miriam's experience during the seven days of her punitive confinement (Numbers 12:15). Let's say that in playing out this scene Miriam calls out to God, an outcry, a plea, a petition, a questioning, etc. Your task, as the director, is to provide your usual support, echoing and interviewing as you see fit. But then you could ask Miriam, "Miriam, does God answer you? Does God speak to you?"

Usually the answer I get to this question is "I don't know." The player is often so locked in the condition of the mortal character that she, in this case Miriam, has not yet tuned in to God. You can at this moment—and this is your option—invite Miriam to leave her part and to play God.

This is done by saying something like, "So let's see if God hears Miriam's cry." To the person playing Miriam you say, "would you be interested in knowing whether God hears this prayer?" If no, then you need proceed no further; if yes, proceed as follows: "Stand up and cross over to this chair here." (And you provide a chair for her to sit in as God.) She does and sits down. "Now you are God, and you have just heard Miriam crying out to you, saying, 'How could you do this to me?" (or whatever it is that Miriam said. Note: Your task here as director is to play her role— or at least say her words appropriately inflected—so that "God" can hear them.) After having echoed Miriam's cry to God you address God, saying something like, "So, God, do you hear Miriam speaking to you?"

The answer is usually, "Yes."

"And do you speak back to her, even though in her ranting and upset she may not be able to hear you right now?"

The answer is usually "Yes."

"And what," I ask, "are you saying to her?"

"I want her to know that..." And here you will interrupt and invite "God" to speak directly to the empty chair in which Miriam had recently been sitting.

"I want you to know..." you provide.

"Yes, Miriam, I want you to know that I hear you, that I am sorry for this punishment, but at this time Moses needs your support. Why were you objecting to his having some comfort with the Cushite woman?"

To answer this question I role-reverse "God" back to "Miriam." The woman playing the part leaves God's chair empty and sits back down in Miriam's chair.

"So," I will say to Miriam, "God does hear you, and God has said that He or She is sorry for your punishment but wonders why you were objecting to Moses' having some comfort with the Cushite woman. Can you tell God why?"

"Well, the reason is I don't have anyone for myself. I was jealous. What do I have? Who do I have? I have no family, no lover. I gave everything to Moses and to the people. She has taken my place as Moses' special confidante."

"Come sit back over here," I say to Miriam. "Let's see what God has to say to you." And again Miriam crosses over and sits in the chair as "God."

"So, God, you have heard Miriam. She has spoken of her jealousy, of feeling unappreciated, supplanted. What do you have to say to her?"

"Oh, Miriam, no one can replace you. Your sacrifice has been supreme, even if it has been unrecognized. But I recognize it. You will be remembered as long as Moses will be remembered, and women will always look to you for strength and inspiration. In fact, the way you bear this punishment from me, which seems unjust to you, will give women—and even some men—the strength to bear things they can't understand. I will be with you in your affliction." God seems finished.

"And now, one last time, let's go back and sit as Miriam and take in what God has said." I reverse this player back from God to Miriam. Once again I repeat the words of God to her so that she can take them in. "Is there anything further you want to say to God?" I ask.

"No," she says, "I can take this punishment. I understand." Then I put aside the chair in which "God" sat.

The reason I do not invite someone else to play God, as I might usually do in Bibliodrama when there is a part to be filled, has to do with how very personal the dialogue between God and each person can and should be. The person playing Miriam—this particular Miriam—will hear God in her own particular way and perhaps needs, or certainly deserves, the chance to imagine herself as God speaking to Miriam. Someone else's version of God at this point, however helpful or forceful, can never fit a player as accurately as her own version. For that reason, in God encounters I invite the player to assume the role of God and conduct the interchange as I have done above.

Sometimes, if such a conversation starts to seem circular or repetitious, I will say to Miriam something like, "Well, you know, Miriam, this God whom you have drawn out to talk is also a busy God. What is one last thing you want to say?" And then in one last role-reversal, "God, what are your last words to Miriam?"

There are, of course, whole scenes that can be developed with God as the central figure or protagonist. Such deo-centric dramas require a willingness on the part of the group to play in such ways.

Appendix 3: Participant-Centered Bibliodrama

As I made clear at the beginning of the book, the particular version of Bibliodrama presented in *Scripture Windows* uses role-playing to gain insights into the biblical text. In that focus, this form of Bibliodrama is part of what I think of as the text-centered school of the form. The Bible comes first; we, as players, serve it.

However, my own work has, at times and under certain circumstances, taken a very different direction and orientation. This other side of my work I call participant-centered; I have also called it "the Psychodrama of the Bible." In this form of bibliodrama (and here with a small "b") the Bible does not come first but is used as a warm-up for group and personal work—in short, for the purpose of self-exploration. Bible comes second, and that is why I would reduce Bibliodrama's capital B to lower case. In this form, as bibliodrama, it can only be conducted in small groups, for depth of this sort requires a much more complex development of group trust and group process than is required by text-centered Bibliodrama. In this form bibliodrama moves toward therapy.

In reality, of course, these two different approaches overlap and intermingle. There is no pure form of text-centered Bibliodrama because in it the interpretive agents are people who bring themselves to bear on the Bible in very personal ways. In their acts of play they stir up their own and one another's histories, memories, and associations. Every act of a biblical role-playing has its interior resonance. The director who attempts to suppress such implications, or who is naïve about their power or importance, runs the risk of blindly bumbling into places where angels might fear to tread. On the other hand, even the most participant-centered bibliodrama can shed a powerful light on a biblical passage. **What is important is that the director have her or his own intentions clear in embarking on this work with a group; the director has an ethical obligation to make these intentions clear to the group.**

In fact, this intention should be made clear in the publicizing and in the formation of the group before it actually begins. Because Bibliodrama-bibliodrama does span such differing purposes, people need to be aware up front of the nature of the work being offered. Some people, exposed to both schools, may come to a bibliodramatic session expecting one thing only to discover another. As this method becomes more widely a part of both the religious and the therapeutic worlds it is necessary to make clear which vector the method is set explicitly to explore. It is particularly necessary to spell out this intention when using the Bible as a pre-text for personal exploration, as a warm-up for transformational and therapeutic work.

A group constituted for the purposes of using bibliodramatic means for the ends of self-exploration will understandably require a much higher degree of professional skillfulness and clinical responsibility from the director. S/he must, therefore, have some solid clinical training. Clearly I have not written *Scripture Windows* for such practitioners. For those interested in acquiring these skills, professional training in a mental health field is a sound idea with some adjunctive training in Psychodrama or Drama Therapy. Specific supervised training opportunities in both these disciplines are not hard to find.[21]

Finally, there are other schools of bibliodramatic thought and discipline, though, as of the writing of this manual, I have only a hearsay relation to them.[22]

---

[21] Interested readers may contact the author through www.bibliodrama.com to learn of training opportunities under his direction.

[22] I am indebted to a correspondence with Professor Bjorn Krondorfer of St. Mary's College for some extremely helpful perspectives and references. I have acknowledged him elsewhere for his informed reading of this book in manuscript form and for his book *Body and Bible* (see bibliography). He was good enough to point me toward work in Germany and Finland that features this form of participant-centered bibliodrama (in Europe apparently always with a small "b").

Appendix 4: Troubleshooting

1. What to do
if someone will not stay in role

The signs that someone will not stay in role are easy enough to spot. A person will break out of character verbally, make asides in his or her own voice, laugh, or even cry in ways that cause you to question whether these affective expressions belong to the character being played or the

---

What follow are his citations and notes.

Gerhard Marcel Martin, *Sachbuch Bibliodrama: Praxis and Theorie* Stuttgart: Kohlhammer (1995). According to Krondorfer, "Marcel Martin is generally known in Germany as the 'father' of bibliodrama, and he produced numerous articles and entries into dictionaries on bibliodrama since the late 1970s. In his new book, he defines bibliodrama as 'the open-ended program of an interactive process between the biblical tradition and 12 to 18 group participants under the direction of one or several bibliodrama facilitators. It is experiential and text-oriented."

Jurgen Bobrowski, *Bibliodramapraxis*, Hamburg: Rissen (1991).

Antje Kiehn et al. (eds.), *Bibliodrama*, Stuttgart: Kreuz Verlag (1987).

Heidemarie Langer, *Vielleicht sogar Wunder: Heilungsgeschichten im Bibliodrama*, Stuttgart: Kreuz Verlag (1991).

Samuel Laeuchli, Die Buhne des Unheils, Stuttgart:Kreuz Verlag (1988) and *Das Spiel vor dem Dunklen Gott*, Neukirchen-Vlugn: Neukirchner Verlag (1987).

One of the interesting things Dr. Krondorfer pointed out to me in a letter is that all these books are written from "a Christian perspective.... In Europe, it seems that there is only a Christian method and hardly anyone knows of similar experiments on the Jewish side."

person doing the playing. At such moments it is generally a good idea to address this occurrence.

But first let's be clear about *why* a person does not stay in role. The reason is almost always because of anxiety. Breaking out of a role is the quickest way to short-circuit a process the participant is fearful will lead to some act of self-disclosure or self-awareness for which he or she is unprepared. This anxiety often operates on an unconscious level. For this reason **it is important to approach all breaks in role with the utmost respect; you have no idea what is going on in the participant, and no railroading, no harshness, no demand for playing by the bibliodramatic rules can do anything but increase the level of anxiety that is already simmering.** Sometimes humor of the most gentle sort—never of the threatening or ridiculing kind—will help a person to either step back into the role more fully or move out of it gracefully. Sometimes, when you are unsure about this, you can check in with a participant: "Are you still Joseph (or Miriam, or another character's name)?" And if a person says, "No, I guess not," then you can ask, "Do you want to stay in this part, or would you like me to invite someone else to play it for a while?" Such an approach looks at the breaking of role as a sign of discomfort, and the appropriate response is that of a host who, seeing a guest feeling ill at ease, seeks to restore some sense of safety.

2. *What to do if group members are inappropriate or distracting*

Just as players may become anxious in the interpretation of roles, so group members may feel some nervousness about issues being touched upon or feelings being evoked. Because Bibliodrama is a spontaneous process in which participants speak and act without much forethought or self-editing, it can give rise to the unexpurgated. No small part of its vitality comes from the relationship of bibliodramatic play to the unconscious, or at least to material usually suppressed in social situations. In those social situations we do not usually play out scenes of death or banishment, arguments with God, or confrontations with siblings, nor any of the archetypal themes the Bible is full of. You should bear this fact in mind and regard interruptions and distractions as being signs of unease with the content or the process of the production.

But whereas the director is often right to halt the proceedings when a player drops out of role, it is not always wise to do this with all distractions and interruptions. Though there is an understandable and natural resistance in any group to this kind of work, it is not always a good idea to stop the play to give this element of resistance its head. Resistance can quickly feed on itself to the point where the Bibliodrama can be stalled and then permanently derailed. If you give too much airtime to elements of the group that are countering the trance with cavils or questions, asides, whispered conversations or comments, jokes, or any physical activity that calls attention to itself, then participants will be distracted from the work in progress, and your own authority will be undermined.

The best tactic—a real challenge to your spontaneity—is to see whether you can in some way draw the resistance into the drama. On one level this may be done by casting the resistant group members as people who might be resistant within the drama itself, or parts of the players, as yet unspoken, that might feel negative, angry, or disobedient to the story as it is unfolding.

Two brief examples:

☞ You are doing the scene in which Abraham banishes Hagar, and two group members, not in role, start to talk to each other. Attention shifts toward them. You might say,

"I wonder if you two could play the part of two members of Abraham's camp who are seeing this scene take place; I wonder if we could overhear your commentary on what's happening. Maybe you could express a little outrage at this; or maybe you are glad to be rid of Hagar and Ishmael."

This gambit accomplishes a number of things at once. First, it signals to the distracters that I have noticed them and that I want to include their energy in the drama. Second, it offers some constructive ways to deal with what otherwise might be free-floating negativity in the group. Third, it is a way for me to maintain my control as director over the process.

More often than not, this approach works. At worst it may be felt as a reprimand; at best it is a way of helping people take a step into participation. Usually it serves to refocus us all on the production.

☞ Another example: Miriam is alone in her tent, isolated and punished with white scales on her skin after arguing with Moses (Numbers 12:15). Again distractions, titters, and whispers. This time I say to these people, "I wonder if you might possibly speak out as parts of Miriam."

In response one person says, "What are we doing here?"

I reframe it or echo it into the process by saying, "Yeah. I'm a part of Miriam sitting here, and I wonder what the hell we're doing here. This is ridiculous. Some people out there are treating this like a game, but it's my skin, literally, we're talking about here."

Or the person says, "I think it's unfair that Miriam is treated this way." (*Clearly not in role, but speaking as a commentator.*)

I take this and say, "I am a part of Miriam that is outraged by the way I am being treated here. After all I have done for my brother and for the enterprise of this God!"

It is not always possible to think so nimbly on your feet, but you will learn to as you gain skill in fielding resistance.

There are times when the distractions merit a more frontal response. "May I ask you please to give your support to people who are trying out this form of study, even if you aren't interested in doing it?" What is crucial is not to be so attached to the production that you allow yourself to become annoyed or angry at the parts of the group that are not so quick or willing to play along. How the director handles the resistance in the group is one of the most important criteria by which, albeit only subliminally, perhaps, the group estimates the trustworthiness of the director. **Resistance always deserves respect; it is a sign that the ego feels itself in danger, and the ego can only be made to relax its grip when it is reassured of its safety.** To force a person or to shame a person into participating can only backfire in the most destructive ways.

3. *What to do if someone uses qualifiers like "maybe"*

Again you should see the use of phrases that indicate an incomplete playing of a role as an indication of anxiety and resistance. In some cases people may not yet fully understand what is meant by role-playing; but usually such qualified ways of playing a role ("Maybe I feel..." or "Perhaps I would say as Joseph that he is feeling..." etc.) indicate that a group member is having a hard time getting into the role.

In such instance, I usually use a gentle confrontation or echoing to shift them more firmly into the part. "No maybes here...I know exactly how I feel in this moment. I feel..." and I will leave this blank space for the person to pick up the role with a little more focus and energy. Or I may say to the player, "Hey, you are Joseph. Tell us what you're feeling."

This kind of approach usually works to bolster the confidence of the player, to make it clear that I want him or her to make a commitment in the playing. Sometimes when a player says, "I don't know how Joseph is feeling," I will counter with, "You are Joseph, and perhaps you are feeling things that it is hard to talk about or even strange, but I think you know how you're feeling. Are you feeling scared?" (if I think that's what might be going on) "or angry?" (if I want to suggest that as a possibility). In this way I coach and support the player in looking inside. I also reserve the option of asking others in the group, in the spirit of doubling, to help us understand what Joseph might be feeling and in that way let this player off the hook.

Often, of course, people who have a hard time finding words for feelings in character have that same difficulty in life, so the patient act of coaching, of supplying some possibilities, may be helpful both in the realm of the drama and in the realm of their lives. But in all such matters where resistance, discomfort, or anxiety are at work, the tone and style of the director must reflect a genuine concern and compassion. **Remember: Process is more important than production. You do not want to sacrifice the feelings of your players for the sake of the show.**

4. *What to do if someone becomes emotionally overheated*

This is the question that is most often asked by new and would-be practitioners. So much of what I have written about in this book has to do with warming people *up*, not cooling them *down*. Yet the skillful director will be as able to help people distance themselves from their emotional involvement in the drama as he or she will be in helping people to engage more deeply.

The easiest way to think about cooling down the process is to offer the player a chance to step out of the part. So for someone who is starting to change color, whose words become agitated, in whose eyes tears are shining—all signs of a fuller degree of emotional engagement in the part—I might want to say something like this: "It seems to me, Joseph, that this scene with your father is bringing up some feelings for you. Do you want to go on, or is this enough?" Even though the question is framed to the person in the role (I speak to Joseph), it is actually a gentle way of breaking the trance and inviting the person playing the part to *think* rather than feel for a moment. He or she also has to make a conscious choice about staying in or stepping out of the process. If it seems that "Joseph" doesn't really hear me, I might then use the person's name, further breaking the trance, and say, "Thomas... Thomas..." and Thomas, who has been playing Joseph, blinks and then smiles somewhat shyly. "So, Thomas," I go on, "it looks like this little scene you're doing with Joseph is moving to you. Do you want to go on?" Again the choice is given.

But the cooling down of the process may occur far earlier than this and in ways that head off the acceleration of feeling. This braking process is done by moving from emotion to intellect. **The law at work here is that the more the head—the intellectual faculty—is involved, the less the emotions will be stirred and engaged.**

So at any point in the drama I can ask a player what he *thinks about* a situation as opposed to how he *feels* in it. I can brake the momentum of the work by offering a comment on the passage: "You know, this scene has always made me wonder why Joseph never tried to find out if his father was still alive." Or I can bring in the cognitive by calling up a traditional commentary; by asking if anyone knows what a particular English phrase is in the Hebrew; or by any number of such interruptions that look for information, solicit ideas, invite a historical perspective, require knowledge, and so diminish the affective process and unhook the imagination.

5.*What to do if someone tries to take over a Bibliodrama*

There are certain kinds of participants who understand immediately how the game of Bibliodrama is played and who bring to it a tremendous hunger to be on stage, and sometimes even an ability to play a starring role. The best of such people respond to a director's gentle requests for restraint; the worst are so starved for attention, are so incapable of sharing the process with others, that they cannot be reminded, in the usual appropriate ways, to wait, to let others play, and to take up less space and time. Though these people are few and far between, they are always great challenges to your role and authority.

A few suggestions:

- If you know this person intends to be in your group beforehand, you can take him or her aside and ask them directly to be mindful of your desire to include others.

- You may think ahead and "reserve a role" for this participant, and again tell him or her before the group that you have a special part in mind.

- You may, again beforehand, invite this person to act as your assistant director with words like, "You know, this is not an easy group for me to work with"—or "I am not feeling on top of my game today"—"I wonder if you could help me. There are a few very quiet people I'd like to draw in. Maybe you could help me make sure their contributions get heard."

- If you do not know this person beforehand, then you will learn what you are up against only in the course of the drama. Your failure or refusal to keep recognizing a raised hand, a constantly waving hand, may make this person more aggressive or even intrusive. The best solution I have found is to give this person a supporting role and, in effect, leave him or her stuck in it.

For example, in the Garden of Eden story, let such a person be the Tree of Knowledge. Tell them at the beginning that this is a very important part and that you will want to hear from them at the end of the story (and be sure you leave the time to do this). To find this minor role requires some quick thinking on your part, but there is almost always a physical object or a secondary character through whose eyes a story might be seen and who in the end can be interviewed for their take on the story. The quarantine of a small part is often the most effective way to manage someone whose need to be heard all the time threatens to take over the drama.

- Finally, it may happen that the only thing left to try, when all else fails, is a direct approach: "You know, Irwin, I feel a little overwhelmed by your energy. I appreciate what you have to offer, but I'd like you to... (appropriate verb here: slow down, make room for others, listen more, etc.)"

6. What to do if someone wants to bring in traditional commentary

Often there are a few people in a group who are knowledgeable or who like to show off how learned they are. Understandably such people are often the very ones who find the "touchy-feely" approach of

Bibliodrama, its way of drawing upon imaginative and affective faculties, somewhat threatening. Their resistance is expressed by a tendency toward the pedantic and the argumentative, or by wanting to tell you what one commentator or another said about the passage. Often these participants have the Bible open in front of them at all times.

Again, respect is the watchword: respect for their level of tolerance for this kind of study-process and respect for their commitment to learning. You need to recognize that they have a real contribution to make. The question is how to engage them in a way that does not break up the trance-momentum.

The first thing I do is to stop them from launching into too long a discourse. Once I recognize where they are coming from, I might say something like this: "I appreciate what you are telling us, but I wonder if you could wait with those insights and questions until we have finished this part of our study of the text. I am definitely reserving time at the end for a very different kind of discussion, and then what you have to say will be very important."

Sometimes I am able to say, in a joking but non-put-down way, "Ah hah! we have Rashi with us today (or Augustine, etc.). Rashi, please tell us what you have to say about this passage," and in this way, clearly, I am inviting the commentator to play a role, the role of Rashi, and thus keep alive the imaginative spirit of the play.

And there are times I have to be just plain firm. "Look, as I said at the beginning of the class, we're trying a very different approach to biblical hermeneutics (good time to use big words, just to remind this person that you're no dope). I'd appreciate the chance to (or I ask for your courtesy so that I can) complete this particular process. There will be time at the end for questions about the approach itself as well as specific insights. OK? Thank you."

7. *What to do if...*

I cannot anticipate all the situations in the face of which the director may inwardly be screaming, "Help!" But the bottom line is this: If you frame your work as an exploration; when you hold gently yet firmly to the process and are willing, if you sense the resistance in the group warrants it, to let it go and to return to the more familiar ways of talking about biblical stories; if you are able to be humorous with yourself, admit you're not sure what to do, appeal to the group for support or advice; if, in short, you stay human and don't try to come across as more polished or proficient than you really are; then you can meet whatever comes up with tact and grace. Directors get themselves in trouble when they cannot admit to themselves or the group that they might be in over their heads or might be confused as to where to go next. Bibliodrama can and should be a collaborative process, and it is always safer to appeal to the group to help you think through any particular crux or uncertainty than it is to feel you must maintain the spell or the control and bully forward. Remember, this way of studying text is, in essence, play—and it should be fun.

Appendix 5:
Bibliodrama From The Pulpit

Generally speaking, the two biggest differences between doing Bibliodrama from the pulpit as opposed to in the classroom are the size of the group you are working with and the time frame you have to work within. Where class size may vary between four and thirty, a congregation may be as large as five or six hundred. (I have worked with a group that size on a few occasions, so it can be done.) And rarely do you have time for anything but a shorter exploration.

Also, in a classroom, one can move people fairly easily in and out of role, onto the stage and then off it again. In a large sanctuary space, however, where it is sometimes hard to hear or see, it is rarely a good idea to get people out of their pews to play. **I almost always choose to do Bibliodrama from the pulpit as voicing and echoing and interviewing.** In that form I warm up the congregation through a certain amount of storytelling, bringing them into the story as it is happening to the characters, as an unfolding whose ending the characters (and we) do not yet know. I look for a point where I will stop telling or reading, where I can begin to play; I look for the exact moment at which the Bibliodrama will begin. The transition might be announced in the following way:

> So now we come to the moment when Moses is a young
> man and, quote, "HE WENT OUT TO HIS KINSFOLK AND
> WITNESSED THEIR TOIL," end quote. We are in Exodus 2,
> verse 11. I want you to be Moses, and I want you to tell me
> some of the things you are seeing and feeling and thinking
> as you go out and witness the toil of your kinsfolk.

The moment I have chosen is rich with ambiguous and complex possibilities. It is the turning point of Moses' life; it will bear the weight of a good deal of conjecture.

(Notice that I put the story into the present tense as well as putting people into role. The introduction here makes the story into something that is unfolding, and if people try to get ahead of the story, I will remind them, "That hasn't happened yet.")

Gradually people respond with upraised hands. They voice Moses in this moment, and I echo them. Sometimes I ask a follow-up question, briefly *interviewing*, but more often I simply pile up the possibilities. Then I will go on to the next moment, saying something like:

> So, Moses, it is said of you that you see, quote, "AN EGYPTIAN BEATING A HEBREW, ONE OF YOUR KINSMEN," end quote. What is this like for you? (Again voicing and echoing.) And then it is written, quote, "THAT YOU LOOK THIS WAY AND THAT, AND SEEING NO ONE ABOUT, (YOU) STRIKE DOWN THE EGYPTIAN AND SLAY HIM." Clearly this is not a totally impulsive act. You look around this way and that. Again, Moses, I ask you to tell me what is going on in these moments.

And so it goes, and because I am not a rabbi, a priest, or a minister, I do not need to move this text toward a homily. I can present it as an example of a kind of new reading. I can bring this participatory experience to a close simply by remarking on the hidden richness of the biblical narrative. I can cite other commentaries to show congregants how we have anticipated and extended the reflection of the past; or I can move to another biblical moment, when Moses strikes the rock after the death of Miriam, and compare the passages. There are many ways to close or to continue this work from the pulpit.

Sometimes I will divide a group up and have different sections of the congregation play either different characters or different aspects of the same character.

For example, in a scene where Jethro is bringing his daughter Zipporah and his two grandsons, Gershom and Eliezer, to Moses in the wilderness, I might have a quarter of the congregation to my far left represent Jethro. I might ask the next section moving toward the right to be Zipporah; the next section would be Gershom; and the section to my far right would be Eliezer. I would begin by putting each section in role and then questioning each section about the feelings of their character. Whose idea was it to go? Why? How do you feel about leaving, about seeing Moses, etc.?

Or, where I sense the possibilities of a strong internal conflict in a character, I might divide the congregation in two parts, each part to represent a side of that conflict.

For example, looking at Abram's call to go to Canaan—which involves leaving his father behind—I might look at the part of Abram that wants to go to Canaan and the part of him that does not.

In working with a large group it is best to have a portable microphone and circulate a little bit in the audience. Your mobility will stir up the energy in the audience. You cannot get to everyone; many people will be landlocked in their pews; but your moving about helps relieve the static, frontal quality of many pulpit experiences.

I have found that a really large group can sustain this kind of bibliodramatic play for longer than you might suppose. Depending on the text chosen and the energy of the group, and in particular how on you are in your echoing, the energy can build and be sustained for more than the twenty minutes or half hour usually allotted to a sermon. On the other hand, a few minutes of bibliodramatic play from the pulpit, as part of a sermon, can engage listeners in an entirely new way. Many rabbis and ministers are already in dialogue with their congregations during sermons; increasingly this is the case. Bibliodrama slides easily into that dialogical form.

Appendix 6:
Some Conventions for Closure

The understandable concern of every director is how to bring a drama to a close, and in particular how to make that close satisfying from an aesthetic and an emotional point of view. If the drama has taken us into difficult feelings—grief, anger, a sense of loss or vexation—then you want to bring people back "up," so to speak, and do so in a way that feels authentic to and integrated into the drama. But what to do when there are no happy endings?

I have spoken more than once about the fact that the Bibliodrama takes place within the environment of the Bible. Among other things, this means that there are resources available to the director, resources of healing and affirmation, that this spiritual text provides. Closure often taps in to those resources.

1. Prayer: One of the most potent of these is prayer. At any moment a character in the Bible may be imagined in prayer (even inner and unconscious prayer); at any moment a character may be invited to pray. Many Bibliodramas end with characters leaving the stage after voicing their prayer for themselves or for others. And even when a character is left feeling utterly alone and unredeemed—Cain, for example, in his exile, or Sarah in the grips of Pharaoh—the spiritual resources of the Bible may be brought to bear. There is always, for example, Job, who can be brought in, if not for comfort, then at least to say, "You are not alone." If one cannot pray for oneself, one can be invited to pray for others. "Cain, what is your prayer for your children and for the generations to come?" "Dinah, if you have a child from this event, what will your prayer for it be?"

2. Stand By Me: Another aspect of closure, hinted at above, is to ask the biblical character who else might stand with him or her in this moment. Other characters in the same drama might wish to speak to a character who feels isolated or alone. Often compassion is felt by many people in the group, and they are only looking for a form in which to express it. Or you may ask that question of the group: "Who else from the biblical tradition might stand with Joseph in his exile?" Ishmael comes forward; Esau, too. "Who else stands with Sarah in her loss of her son?" Rebecca and Hannah come forward. "Who stands with the drunken Noah naked in his tent?" David is there lamenting the loss of Absalom; Job stands there as well.

3. Divine Consolations: Then there is the possibility that God may have the final word in a Bibliodrama. Or some figure from the heavenly host. When you invite an angelic or heavenly voice ("Are there any of God's helpers who would like to say a word to...at this moment?") you shift perspectives, and you help your group to find a way out of what might otherwise feel like a dismal state.

4. Distance: Sometimes nothing will entirely lift the gloom or the sense of loss a Bibliodrama might evoke. Then a series of steps from the drama back to our own identities may be in order, steps that distance us from the feelings in the role-play. The characters need to be disengaged from us, we from them. The empty chairs in which they first sat must be neutralized and made empty once again. Participants can be invited to stand behind those chairs and speak their own words of comfort to the figures they played. As a group we can analyze them a little; we can remind them of a future they do not yet see. We can even tell them that ages and ages hence someone will step into their shoes and understand, as if for the first time, how deeply they suffered their condition. Then group members may take their seats again in the audience. You place the chairs aside, affirming that they are only chairs again. You may open the Bible and invite the group to imagine the characters there as in a kind of many-roomed mansion. They have been there a long time. They are waiting for us. Then the reviewing can begin.

5. Quiet and Music: When such gentle and prolonged closure is required, the reviewing often begins on a reflective, quiet note. Sometimes a chant or a shared piece of music will help gather the group back into an awareness of one another as we meet again in this reality. Sometimes movement, a formed circle, a meditative walk around the room will accomplish this transition. Sometimes the simple opening of a window serves to dispel the gentle trance—in some ways like a dream— and remind us of the life that still runs busily around and inside us.

Epilogue:
A Critique Of The Method

Here at the end I want to say a few words about what I think are the limitations of the form of Bibliodrama that I have been describing and advocating in this book.

Bibliodrama, as expounded here and manifest in my practice of it, is characterized by three defining qualities. These are: its great reliance on the personality and therefore the biases of the director; its adherence to certain aesthetic principles (of form and shape and closure); and its subservience to the text rather than to the experience, the fantasies, the extravagances of the participants. Each of these factors shapes Bibliodrama and gives it a particular cast. Each of these factors has its liabilities for the politics—in the broadest sense—of bibliodramatic practice.

In the first place, the role of the director as spelled out in this manual is in many ways as dominating and determining as the role of the priest or rabbi whose place, in a sense, the director usurps. Yet the director does not have the overt or recognizable public affiliations, does not bear the impress of an institutional sanction or ordination that might confer some legitimacy on his or her work or at least lend some clarity to the director's role. Thus the bibliodramatist may be viewed, indeed may operate, as a loose cannon among the keepers of the canon. He or she operates without oversight and without responsibility to some certifying, credentialing body.

All the dangers of the *auteur* attend the bibliodramatist, dangers of ego, power, coercion, and corruption. *Auteur*, deriving from the same word that gives us the word authority, belongs to a model that may end up as authoritarian. In that model, individual efforts are often subsumed under an authorial agenda. Though in its process Bibliodrama appears to be a pluralistic, polyvocal, and open-ended exploration of story, it can be in practice the work of a mastering directorial consciousness that, in ways the director may often be unconscious of, controls group process, closes off certain kinds of interpretations, and privileges others.

In the second place, and in my own case in particular, my predilection for a rather conventional dramatic aesthetic—in which there is character, conflict, insight, and some sense of resolution and closure—may easily blind me to the messier energies that are evoked by the opportunities to play roles in an improvisational process. The model of Bibliodrama set forth in this book can make the practitioner too much a slave of the theater. If one is too interested in pleasing an audience, or those members of the group who need linear development and look for a well-made play, one can sacrifice the genuinely exploratory, transgressive, unintegratable elements of improvisational exploration on the altar of aesthetic form.

In the third place, the primary emphasis of text-centered Bibliodrama is to serve the canonized narratives. Certain questions about those narratives, certain counter-textual possibilities, certain passionate protests cannot always be contained within the role-play. Admission to the theater of Bibliodrama requires a certain basic acceptance of the Bible as it stands. The kinds of power stances, gender biases, social relations, racial assumptions enshrined in the Bible are not easily challenged by a method that begins by accepting the stories as they are and working within their unyielding frameworks. Radical as Bibliodrama is in some respects, it is also a method that can be seen to buttress the status quo. And that status quo has favored and still favors certain educated elites.

Not only does Bibliodrama serve the canon, it does not serve the participants in the fullness, complexity, contrariness of their participation. Though Bibliodrama, as I practice it, attempts to walk a fine line between its honoring of the text and its honoring of the participants, it can also be accused of falling between two stools. Certainly it can be accused, in its inability to serve two masters, of choosing the past over the present, the object over the person.

Two other matters need explicit mention. Bibliodrama is not only pluralistic, it is relativistic in its orientations. It undermines certain absolutes, and while there are those who find this subversion healthy and appropriate, there are others, perhaps unaware of just how decentralizing and destabilizing the bibliodramatic process can be, who may feel their connection to tradition and authority being, albeit implicitly, challenged. In the force field set up by bibliodramatic exploration the question of the legitimacy of interpretation, what makes one interpretation more valid than another, raises its head. The bibliodramatic environment demands tolerance as it unleashes people's powers of playful and passionate interpretation. In inviting the imagination to reengage in the study of texts, Bibliodrama sets loose an energy that is both vital and wild.

Finally, as a discipline—if that word can be used at all for something so young and idiosyncratic—Bibliodrama lacks its critics, lacks a cautious, skeptical, vocal community of intelligent practitioners and peer review. Though performed in the open and not behind closed doors, Bibliodrama too often seems magical and invites people to suspend, perhaps too much, the critical disbelief that is a sign of caution and of maturity. What Bibliodrama will need if it is to grow strong is to submit to challenge and question; it must be forced—as must its practitioners—to examine assumptions, to tease out the implications of its strategies, to look hard at its ethics, its goals, its styles. With the publication of this manual and the development of various training opportunities this work is becoming part of the public domain. There can never be an armor that shields us from abuse, folly, or irresponsible extremes, but the best protection against them is the creation of critical colleagueship and review. Those of us who are drawn to learn and practice this method are obliged to remember that to play with Bibliodrama is to play with fire.

Afterword

We cannot close this story without speaking of its sequel.

In 1998 we were invited to Germany to present our version of Bibliodrama to a group of European theologians, educators, and pastors who had, quite unbeknownst to us, formed a movement of the same name.

We quickly discovered the similarities and the differences. What the "Pitzele" and European forms of Bibliodrama had in common was their focus on the uses of imagination as way of opening fresh interpretations of the Bible. The difference came in both the method and context.

European Bibliodrama made use of the biblical text as a pre-text for deep spiritual self-exploration in small groups that stayed together for several days. In an atmosphere of a retreat, guided by trained leaders who made use of a variety of methods—role-playing only one of them—participants engaged in shared and solitary explorations.

Our form of Bibliodrama had grown out of the three-way intersection: the methods of psychodrama, the license of the Jewish tradition of midrash, and an audience initially of rabbis who recognized even before we did the potential role of this work in animating their congregations.

Perhaps the most important difference, however, was the number of people who could participate in such a Bibliodrama. The "Pitzele" method could be used with very large groups; it could be used from the pulpit, in the classroom, in the seminary and in interfaith contexts; it could engage people of differing backgrounds and ages. And it was this range that impressed Uta Pohl-Patalong and Frank Muchlinsky, who were both members of the European Bibliodrama cohort. They wished to learn more. And so a new chapter in this history began with our return to Germany the following year to offer the first of what became several training programs. By the end of the 1990s Bibliodrama had been renamed "Bibliolog" to distinguish it from European Bibliodrama. (See: https://

de.wikipedia.org/wiki/Bibliolog)

In 2005 Uta published a book in German entitled *Bibliolog*. In it she adapted *Scripture Windows* to the work she and Frank had initiated and that was spreading in ever widening circles through Germany and Austria. But as interest in Bibliolog reached non-German-speaking countries, an English version of Uta's book became necessary. To that end her book was translated into English: its title is *Bibliolog: A Creative Access to the Bible*. It is available on Amazon.

We recognize that Uta's book is a superb and thoughtful piece of work. Though it is not a translation of *Scripture Windows*, it makes many references to the book. It thoroughly understands the method, offers focused and vital ways of learning and teaching it, and has numerous examples of its application. The last section contains accounts of Bibliolog in different settings and in the words of different practitioners. It captures, in a way *Scripture Windows* does not, the versatility of styles and contexts in which this method can evolve. For those who find *Scripture Windows* a helpful introduction to this method, we urge you to get your hands on this book also. It will expand your horizons and take your practice to another level.

Postscript

I have to thank the women of Germany who were in our Bibliolog classes for helping me to step out from the comfortable assistant role I developed in the USA Jewish community working with Peter. These women persistently wanted to hear more from me and appreciated my value as a group leader and teacher.

Because of this expansion of my role in Germany I developed new ways of thinking about training. My anxiety as a relatively inexperienced director turned out especially to be a valuable asset. I was able to model directing a Bibliolog as a beginner in a way that students could easily relate to. I revamped our way of giving feedback to these novice directors, focusing on what they did well and what special gifts only they can bring as a director. This counteracted the tendency to compare themselves to Peter's fluid directing. Being able to see that the tools look very different in different hands helped underscore the improvisational nature of Bibliolog and lessened the tendency to think there is one right way to direct. An important lesson for students and teachers.

Bibliodrama/Bibliolog is richer for these learnings.

—Susan Pitzele

Acknowledgments

In reflecting back over almost fifteen years of practice as a bibliodramatist, I am aware of how many people I have to thank. Bibliodrama, as I have come to practice it, has developed as a dialogue between myself and a varying community. Each time I share this work I learn something about the craft. It is impossible to acknowledge all the people who have helped me understand more clearly what Bibliodrama is about. But certain colleagues and friends stand out who have encouraged the work and helped me to teach it and to write about it.

Rabbi Eli Spitz, always a generous colleague and one of the first to find uses for Bibliodrama in his teaching, has cheered me from the beginning. He is joined by a whole host of rabbis who have invited me to share my work with their congregations; in those contexts text-centered Bibliodrama was developed and refined. Among the most consistent champions of this work has been Rabbi Jack Moline, a signal friend to my journey as a Jew and as an artist in this form. His enthusiasm for Bibliodrama, his expert grasp of its uses, gave me an early indication that the method was transmittable. Rabbi Burton Visotzky, Professor of Midrash at the Jewish Theological Seminary, gave my work his blessing, and through him the blessing of a tradition, at a time when I was very unsure about myself. His pat on the back has been of lasting value.

The same is true of Rabbi Norman Cohen. He frequently asked me to share my work with his classes, in his course on Modern Midrash at Hebrew Union College. He was instrumental in getting me invited to teach in the Doctor of Ministry Program at HUC, where for a number of years I taught Bibliodrama in a yeasty interfaith context. Rabbi Kerry Olitzky, then the dean of that program, gave me the support and freedom I needed.

I was also invited to teach at the Whizin Institute at the University of Judaism on a number of occasions. Ron Wolfson and his extraordinary staff welcomed me and my work. It was there I met Joel Grishaver, who, long before he became my publisher, was both a friend and a collaborator. Joel's brilliance lit up Bibliodrama in all sorts of ways for me. Together we taught at the Whizin Institute and learned from each other. Bruce Whizin, one of the chief architects of the Whizin Institute, was immediately taken by Bibliodrama, participated as a player in some of the most fruitful sessions I ever conducted, and, on a number of occasions in person and in writing, shared his insights into what makes Bibliodrama tick. To him and to his wife Shelley I owe much for their friendship and keen interest.

Dr. Ann Ulanov, chair of the Department of Psychology and Religion at the Union Theological Seminary, invited me to join her staff as an adjunct. Courses I taught at Union were laboratories for the deepening of this method. Dr. Chris Leighton, director of the Institute for Christian and Jewish Studies in Baltimore, has also given me invaluable opportunities to share this work in an interfaith context; his thoughtful reflections on Bibliodrama helped me grasp more clearly how Bibliodrama could serve the Christian community.

Certain peers in this work stand by me as I continue to develop. Jonathan Schreiber, Wexner fellow and ardent educator, quickly made Bibliodrama his own and shared with me his original ways of teaching it. Shawn Israel Zevit, one of my students and now one of my teachers, served on the faculty of the first Bibliodrama Training Institute. Barbara Breitman was also on that faculty and helped me think about the politics of Bibliodrama. Rabbi Sue Fendrick is another friend to this work and now a colleague in the teaching of it whose perspectives I deeply value. Phyllis Ocean Berman, a gifted student and a superb teacher, was one of the first people who, by the speed with which she learned Bibliodrama, gave me confidence in my ability to teach it. Many of the students who attended the 1996 Bibliodrama Training Institute—affectionately called BTI1—gave me their feedback about the manuscript as a manual. Many of their suggestions are now incorporated into this final version. Among them, Lev Herrnson's have made the greatest impact on the present book. Rabbi Paula Goldberg gave me the benefit of her processing of a powerful bibliodramatic experience of which she was part, and I am grateful for the time she took to teach me more about the experience of the participant.

Then there are those who, in being friends on a personal level, are friends to the work I do as well. Foremost among these is Larry Winters, who read the manuscript, made helpful suggestions, and has listened through the years as I grew in confidence as a bibliodramatist. Alicia Ostriker, poet and teacher, has shown me new ways of being a poet in this form; her reading of the book in manuscript encouraged me to stay loose as a writer. Rabbi Rachel Cowan, both as a friend and in her capacity as an executive of the Cummings Foundation, has championed me and this work from a very early point. A grant from the Cummings Foundation made BTI1 possible.

The manuscript of *Scripture Windows* benefited from a number of readers. Professor Dick Hathaway, as he has done before, gave me the benefit of his critical intelligence. Rabbi Neil Kurshan read an early version of the manuscript and made comments that helped the next version to be clearer. Jo Salas, writer and sister, also read an early version of *Scripture Windows*; I have woven her suggestions into the fabric of the book. Professor Bjorn Krondorfer read the manuscript and gave me the benefit of both his eye and his years of experience as a bibliodramatist. He has acquainted me with the work of European and Christian bibliodramatists. His different orientation to this work has made me see my own all the more clearly by contrast: an invaluable dialogue.

Then there are the four people whose names are prefixed to this book and who form the inner family of support for Bibliodrama. Zerka Moreno ushered me into the world of psychodrama; from her I learned many of the skills upon which I built the craft of Bibliodrama. Rabbi Steve Shaw welcomed me year after year to teach at his Rabbinic Institute. There I was able to learn from men and women who were daily in touch with Jewish and congregational life. In teaching Bibliodrama at those Institutes I had the chance to learn and grow from students and fellow faculty members alike. Rivkah Walton has had the deepest influence on my work as a teacher of Bibliodrama. Almost singlehandedly she designed the curriculum for BTI1 and critiqued my work there. Her readings of *Scripture Windows* have aided its evolution in structure and design. Her enthusiasm for Bibliodrama has convinced me to continue to try to develop ways of transmitting it. Lisa Goldberg gave *Scripture Windows* its most thorough read. Everywhere she freed my prose of awkwardness and didacticism. The flaws that remain can only be charged to my account. Lisa made me aware, in ways I had not been before, of how much art and tact are involved in editing.

And two final acknowledgments:

I thank my wife, Susan: reader, companion, clear-eyed critic, and *sine qua non*. She has accompanied me on the whistle-stops of my biblio-dramatic campaigns. She has always loved me in this work and this work in me.

And thanks to my father, who died in August of 1996. More than anyone, he gave me the respect and love I have for the written word; more than anyone, he showed me the delight and value of the imagination.

CPSIA information can be obtained
at www.ICGtesting.com
Printed in the USA
BVHW031752170519
548586BV00002B/199/P